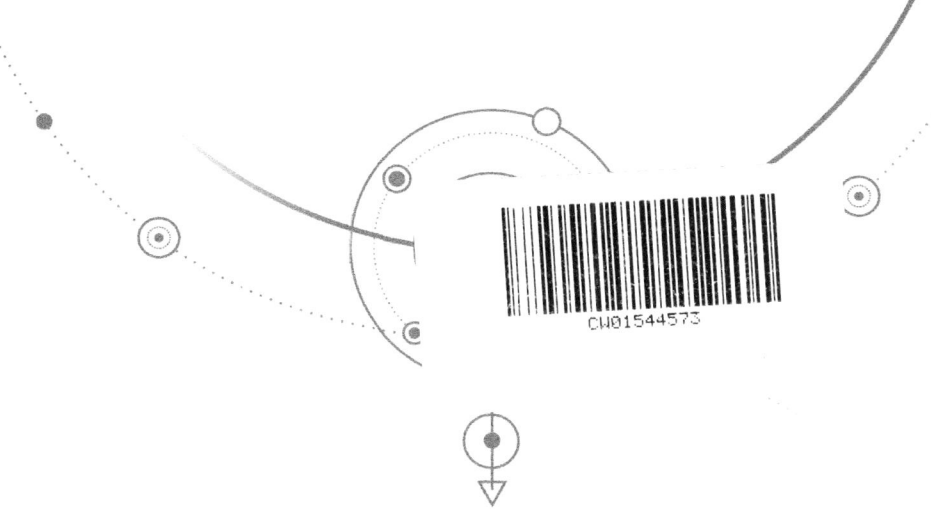

72 KEYS TO MANIFESTATION

An Ancient Path of a Modern-Day Alchemist

A profound guide to finally manifesting the life you want.

Mariya Nurislamova

© Mariya Nurislamova 2021

All rights reserved. No part of this publication may be reproduced, distributed, or transmitted in any form or by any means, including photocopying, recording, or other electronic or mechanical methods, without the prior written permission of the publisher, except in the case of brief quotations embodied in reviews and certain other non-commercial uses permitted by copyright law.

The advice and strategies found within may not be suitable for every situation. This work is sold with the understanding that neither the author nor the publisher are held responsible for the results accrued from the advice in this book.

ISBN Paperback 979-8-9850663-0-2
ISBN Hardcover 979-8-9850663-1-9
ISBN Ebook 979-8-9850663-2-6

First Edition

Cover Design by Jorge Riera
Editing by Sandy Draper
Art Direction by Morgane Leoni

Website: www.thisismariya.com
Email: info@thisismariya.com

Printed in the United States of America.

72 KEYS TO MANIFESTATION

CONTENTS

FOREWORD   8
PREFACE   11

PART I: **THE ENERGY MAGIC BEHIND MANIFESTATION**   17

Key 0 | The North Star   19
Key 1 | The Father Energy, Within and Without   23
Key 2 | Your Power Has Not One, But Two Sources   27
Key 3 | Sun Children   30
Key 4 | The Universe of Two Suns   34
Key 5 | Planting the Seeds   38
Key 6 | The Maze of the Multiverse   43
Key 7 | The Power of Nothing   47
Key 8 | The Law of Three   52
Key 9 | The Quantum Leap   55
Key 10 | Finding Your Original Sound   58
Key 11 | The Stacking Principle   61
Key 12 | The Black Sun Activation   65
Key 13 | The White Sun Activation   68
Key 14 | Getting Rid of Clutter   71
Key 15 | Sun Breathing   76
Key 16 | The Gestation Principle   79
Key 17 | Matter and Antimatter   82
Key 18 | The Amplification Principle   86
Key 19 | Solar Wind Rising   91
Key 20 | The Sun Has a Crown   94
Key 21 | The Path of an Alchemist   98

Key 22 | Bending Time	102
Key 23 | Claiming Territory	107
Key 24 | The Principle of Repetition	111
Key 25 | The Three States of Energy	115
Key 26 | The Many Aspects of Matter	120
Key 27 | Bond with Your Sponsoring Force	126
Key 28 | Sources of Energy	130
Key 29 | The Mirror Universe	136
Key 30 | Cycles of Manifestation: Lunar, Solar, and Earthly	140
Key 31 | Eternal Night of the Black Sun	143
Key 32 | Ancestral Magic	146
Key 33 | Chakras of Abundance	151
Key 34 | The Masculine Code	156
Key 35 | The Feminine Code	161
Key 36 | The Code of Divine Oneness	166
Key 37 | The Secret of the Ankh	171
Key 38 | The Breath of the Ankh	178
Key 39 | Sacred Geometry in Action	182
Key 40 | The Indigo Well	187
Key 41 | In the Flow	190
Key 42 | Portals of Cosmic Alignment	195
Key 43 | Objects of Abundance	199
Key 44 | The Quantum Bridge	202
Key 45 | The Temple of Manifestation	206
Key 46 | The Game of Focus	210
Key 47 | The Triple Helix of Manifestation: Be, Do, Have	213
Key 48 | Manifestation Archetypes: Strategy by Archetype	218
Key 49 | Closing the Energy Loop	224
Key 50 | Imprinting	229
Key 51 | The Earth Star Chakra	234

PART II: YOUR BELIEF SYSTEM AS A KEY TO MANIFESTATION   237

    Key 52 | The Principle of Fullness   238
    Key 53 | The Anatomy of Thought   241
    Key 54 | Thought Loops   244
    Key 55 | Your Mental Aura   247
    Key 56 | Something Borrowed   250
    Key 57 | The Money Chapter   256
    Key 58 | The Great Logos   260
    Key 59 | The Principle of Allowing   264
    Key 60 | Expanding Your Comfort Level   267
    Key 61 | Mastering Faith   271
    Key 62 | The Lesson of Pressure   275
    Key 63 | The Dormant Power of Your Personal Truth   279
    Key 64 | The Universe Starts with You   282

PART III: MANIFESTING ON A PLANETARY LEVEL   287

    Key 65 | Manifesting Through an Egregore   288
    Key 66 | Activating Your Merkaba   291
    Key 67 | The Sacred Flames for Manifestation   296
    Key 68 | Creating Your Manifestation Double   301
    Key 69 | Assemblage Point   306
    Key 70 | Ley Lines, Axis Mundi, and Planetary Alignment   310
    Key 71 | On Anchoring   315
    Key 72 | Your Own Manifestation Code   318

PARTING INTENTION   323
ABOUT MARIYA   324

FOREWORD

Hello friend,

Nothing in the Universe is coincidental. "Coincidence," "chance," and "luck" are labels used by those missing the bigger picture. I believe our meeting is a careful sequence of synchronicities that led you to this point, a culmination of a meticulously planned path; it is also a reflection of who you are at soul level. This book may be the only book on manifestation you will ever need, or a companion volume to similar books you have read. Either way, I hope *72 Keys to Manifestation* brings you a fresh perspective on the energy of manifestation. This book is not for the perpetual skeptic, but the journey will be worth it—provided you keep an open mind.

I am not your guru, because the path you walk is your own. The truths presented in this book are meant to help you navigate the world around you, but by no means are they dogmatic or prescriptive. Beyond all, I want you to listen to your heart for the truths that resonate within you and leave out all the rest. There is no "one size fits all" in manifestation, but I hope this book offers you a variety of concepts and practices to select from.

I know a thing or two about abundance. I think I always have, despite being born into a Russian family of very modest means. And yet it is not the abundance that I achieved in my own life that makes me qualified to write this book. It is not the path I had to walk to get here, to my state of bliss, wealth, and perfect abundance that makes me an expert on manifestation. It is not the eight-figure business (soon to be nine figure) that I built, or my loving husband, or my picture-perfect lifestyle—all those are just some outcomes of the energy that I put out into the world. What qualifies me to write this book is a calling from Spirit—a sacred task that I was given by the energies of light to bring forth this ancient wisdom back into the limelight.

Despite my being called to write *72 Keys to Manifestation*, it wasn't an easy book to pen. It forced me to reassess my self-given labels and re-emerge as the one I came here to be. Until now, I have referred to myself as an "entrepreneur," but who I am at my core is perhaps very different. You see, I communicate with Spirit every day. My path has been informed by insight and intuitive guidance every day since my awakening in the summer of 2018. My life hasn't been the same since.

This book is just a small glimpse into the world of deeper understanding, the world I dove into headfirst after my awakening. These pages have been channeled from

Spirit—cover to cover. There is very little authorship I can claim of the concepts and practices offered here. I am but a vessel. I am but a scribe. And it is from a place of love and surrender that I have written this book for you. I hope you find it helpful in the next chapter of your manifestation journey. I hope it can serve as a guide and reference material for you for many years to come. Since the moment that my "special" abilities made themselves known (at this point, I am clairaudient, clairvoyant, claircognizant, and clairsentient), I have been handheld and guided by Spirit and higher consciousness every step of the way. And I would like to do the same for you.

Here is to you, my friend, and the next step in your personal abundance journey and unlocking your full potential. We'll do this together. If only you knew what an honor it is for me to guide you into a better future.

Much love,

Mariya

INTENTION

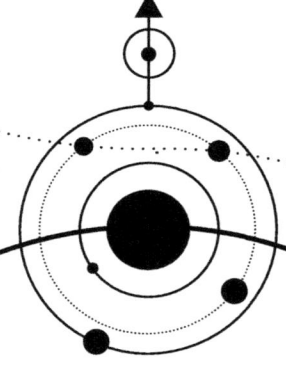

*To all the seekers out there,
with the greater good of this
Universe in mind:
May this book be your personal well of
abundance, and may it spread bliss from you
to every being that crosses your path.*

*That is my intention for you
and for the world.*

PREFACE

Let's start with the basics. Some of the things you read in this book might seem "out there." I ask that you keep an open mind. Manifestation, simply put, is a pointed direction of creative energy from a non-physical space into a physical object or state, and as such it is both an art and a science. But above all, it is a practice, a ritual, and a lifestyle. That is why I wrote this book as a practical guide with plenty of exercises to help you fully experience the concepts presented here.

While manifestation is a discipline and a practice, it is first and foremost an energy practice—a skill of transforming your physical, emotional, and mental energy into your desired outcomes. In the following chapters, we will treat manifestation as such—an energy discipline. On that note, anyone attempting to master manifestation is essentially an alchemist in training. While the alchemists of old attempted to transform lead into gold, as a modern-day alchemist, you can learn to transform your energy into anything your heart desires. Manifestation is thus the science and art of transmutation.

Below is a quick overview of the journey we are about to embark on, so you can easily navigate the book. My vision was for you to master manifestation in 72 days – one key per day. Each key addresses a separate topic and contains a practice or meditation to help you integrate the newly found understanding on a deeper level. The book is divided into three sections that collectively provide a comprehensive overview of the discipline of manifestation.

In Part I, The Energy Magic Behind Manifestation, we'll address your energetic body and energetic state. The rest of this book won't be as effective unless you first address the basics. This is the most important section of the book and the one that most other books on manifestation often don't fully address.

In Part II, Your Belief System as a Key to Manifestation, you'll work with your belief system and anything that might be preventing you from experiencing your full abundance—all day, every day. Chances are, you inherited a slew of beliefs around money, abundance, work, and happiness from your parents and society at large. Given the state of the planet today, I am willing to bet that some of those beliefs don't serve you. We will explore how to find your limiting beliefs and, most importantly, how to transform them into a narrative that is positive, automatic, and prolific in its power. The Keys in this section will help you rebuild your mental network into something that works for you, not against you.

In Part III, **Manifesting on a Planetary Level,** the Keys will be devoted to the very few of you working on manifesting things on the planetary level. This one's for you—star seeds, indigo children, warriors of light, and all who know they came here for a bigger purpose. Please stay tuned, as this section addresses some of the hidden, ancient knowledge that has been the domain of the few until now. This knowledge is seeking to make itself known now, so I chose to serve as a vessel for bringing it into this time-space reality so you and I can change this world together.

A FEW SUGGESTIONS BEFORE GETTING STARTED

Every key offers at least one meditative experience, practice, or ritual to help you consolidate the learnings. Here is some practical advice on how to best prepare.

CREATING A HEALING SPACE

Practices are most impactful when done intentionally. This means the setting really matters. Make sure you reserve some alone time to do the exercises in this book. You may choose to bring some "objects of power" into your healing space to make it even more impactful and magical. I love using crystals, and I find that citrine, amber, and sunstone work best for manifesting, so consider having them in your healing space. You may even want to hold a crystal as you meditate to help focus your energies further.

I also like lighting a candle or two since the energy of fire effortlessly clears away any blockages or stuck energy from the room. Aroma is also important, so you might want to burn an incense cone or stick. Sandalwood, frankincense, cedarwood, cinnamon, or jasmine are perfect for manifestation work, but you can go with any other fragrance you prefer.

Before starting the practice, consider smudging your space to clear away any negativity or unbalanced energy. To smudge your healing space, you will need some white sage, mugwort, or *Palo Santo*. Light the tip of your smudge stick and let it burn for a few seconds, then extinguish the flame and allow the stick to smolder. You may want to have a small plate or abalone shell where you can place your stick safely so its smoke can fill the room. You may also want to do a quick lap around the room to smudge the space evenly, carefully stopping in each corner since that is where the negative energy tends to gather.

Setting up energy protection is also a good practice. I find that black tourmaline, black obsidian, and black kyanite are most effective in offering energetic protection. Simply place a small stone in each of the four corners of your room to create a protection grid around you.

MEDITATION TIPS

Most of the practices in this book take the form of a guided meditation or visualization; the following guidelines will help you get the most out of them:

- △ Make sure you are well rested before taking on a new practice. Manifestation work requires ample energy, so ensure you are not accidentally depleting your resource.
- △ You can do most of the practices sitting or lying down; just make sure you are comfortable staying in this position for some time.
- △ For further protection and energy amplification, before starting the practice, imagine a pyramid of white light around your body. Know this is an ancient symbol of Divine protection; you are safe and sound within its borders.
- △ Once the pyramid is in place, start breathing deeply through your belly. Generally, ten breaths are enough to get you to relax and embrace the energies coming through, but if you feel stressed or overwhelmed, you may want to do additional breaths. Allow your thoughts to come and go freely, like the waves of the ocean. Don't hold on to them—they will be there once your practice is over.
- △ If the practice requires you to "see things," it may be helpful to activate your third eye before starting. The third eye is located in the center of your forehead. You may want to imagine it as a pulsating sphere of violet light. With each breath, imagine the sphere expanding and starting to rotate faster and faster, clearing away any dark blockages that may be in the area.
- △ Lastly, trust that you've got it, and surrender to the process.

GROUNDING YOURSELF AFTER PRACTICES

If you feel lightheaded after energy work, you may consider a simple grounding exercise before closing your practice.

1. Plant both of your feet firmly on the ground.
2. Starting from the back of your head, imagine your energy beginning to flow down your spinal cord.
3. When your energy reaches the tailbone, allow it to split into two streams and go down your legs, finally coming out through the soles of your feet.
4. Imagine this energy transforming itself into the roots of a mighty tree going deep into the Earth.
5. Picture the roots stretching toward the very center of our planet and being fully planted there. Feel the power of being connected with and planted into the Earth.
6. You are safe; you are secure; and you are now fully grounded.

JOURNALING

It may be beneficial to keep a journal of your experiences as you work through the various practices of the 72 Keys. You may often get unexpected insights or intuitive hits as you go through the exercises. Make sure to write them down in case you want to go back to them in the future. A journal is also a great place to keep track of your intentions and goals so you can focus and bring even more momentum to your manifestation work.

DREAM BOARD

To be an effective manifestor, it is important to get clarity around what you want to manifest. Creating a visual dream board is a good place to start. That way, when you get to the practices, you will know exactly what your vision for your future is.

One option is to create a Pinterest board of what you want to manifest in the next one to three years. An ideal dream board includes both immediate and long-term goals, so the Universe has some breathing room. But it is also important to know your

North Star—if you had to pick one major thing to manifest, what would it be? That will become your focal point for all your manifestation work.

You can also choose to do a physical dream board using scraps from the old magazines or printouts of your favorite images from the Internet. Placing this board in your bedroom is a good idea since it leverages the Law of Amplification—you will repeatedly come in contact with the board, which will make it easier for you to manifest.

PICK YOUR FAVORITE PRACTICES

Once you finish reading the book, your manifestation journey is far from over. There is always more goodness to manifest. I recommend jotting down your favorite practices so you can introduce them to your weekly/monthly routine for even better results in the future.

A NOTE ON GENDER

This book uses the terms "masculine" and "feminine" a lot to discuss energy related concepts, this is done for the sake of simplicity and ease of understanding. It is my belief that our soul experiences the full spectrum of masculine and feminine energies as we go through incarnations. We are all at soul level gender fluid. In fact, at soul level you are both masculine, feminine, both and neither at the same time. Whatever gender you identify as currently, whatever path you have come to experience, know that inside you have both energy types – the masculine and the feminine, albeit most likely in different measure. I hope you can keep an open mind when reading this book and get creative when applying the concepts presented in later chapters to your unique self and your unique path.

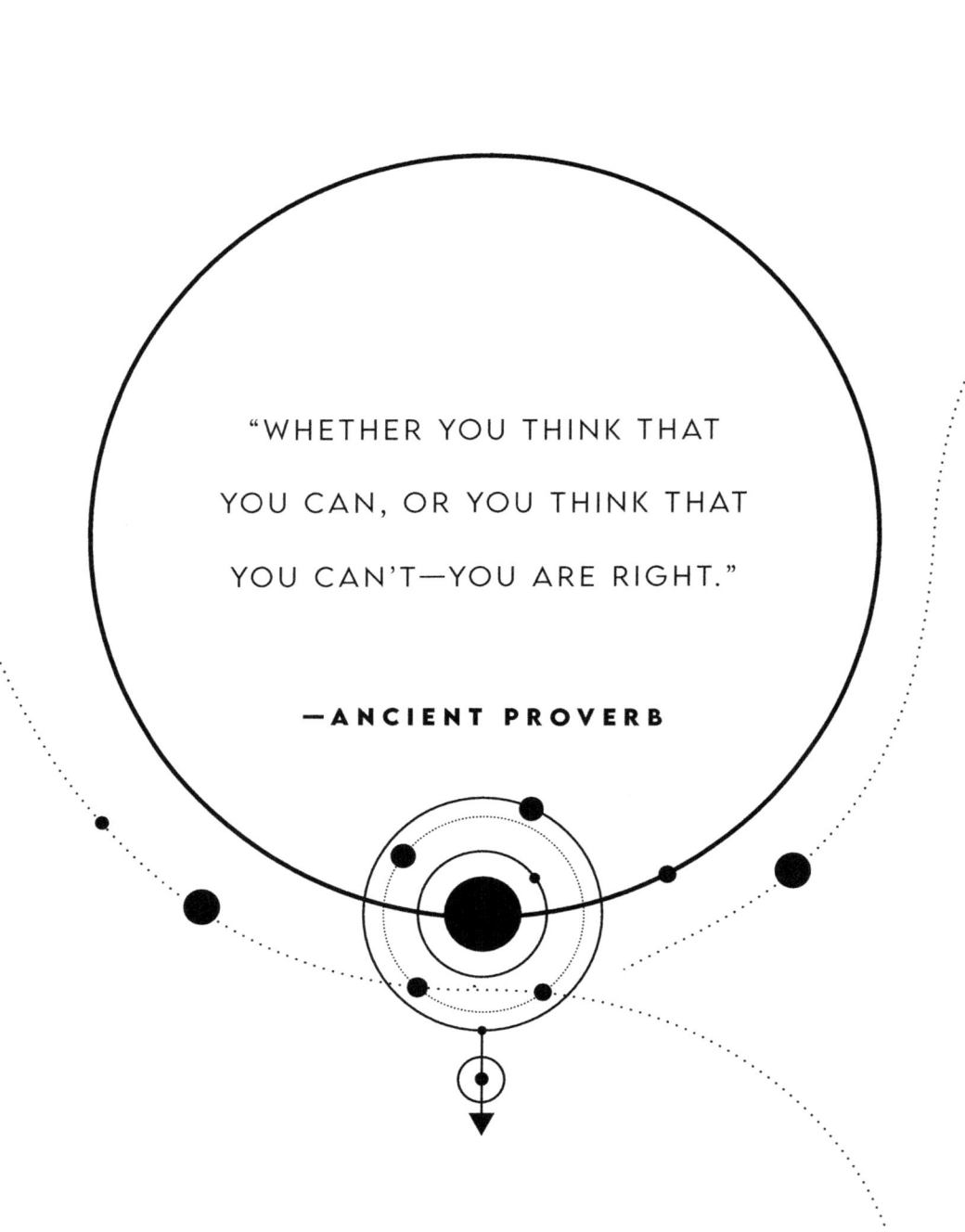

"WHETHER YOU THINK THAT YOU CAN, OR YOU THINK THAT YOU CAN'T—YOU ARE RIGHT."

—ANCIENT PROVERB

PART I

THE ENERGY MAGIC BEHIND MANIFESTATION

There is enough Divine spark in you to manifest anything your heart desires. I know this to be true, and I know how to help you get there. However, heeding the warning of "being careful what you wish for" is critical in manifestation work, less you spend precious time manifesting something that wouldn't serve you at all.

I have taken the liberty to write Chapter Zero, hoping it will save you decades of pursuing the dreams that are only masquerading as your own. Finding your unique path and stepping into it fully is the single biggest act of self-love. I have written the following chapter for you, as an orientation in the vastness of the Universe. This is Key Zero—the absolute beginning of your journey, the quiet before the storm, the space between an exhale and an inhale. Key Zero is what must happen before you get to the sacred act of manifesting.

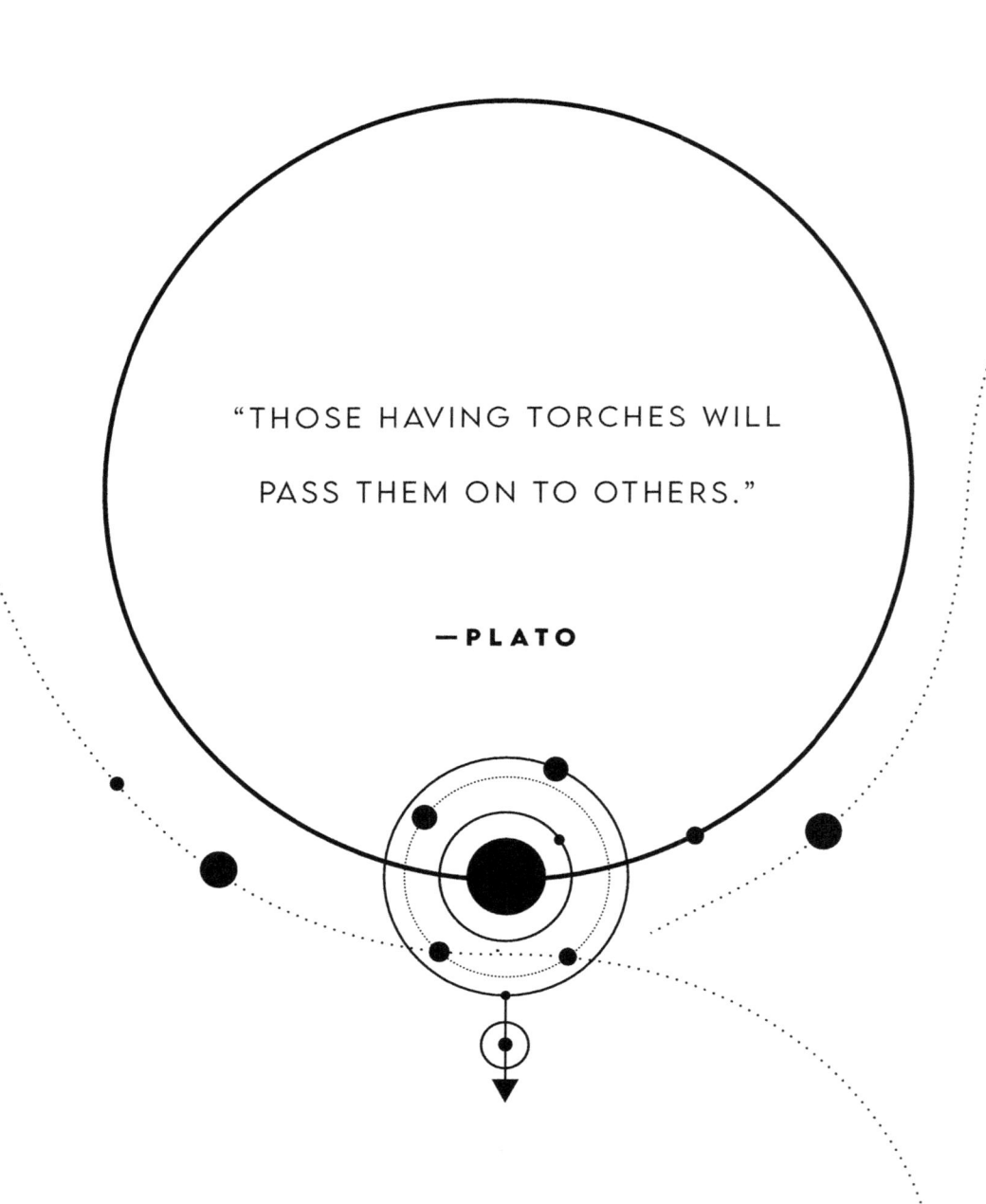

"THOSE HAVING TORCHES WILL PASS THEM ON TO OTHERS."

—PLATO

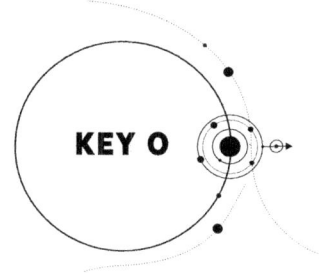

KEY 0

THE NORTH STAR

For generations, humans have used the North Star (or *Stella Polaris*) to navigate their way through the tumultuous oceans. Plenty are the stars in the sky, but only Polaris perpetually points to the north. Coincidentally, the spiritual and energetic meaning of Polaris goes a notch beyond being a simple navigation tool. The light of Polaris is the guiding light of cosmic magnitude, which connects you to the Higher aspects of your being and brings you closer into alignment with your unique, unparalleled path. There are many paths you could choose to walk. Perhaps each of them has inherent value, but only one path is most optimal for you in this lifetime. This path is a sacred contract between you and your Higher Self. This path is a careful brushstroke within the monumental painting of all of your incarnations from the beginning of time. This path is your unique flavor of adventure—the only thing that leads to true contentment, happiness, and peace of mind.

Polaris has been on a mission to light the path for all the seekers on Earth for more than 2,000 years. It will remain here for many more generations until the next major North Star, *Vega*, takes its place. But that will be a whole new Earth, and a whole new set of challenges. For now, the steady light of Polaris is the only guiding light you need to show you the way.

Polaris is a midpoint between this reality and the realm of Spirit where your Higher Self dwells. It is a beacon and a compass that, when activated, will always ensure your actions are aligned with your highest good and are pointing to your own true North—the direction where your personal evolution awaits.

Once your connection to the North Star is activated, you will use it to stay on track because it is aligned with your goals. Below are a few simple ways you could leverage your connection with the North Star and its guiding energies to bring you closer to the life you want.

PRACTICE: DAILY ALIGNMENT WITH THE NORTH

Any time you face north, you inadvertently open a direct line of communication with the North Star. This allows the star to impart its healing and guiding energies straight into your higher chakras. Take a minute every day to face true planetary north and imagine the North Star up in the sky. Visualize being fully aligned with the star. Picture how its energies are giving you a much-needed tail wind, propelling you forward. Imagine the clarity that comes from this alignment. You may also want to align your work desk and/or bed to the north as it allows you to stay in the flow of this guiding star as you are working or sleeping. Facing true north is a practice, a ritual, and a habit. When you achieve alignment with the North Star, you will find that decision making becomes easier, your intuition is heightened, and opportunities keep knocking on your door.

PRACTICE: QUICK GUIDANCE

For quick in-the-moment guidance from the North Star, close your eyes and imagine breathing into your third eye area (it is located in the center of your forehead, just above and between your eyes). As you do so, feel how your third eye area expands and becomes activated. After ten expansive breaths, focus on the image of the North Star in your mind's eye and ask a question. The answer is bound to come in one form or another—a sign, an intuitive hit, or a deep knowing. Moreover, it will be fully aligned with your path and your greater good.

PRACTICE: AUTOMATIC WRITING

If you have questions about your path, you can use a simple technique called "automatic writing."

1. Close your eyes and take a few moments to connect to the North Star in your mind's eye.
2. Picture a stream of light stretching out from your body toward the center of the North Star, then looping around and coming back to you.

3. Allow the stream of light to travel the loop you just created at least three times to solidify your connection with the star.
4. When you're ready, open your eyes, take out a journal and write down a question—anything you want to ask. Then write the words: "Answer from my North Star."
5. Allow the answer to come freely and spill out onto the page.

You will be surprised at the accuracy of what comes back. You can have a whole conversation with the North Star this way—asking any follow-up questions that you'd like. This is a simple yet effective technique if you have questions about your path in life.

PRACTICE: NORTH STAR ACTIVATION—THE TRIANGLE OF POLARIS

For this meditative practice, you want to be facing north to ensure a seamless connection with the North Star.

1. Close your eyes and settle into your body. Start with a few deep breaths, allow them to cleanse your mind from traces of internal dialogue.
2. Focus on the image of the North Star high up in the sky. There is something pure and pristine about its etheric glow. Something familiar, as if you have always been aware of its presence. Watch as the North Star begins to pulsate, sending you a wave of light vibrations. As the light emanating from the star reaches you, notice that it enters your body through the middle of your forehead—your third eye area. Allow this process to take place naturally. Notice that your third eye center is becoming saturated with the star's energy, and, as it happens, your third eye starts to pulsate just like the star itself.
3. Watch as the star's pulsations reach your heart space. Let your heart bask in the healing light of the North Star, absorbing as much of it as possible. Allow this process to unfold naturally. Take your time; don't rush it. When the process is completed, your heart will start pulsating with the North Star's energy.
4. Watch as the triangle of light forms, connecting the three pulsating points into one cohesive geometric shape. One point of the triangle is the North Star, the second point is your third eye, and the last point is your heart space.

Picture the energy of light circulating through this triangle, coursing back and forth between you and the North Star. Familiarize yourself with the energy of the star, allowing it to come and go freely, becoming activated in your body. Let the light travel through the triangle faster and faster until it reaches the speed of light.

5. When you are ready, picture the triangle of light bursting into a trillion smaller North Stars, showering your whole body from the top of your head to the tips of your toes. Allow the tiny North Stars to enter each cell in your body—one North Star per cell. Let each of the tiny stars transform your cells from within. May the healing energy of the star rewire and reframe your whole body, aligning you to your true North, your unique path, your mission in life. Allow the star's energy to settle into your body and stay there for the remainder of your time on Earth.

Now that you are one with the star, it can guide you into your best future yet. Trust this guiding light within; trust yourself to make the right choices. And when in doubt, you can always ask the North Star for answers.

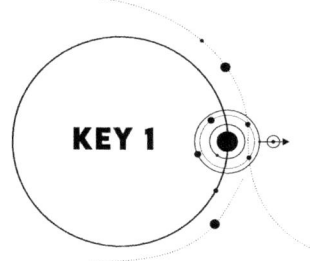

KEY 1

THE FATHER ENERGY, WITHIN AND WITHOUT

All the energy that has ever existed has a source. Energy doesn't appear out of nowhere, and neither does it dissipate into nothing—it simply flows from one state to another, molding and shaping the Universe along the way. Manifestation is a game of mastery—of taking energy and wielding it to create the things you want to see in the world.

Each of you was born with a unique combination of energies—your innate energy pool. This pool is composed of the energies across the full spectrum of the rainbow, all of which represent different aspects of Creation and various facets of your personal power. From this perspective, you are a walking rainbow of light moving through reality while creating it simultaneously.

Not all energetic frequencies are optimal for manifestation, however. Each stream of energy you carry is a specific reflection of Source consciousness and is meant for a unique purpose. Some energies are tuned in to love, others to creation, and still others to survival or enlightenment. Collectively, these energies represent the fullness of who you are. Manifestation energies are represented by two primary colors—yellow and gold. Yet they also form a spectrum of all the hues in between, starting with creamy-yellow and moving through canary and deep yellow to culminate into effervescent pearlized gold. As a naturally born Creator, you have all of these manifestation energies to some degree. However, if you already have them, how come you don't always get what you want in life? How come your manifestation is so slow that it barely feels real?

Your personal power, your confidence level, as well as your manifestation potential all depend on exactly how much yellow-gold energy your personal spectrum contains. And while everyone has some manifestation energy, plenty of people don't have enough. You may not be able to impact how much yellow-gold spectrum energy you came to Earth with, but you can certainly impact what you do with the amount that you have.

The quality and quantity of your yellow-gold spectrum energy directly correlate to your relationship with your biological father. Your father will contribute his manifestation pool to form yours at the point of conception. That is why the ability to manifest (or a lack of thereof) tends to run in families. The energies of the yellow-gold spectrum are quite volatile and are easily depleted. Therefore, it is critical to replenish them. While you are incarnated, the closest source of the yellow-gold spectrum energies is your biological father. That is why the number one precursor to perfect manifestation is a healthy relationship with your father. This way, you can always tap into his energy resource and replenish your own stream. Don't worry, this is a symbiotic relationship—you are not feeding off your dad in a parasitic way. It is a natural flow of energy, and one of the laws of this time-space reality. However, if your relationship with your father is strained or non-existent, you are subconsciously cutting yourself off from getting access to the manifestation energy pool and vastly limiting your ability to have the life you want.

At birth, you were assigned an energetic cord that connects you to your personal well of power. This cord is yellow, and it starts right around your belly button (that is why we don't like it being touched, since everyone who touches our belly button has access to our lifeforce). Your belly button is the gateway to your power—and thus is one of the strongest energy points of your body. The yellow cord connects your solar plexus chakra to your father and his father before him, reaching back right to the very beginning of your ancestry line. But it doesn't stop there. It also connects you to the energy of the Sun—the closest representation of Source energy in the Solar System.

The Sun is your ultimate ally on the road to manifestation. This celestial power can help you achieve anything you want—anything at all if you only allow it to. However, you cannot get to the Sun and truly feel its power coursing through your body unless you first connect to your father. And I don't mean a simple phone call. You might talk to your dad daily while remaining completely unattached to the nurturing and powerful source of his solar plexus.

The number one step on your road to abundance is reconnecting with your biological father and mending and nurturing that relationship. This is your rite of passage—your foundational stone. Forgo this step, and it can be much harder to reach your full manifestation potential. That is why we are starting here. And that is why even if this is the only chapter of this book that you take to heart, you will move much closer to the life you desire.

PRACTICE: RECONNECTING WITH YOUR FATHER

Here is the good news—you can heal your relationship with your dad whether he is alive or not. This practice will even work if you have never met your father. The exercise for today is incredibly simple, even mundane. But it is exceptionally powerful. Today, you will write a letter to your father.

Start your letter by acknowledging the current state of your relationship. Feel free to use the following prompt to start your letter: "Dad, I know that our relationship has been _____ over the years." The impact of this exercise will be directly correlated with what you put in—garbage in, garbage out, so use the following pointers below to help you craft a healing letter.

- △ Be honest and specific in describing the relationship you and your dad have had over the years.
- △ Acknowledge how you feel about your dad today. The good, the bad, and the ugly.
- △ Thank your dad for the three greatest gifts he has given you. The three greatest lessons, or some special talents that you have developed thanks to your dad. His energy is quite literally inside you; it created you, so you most certainly have things to be grateful for.
- △ Think of and write out the three greatest wounds you received from your dad, even if they were unintentional. If you had a great relationship with your father, this might be a very hard section to fill in, but I promise you: unless you get this out in the open and outside of your subconscious, you cannot move forward.
- △ Forgive your dad for everything he did that wasn't a positive influence in your life. Write out the words of forgiveness
- △ Acknowledge that you wouldn't have grown up to be the person you are if it wasn't for your dad's lessons and for the special place he always held in your life. (This is important and true, even for those of you who grew up without your biological father. His energy has been formative in your life, and it is time to acknowledge it.)
- △ Tell your dad that you love him very, very much, and you are proud that he chose you as his child. Tell him that he was a perfect dad for you, and you would not have chosen anyone else for that role.

When you have finished writing your letter, use the following activation practice:

1. Close your eyes for a second and watch the yellow cord that connects you and your father pulsating with beautiful golden energy.
2. See it becoming stronger, thicker, and brighter.
3. See new golden strands appear where there were none before, and watch your connection deepen.
4. See your dad smiling at you, his eyes full of love. See him hug you and tell you that he loves you very much. For it is the truth, and has always been the truth.
5. See this golden cord that connects you to your father stretch and move through time and space, connecting you both to the very core of the Sun—its timeless cosmic energy that permeates everything in the Universe.
6. Feel the energy and the love of your Divine Father in the sky, the source of all your creative energy, coursing and pulsating through your body. This source has enough energy to last you many lifetimes, and it certainly has enough to enable you to manifest whatever you desire in this life.
7. Allow this golden energy to fill your body as if it were a vessel, as if you could hold on to that energy and make it yours. Drink up this beautiful golden elixir until you feel sated and until you are full to the brim. Feel this energy inside your body, inside your muscles, and inside your bones. Remember this feeling of being entirely in sync with your father's energy—within and without—for this is the source of all your power, and your greatest tool on the path to abundance. And know that if you feel full right now, it only gets better from here.
8. If you feel called to do this, read the letter to your father aloud. You can do this whether your dad is alive or not.

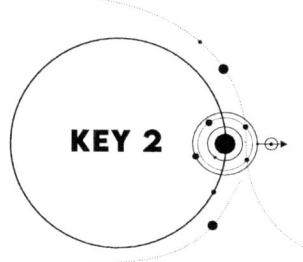

KEY 2

YOUR POWER HAS NOT ONE, BUT TWO SOURCES

The two sources of your manifestation power are ancestral and celestial.

Let's explore your first power source. **Ancestral power** is determined by the genetic energy imprint of your DNA and represents the gift of power left to you by your ancestors. Despite years of DNA research, most of the human genome is still a mystery to science. Since genetic material is a part of every cell in your body, your DNA serves as the primary Law of the Land within, governing things like your weight, health, and phenotype—but it doesn't end there. DNA is responsible for your energetic composition—or the quality and quantity of energy flowing through your Etheric (Energetic) Body. We all start with a set of cards we are dealt at birth, but there are several ways to increase the natural flow of energy through your body regardless of your genetic predisposition. Later in this book we will be addressing some of them, but we have to start with the basics first.

The yellow polarity of the yellow-gold energy spectrum directly impacts how quickly you can achieve goals, the caliber of the goals you set for yourself, and your overall levels of persistence, confidence, and assertiveness. If your yellow energy pool is lacking, you will experience a loss of power related to setting and achieving goals. You may also shy away from ambitious projects and experience scarcity in at least some areas of your life. Understanding the quality and quantity of your yellow energy pool is the first step in assessing what you have to work with and what needs to be improved. Your yellow energy is the fuel that can enable you to move with intention and speed or stop you dead in your tracks. The good news is that you can amplify your natural energy levels with the tips from later chapters.

The second source of your manifesting power is **celestial** in nature. It consists of three major streams:

1. The energy of your Spirit (or Higher Self).
2. The energy of the Sun.

3. The energy of the Source—the greater consciousness that connects everything in the Universe.

This type of energy is translucent gold in color and represents the most potent creative force you can access. Nothing is impossible if you leverage this energy when manifesting. Many of us are deficient in this energy type since the ancient knowledge of connecting to Higher Realms and the Sun consciousness has been neatly tucked away in the libraries of various secret societies or reduced to myth. Reclaiming this energy can be game-changing. It could transform your perception of what's possible overnight. And it is my intention that each and every one of you can connect to and benefit from this abundant stream.

True magic happens when you combine the two energies into one symbiotic stream—the material energy of achievement with the high spectral energy of creation. In today's practice section, we'll be working with these two streams.

PRACTICE: THE TWO GLASSES: ANCESTRAL AND CELESTIAL

Today you'll be working with your inner vision, otherwise known as your imagination. Don't worry about getting this exercise "right." You couldn't get it wrong if you tried—think of this like a mini-meditation, only better.

1. Close your eyes, take three deep, full-lung breaths, and quiet your mind.
2. In your mind's eye, imagine two transparent glasses in front of you. The one on the left contains yellow liquid. The one on the right has golden liquid.
3. Focus on each glass separately. Does it barely contain any liquid, or is it filled to the brim about to spill over? Don't look for the "right" answer—simply observe.

What you see shows how much of each of the two powerful manifestation energies you have. This is a diagnostic of sorts. The size of your glass is your potential—how much you are meant to have under perfect circumstances. The left glass with the yellow liquid represents your ancestral energy and the manifesting power of your DNA. The glass on the right with the golden liquid shows you how much of the higher dimensional creative energy you currently have compared to your full potential.

Now, if your glasses are full to the brim—congratulations! You will be an effective manifestor in no time. If your glasses are close to empty or only half full—don't despair. Working with energy is fairly straightforward. Below I explain how you can replenish each of these energies.

1. Imagine two energy streams similar to waterfalls—one with the yellow-colored energy and the other with the effervescent golden flow.
2. Fill your glasses to the brim using these two powerful streams. Feel the energy entering your body and allow it to take hold there, to find some space where it can stay, and grow roots.
3. Lastly, when both of your glasses are full, picture the two energies floating up and out of your glasses and connecting in a double helix pattern—exactly how the two strands of your DNA connect. This is a very powerful joint stream of energy that is both grounded and limitless.

Keeping the two glasses full is very important. Please bookmark this practice to come back to it at a later date. It is important to refresh this exercise every few months to maintain your most optimal energy state. The energy flow is just that—a flow—and is characterized by high and low tides. Knowing this, it is impossible to fill up the glasses in perpetuity—you will have to perform maintenance work with some level of regularity. Any time one of your glasses gets depleted, just refill it.

This exercise seems very simple, but it is one of the best examples of the spiritual alchemy of manifestation I know, and it is pure, undiluted power.

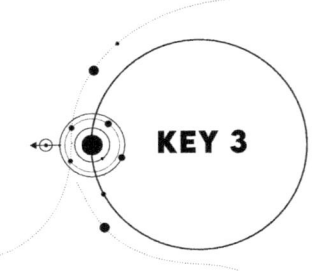

KEY 3

SUN CHILDREN

We, all of us, are Sun Children. It is no coincidence that in our Solar System, every planet revolves around the Sun—it represents the central axis of all movement, all life, and all action. In your journey to becoming an alchemist, the Sun—the Master Manifestor—holds a special place.

Our ancestors knew about the unparalleled, all-sweeping power of the Sun and had numerous rituals to commemorate its energy. They celebrated with dawn, sunset, equinox and solstice ceremonies, as well as Sun Initiation—a ceremonial feast held by many tribal cultures every time a child came of age. Multiple festivities also existed to celebrate the change of the seasons and the Sun's central role in this beautiful spectacle.

Whether we are conscious of this connection or not, our lives still revolve around the Sun. Our crops are nurtured by it, our springs bring us a sense of renewal, and summers promise a healthy dose of vitamin D. Yet we have been taught to think of the Sun as something inanimate—not dissimilar to a piece of furniture, only much larger and, well, hotter.

Did you know that, among other things, the Sun has the power to activate your pineal gland (or third eye)? Now of course, at this point, this knowledge is so well forgotten that most sages are completely unaware of this property of the Sun. For this process to happen, the Sun requires an unobstructed path to the center of your forehead. Yet this generation has been taught to be quite literally scared of the Sun.

Don't believe me? Just look at the wide variety of SPF products in the US and Europe. Yes—SPF blocks the harmful sun rays that have been linked to skin damage, but it also blocks many benefits of the Sun and the energetic exchange it has to offer. Now I am not advocating going SPF-free, but ten minutes a day of unobstructed sun exposure (think morning sun, before 10 a.m.) is equivalent to two cups of espresso plus a dose of healing celestial energy that can empower, protect, and inspire you.

In our fear and misunderstanding of the Sun, we have completely lost our ability to be truly nurtured and supported by it. The Sun is our Celestial Parent; at this moment in time, it displays the planetary father energy—the energy of the pure and all-loving Divine Masculine.

We started this book by addressing your relationship with your biological father—the most immediate masculine energy that gave you birth. The Sun is next in line and definitely not any less significant. If you would like to become the power manifestor you are meant to be, understanding and healing your relationship with the Sun is the inevitable next step.

PRACTICE: DIAGNOSING YOUR RELATIONSHIP WITH THE SUN

Let's start this practice session with a short diagnostic. Below you will be offered some rules of thumb to determine how strong your connection to the Sun is. As you read through each sign, make a note of whether or not it describes you.

Signs that you have a weak or sub-optimal connection with the Sun (you don't have to display all the signs):

- △ You are allergic to the sun or burn easily.
- △ You dislike or are scared of the fire element. You don't like fireplaces or bonfires and don't care for candles.
- △ You have resentment toward your father/grandfather or any other male relative.
- △ You dislike the color yellow and don't wear it.
- △ You dislike or are not drawn to objects/jewelry made of gold.
- △ Your house/apartment has little natural sunlight, and you are okay with it.
- △ You prefer cool places and dislike the summer heat and beach vacations.
- △ You feel tired a lot.
- △ You lack confidence in key areas of your life.

Signs that you have a strong connection with the Sun (you don't have to display all the signs):

- △ Your skin tans easily and evenly.
- △ You have freckles.
- △ Your natural hair color is red.
- △ As a kid, you drew the sun a lot.
- △ You have always had a special affinity toward large cats, especially lions.
- △ You like the smell of sandalwood, citrus, and cedar.

- △ You have a great relationship with your father and other male members of your family.
- △ You like being in the sun and enjoy the summer and hot weather in general.
- △ You like yellow and/or gold objects.

If you have found signs that your connection to the Sun is not entirely optimal, you'll need to do some work using the following practice.

PRACTICE: FORGIVENESS AND SUN CONNECTION

To develop an optimal connection with the Sun, you'll need to use the following steps:

Step 1: Forgive your father for any wrongdoing or trauma he may have caused

Unfortunately, this is not a step you can skip. An effective practice here can be writing down a list of all the things you need to forgive your father for and then burning that list using the flames of a yellow or white candle. As your list burns, feel the pain leaving your body and making room for a new kind of energy—the energy of love and acceptance toward your father.

Step 2: Establish a direct line of communication with the Sun

This practice will require spending a few minutes in a meditative state. It is one of the easiest and most effective practices to nurture and grow your relationship with the Father Sun.

1. Close your eyes, take a few deep breaths, clear your mind from all the clutter of your daily thoughts, and focus on watching your breath enter and leave your body.
2. Imagine standing in a beautiful meadow and being surrounded by nature. The wind is ruffling the leaves of the nearby trees, and you feel completely and utterly safe.
3. Look up into the sky. Do you see the Sun? You should. If you don't see the Sun, you will need to find exactly what object obstructs your view. It might be the

clouds, a veil, or any other random object that may not even belong in the sky. Take time to remove whatever is blocking your Sun—you are completely in command of your energetic field, so you have a right to make any modifications that feel right.

4. Once the Sun is in full view, you should be able to see a golden thread of light between your belly button and the Sun's center. The key to manifesting with the Sun is establishing a healthy circulation of *prana* (life energy) between you. To enable that, we will try a breathing exercise.
5. Take a deep breath in and think of one thing you are grateful to the Sun for. Hold your breath here for a few seconds.
6. As you exhale, send your breath directly to the Sun's core, where all the magic happens. Hold your breath here, watching how your breath's energy turns into golden dust and settles into the inner walls of the Sun.
7. Notice how a ball of light energy starts to form in the center of the Sun.
8. As you breathe in with power and intention, picture how this ball of light enters your chest and settles down in your belly area. Hold your breath for three counts here.
9. Repeat this breathing practice until you feel a slight tingling sensation in your fingers.

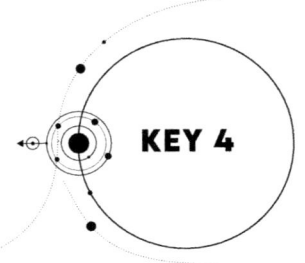

KEY 4

THE UNIVERSE OF TWO SUNS

Did you know that we have not one, but two suns governing our Solar System?[1] There is nothing that quite compares to the power of the two suns, especially when combined. Unfortunately, only a few people are even aware of the second sun, let alone in tune with it. The truth of the second sun was partially known to the Third Reich and was present in some of the regalia of Hitler's regime, albeit this ancient energy and power cannot be used in self-serving ways without massive payback. The true mystery of the second sun can only be revealed to those pure of heart and pure of intention.

The Second Sun, or Black Sun, is a twin sibling of the White Sun—the Sun we are all familiar with. Together they form a binary Solar System—a planetary arrangement with two focal points around which everything else revolves. About 80 percent of all the stars in the Milky Way have twins and revolve around a common center of gravity created by the interaction between their centers of mass. Recently, scientists have found evidence that a mysterious Second Sun was governing the state of affairs in our Solar System.[2,3] And indeed, if you take a look at the facts, certain things about our most immediate cosmic composition don't add up. Think of a leap year, for instance—a poor attempt to fudge the numbers and come up with an approximation of a calendar year. The cosmic math is much, much more precise than that. It may be many decades, if not centuries, before science fully acknowledges the existence of the Second Sun. Still, its energy, if unlocked properly, is one of the greatest assets for anyone looking to build a better life.

---

1   Siraj, A. and Loeb, A. (August 18, 2020). "The Case for an Early Solar Binary Companion." The Astrophysical Journal Letters, 899(2). Retrieved from https://iopscience.iop.org/article/10.3847/2041-8213/abac66

2   Carter, J. (August 18, 2020). "Was Our Sun A Twin? If So Then 'Planet 9' Could Be One Of Many Hidden Planets In Our Solar System." Forbes. Retrieved from https://www.forbes.com/sites/jamiecartereurope/2020/08/18/was-our-sun-a-twin-if-so-then-planet-9-could-be-one-of-many-hidden-planets-in-our-solar-system/?sh=236cdb6c585a

3   Owlcation. (Feb 26, 2021). "The Nemesis Theory: Is There a Second Sun in Our Solar System?" Retrieved from https://owlcation.com/stem/Nemesis-Is-there-a-Second-Sun-in-the-Solar-System

Let's take a closer look at this mysterious star. In truth, the Black Sun is hardly black—rather almost charred purple, like the night sky and stardust combined, and it is powerful, abundant, and full of ancient magic. It is alive with the electric current of deep blue and effervescent purple, and it's rich in life-giving energy, much like its twin. It is the great Creator in the sky, second to none and equal only to the White Sun. Both suns govern the material world—things that have moved from the state of potential to the state of actualized form. In our world of duality, it is important to point out that black doesn't mean bad or evil and certainly has no reference to blood sacrifice and dark magic. Whereas the White Sun represents the day and our conscious mind, the Black Sun represents the night and our subconscious mind. That makes the Black Sun the ruler of dreamscape, healing, intuition, inspiration, rest, rejuvenation, and the collective subconscious. While the White Sun is all about massive action, the Black Sun sets the stage for that action, gathering the resources and strength required for the quantum leap. One is impossible without the other.

Every book on manifestation, to some extent, acknowledges the power of the subconscious in forming our reality. Yet the relationship between the conscious and the subconscious is not well understood. One tactic commonly suggested in manifestation is to change your beliefs by repeating mantras enough times that they "slip into" your subconscious and start helping you manifest the life you want. Repetitions do work, but there is a faster way to fuel manifestation, and that is recognizing and building a connection with your long-lost ally—the Black Sun. The Black Sun governs your subconscious through and through—and contains all the memories and imprints of your past lives, parallel lives, childhood memories, irrational fears, and the "why" behind all of your habits. It truly knows you best. Opening up a direct line of communication between you and your subconscious through the aid of the Black Sun can help you manifest ten times faster. And that is no exaggeration.

PRACTICE: BLACK SUN CONNECTION DIAGNOSTIC

The Black Sun is rooted in mystery, so here are a few of the signs that point to how strong your Black Sun connection is.

Signs that you have a weak or sub-optimal connection with the Black Sun (you don't have to display all the signs):

- △ You have insomnia.
- △ You don't often dream or don't remember your dreams upon waking up.
- △ You have very few or no memories from your early childhood (four years old and younger).
- △ You don't trust your intuition.
- △ You have a hard time making decisions—big and small.
- △ You had to work for everything you have—you never get a "break" from the Universe.

Signs that you have a strong connection with the Black Sun (you don't have to display all the signs):

- △ You have vivid dreams and remember them easily.
- △ You often experience a sense of déjà vu.
- △ Sometimes you experience lucid dreaming.
- △ You have had an out-of-body experience.
- △ You have a strong intuition and sometimes you just "know" things.
- △ You have psychic or healing abilities.
- △ You are left-handed.
- △ You have enough of a strong energy field that technology acts weird around you—perhaps not turning on or becoming glitchy.
- △ People call you "lucky," or you perceive yourself to be lucky—things you want just happen for you sometimes.

PRACTICE: ESTABLISHING YOUR CONNECTION TO THE BLACK SUN

To strengthen your connection to the Black Sun, use the following meditation:

1. Get into a comfortable position and close your eyes. Start with a few deep, slow breaths and let your inner dialogue subside—it will be here when you come back.
2. Imagine staring at a beautiful night sky. It is as black as the deepest shade of onyx with a slight hint of purple. The sky is full of stars. You are far away from

the noise and the lights of the big city, and the night is warm. From here, it feels like you can see the whole of the Milky Way.

3. As you continue to breathe, imagine breathing in the energy and the essence of the stars with each inhale. There is no rush here—the stars have always been and will always be here. Picture your lungs filling with their shimmery calming energy.

4. As you take in the beauty of the night sky, imagine floating up—as if your body was completely weightless. Feel how the night sky envelops you, forming a protective sphere around you.

5. Find yourself inside that sphere, surrounded by the essence of the stars, the wisdom of the galaxy, and the timeless nature of the cosmos. The sphere is not inanimate—it is a living and breathing organism. At first, you don't pay attention to it, but with time you notice small electric currents running through the surface of the sphere—they sparkle with the most beautiful deep blue and purple glow. You feel completely safe and secure, tucked away from all your Earthly troubles.

6. Know that at this moment, you are inside of the Black Sun—connecting with its ancient wisdom and being healed and nurtured by its potent energies. You can share your deepest worries and fears with the Black Sun—it has the power to transmute anything that is no longer serving you. Let it take care of your worries and your troubles. Allow it to show you a perfect path forward. Ask the Black Sun to be your ally, friend, and supporter as you embark on a journey to manifest the best life for you and those you love.

7. When you are ready, ground yourself back on Earth (refer to the Preface). Thank the Black Sun for this healing and beautiful experience, and let it know that you will be back for more healing and more guidance soon.

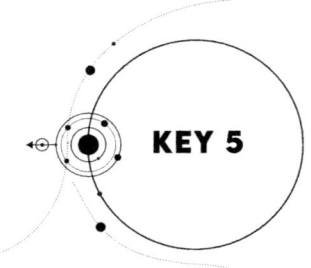

KEY 5

PLANTING THE SEEDS

> *"As above, so below, as within, so without, as the Universe, so the soul."*
>
> –Hermes Trismegistus

An ancient Hermetic principle, one of the Great Laws of our Universe, states, "as above, so below." It speaks to the great synchronicity of everything around us—things big and small. By studying our bodies, we discover the Universe; by discovering the Universe, we learn more about our bodies. Any exploration of the two suns would be incomplete without establishing parallels to your own body. Each planet in the Solar System has a corresponding organ within your body. The organ corresponding to the White Sun is the brain's left hemisphere, and the right hemisphere corresponds to the Black Sun. Collectively, the two suns govern our most vital organ and project forth and react to the life around us.

Despite the brain's two hemispheres being virtually equal in size, we live in a predominantly logical, left-hemisphere-governed world. We need things and concepts to have proof and be backed by science. We thrive when something is measurable; we love phenomena that we can both understand and predict. Of the two suns, the White Sun is currently in a position of power and great visibility. The White Sun rules supreme over the sky—visible in its full glory. We are taught to be logical, not emotional, to perfect our verbal communication, and to back up everything with facts and numbers. Biologically, the White Sun (left hemisphere) rules our right hand—the dominant hand in about 90 percent of the human population. Many of you might find the simple act of brushing your teeth with your left hand incredibly challenging. But is this how things were originally designed? Has this always been the intention?

Things in nature are never random, nor ever simply "wrong." Nature is in balance with itself and all beings around it. So no, nature would have never created the right hemisphere of our brain to be equal in size to the left if we were not meant to use it to the same degree. Let's examine what the right hemisphere is responsible for, paying special attention to what we are sacrificing in a world governed primarily by logic. The right hemisphere is responsible for your creativity, imagination, emotions, arts, intuition, insight, and sense of connectedness to the world around you. But most importantly, and this is where the first veil of mystery falls, your right hemisphere is the gateway to your subconscious mind. It operates according to a specific set of rules and, when understood properly, is just as easy to work with as your conscious mind.

Let's finish up with our science exploration, shall we? Another vital part of our supercomputer brain—the corpus callosum—serves as connective tissue between the hemispheres, bringing them into one cohesive unit. Or at least, in theory, it does. Currently, within an average human, the flow of information is mostly one-sided: the information moves from the conscious mind to the subconscious mind (or from left to right). What's missing is the opposite flow—or the subconscious mind feeding the conscious mind so the two could truly understand each other. Enlightenment, for one, is impossible unless the two sides of the brain are working completely in sync. The pineal gland—the seat of enlightenment and heightened awareness—is located right in the middle between the hemispheres. For it to get activated, two streams of energy are required—the left stream and the right stream. In most of us, the stream from the right hemisphere isn't potent enough to activate the gland, and thus, the third eye remains unopened.

As we move forward in our exploration of the energetic forces that fuel manifestation, it is important to unlock the power of your Black Sun (right hemisphere), as well as the corpus callosum (connective tissue), and let them work for you, not against you, to create the life you want. For some of you, this might involve accidentally opening your third eye. Consider yourself warned.

PRACTICE: ACTIVATING THE BRAIN'S RIGHT HEMISPHERE

One of the precursors to fast and effective manifestation is having both of your brain's hemispheres operating at full capacity. By virtue of your existence on Earth today, you have an underutilized right hemisphere. To revive your relationship with the Black Sun, you will need to force your right hemisphere to become more active. One way to do this is to challenge yourself. Pick an activity you do every day and relearn to do it with your left hand. Every day find more and more ways of how to use your hands interchangeably.

As time goes by and your left hand becomes more equipped to do daily tasks, you will start noticing real shifts in your body and even your mood. You will feel more inspired to create things, you will start becoming more intuitive, and your quality of sleep will improve. And like I said before, you will be a much more powerful manifestor.

If your left hand is already the dominant one—that's great! For you, the practice is exactly the reverse. Either way, you have to get to a place where you have equal command of both of your hands—that is the true key to unlocking your full potential.

PRACTICE: THE BLACK SUN SUBCONSCIOUS-ACTIVATING MEDITATION

In this simple exercise, you will be planting the seeds—uploading the codes of what you want to your subconscious. Using this meditation can encourage both of your brain's hemispheres to work day and night to help manifest your desires. In this instance, one plus one equals ten; such is the power of this connection. This practice also works on strengthening your corpus callosum. Where things generally break down is in the communication between the hemispheres (the two suns). Like all twins, they don't always get along and don't always want to talk to each other, so we need to clear up the pathways and restart that communication. Feel free to repeat this practice once per week for three weeks to solidify the connection.

Before going into this meditation, get complete clarity on the exact object or event that you want to manifest in your life. After this meditation, your desired outcome will become a part of your subconscious and will start attracting people and events into your life almost immediately. Having clarity upfront is extremely important.

You'll also want to make sure you are well rested before doing this practice. This is a cornerstone (foundational) manifestation practice, and it will have tremendous power if you do it properly. You don't want to go into this exercise if you feel sleepy, sad, or upset about something, so ideally, complete it first thing in the morning.

1. Lie down or find a comfortable sitting position. Close your eyes and focus on your breathing. As you inhale, do so in three stages: first, inhale into your belly, then your ribcage, and lastly into your chest area. Hold your breath here for

three seconds, then exhale completely. Repeat five to six times. This will help you get into an active but calm state that is perfect for manifestation.

2. Imagine floating in beautiful dark waters. They are deep and warm and feel familiar to you. As you look up, you see a vast starry sky all around as far as you can see, and you feel completely safe and secure just to be floating in these nourishing, welcoming waters and quietly observing the stars. You feel like a small child, but also infinite, almost eternal. Time doesn't exist here. Nothing is chipping away at your inner peace. There is no need to rush anywhere—no place that you need to be other than here.

3. In this moment, you know that you are surrounded by a force much larger than yourself—one that always was and always will be. Relish in this connection. This isn't new to you at all; you were once born from a place that felt just like this—infinite, beautiful, safe. As you float, making no effort to stay above water, you remember that there is a wish you have—your heart's desire, something that you know will make your life better. What is it? Think of it at this moment. What is it that you would like to manifest?

4. As the images and words are forming in your head, let them settle in and become solid. Using one of your fingers, write out exactly what you want to accomplish across the vast starry sky. Use bold strokes and notice how every word you write appears in the sky in the most radiant gold script imaginable. Your words glow, shimmer, and come alive. What you just wrote has a frequency—an energetic imprint that is one of a kind. And the vast sky welcomes that vibration fully—it rejoices in this newly found direction. It wants to help you get what you want and pledges its allegiance to your cause.

5. Watch as the golden words you wrote in the sky solidify and become an integral part of this beautiful scenery. They are now forever etched within your subconscious and are starting to come true. You want to thank the dark waters and the starry sky for being your allies in this, for choosing to help you, and for being in this with you. Their power is now yours. Let yourself stay in this moment for as long as it feels good, admiring the landscape and the new frequency you brought here.

6. When you are ready to depart, picture your body starting to float upward toward an opening in the sky. In a few moments, you reach a point of demarcation. As the starry sky opens up, it gives way to another sky full of sunlight and fluffy clouds. It's like the two skies live together side by side but are separate from one

another—you can see when one ends and the other begins. It is completely up to you to make them one—to make them whole.

7. Feel free to take out a brush and blur the demarcation lines. See how one sky gently merges with the other—they are twins, really, not a threat to each other. See how the two skies are happy with your making changes; they never liked being apart and are stronger together. Now they can communicate with each other even when you are gone. Now they can help you get what you want.

8. Notice that as the two skies continue to merge, you start seeing the same exact words you wrote on the starry sky appear in the blue sky—an exact replica and an exact match. The ink here is deep purple and shimmery, and it looks beautiful in the clear day sky. Now your intention is alive in both worlds—the world of your awake state and the world of your dream state.

9. Thank the day sky for agreeing to be your ally in this and for accepting this new frequency. You have just gotten yourself another powerful supporter. You no longer have to walk the walk alone. There are at least two massive cosmic powers on your side.

10. Stay here in this moment, soaking it in for as long as it feels good. When you are ready, return to your awake state.

11. Don't rush to get back to your daily activities. Rather, take out a notepad and write down the words that you wrote in the starry sky. This is the living and breathing code of your manifestation, and it has true magical power. Keep it in your house where you can see it. Every time your eyes come in contact with this phrase, the energy of your manifestation will keep amplifying.

Congratulations, friend. Today you have planted the first seeds of your new life.

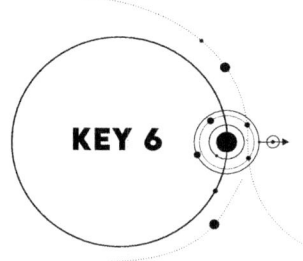

KEY 6

THE MAZE OF THE MULTIVERSE

The structure of the Universe is ineffably more complex than meets the eye. And while you don't need to understand it fully to be an effective manifestor, some concepts are too important to bypass.

At any point in time, multiple versions of you exist in the Universe. Collectively, they form your unique learning experience within a particular incarnation that will eventually go on your permanent record. However, while you are still in this incarnation, they represent the potentiality of all your life choices. Whenever you face a difficult or life-altering decision, you don't actually decide one way or another—your soul chooses both. From your limited perspective, it may seem you move toward one potentiality; however, your soul is keeping a tab on both, choosing to experience them simultaneously.

FIGURE 1: THE MULTIVERSE

As life choices accumulate and we get older, our soul experiences thousands of parallel paths simultaneously, each of which leads to different learnings and outcomes (see Figure 1). Each of these paths requires energy to maintain and nurture. So, in essence, your soul creates more and more splits as you move forward in life. Some directions become obsolete, so the soul erases them, as they offer no further evolution or expansion. The energy freed up in that process then rejoins the original source reserved for this incarnation and awaits further splitting in the future.

When we die, all the learnings from this incarnation are uploaded to our oversoul and stored in our personal knowledge bank—or subconscious. The soul also chooses the most optimal path lived and uploads that path to the *Akashic* field—an informational field of all that was and all that is (the Universal knowledge bank). So in the future, when you refer to a "past" life, you will have only one record per incarnation and not multiple. In other words, at death, the soul chooses the most optimal path from the ones lived to remember while the rest are deleted.

The trick with manifestation is that it requires quite a significant amount of energy, and most likely, you will need to tap into the same resource used to create all these parallel lives. The more parallel lives, the less potential energy you have to manifest what you want in this particular aspect of reality.

I know this information is a lot to process. But don't worry—you don't have to understand this fully or even believe it to be able to use this awareness to your advantage. When working with the multiverse reality, there are two important truths to keep in mind:

1. In the multiverse, everything happens simultaneously—there is no future or past. Everything that happens has already happened as soon as you make a particular choice. It might not seem this way because you are too immersed in the game to see it clearly. However, it doesn't make it any less true.
2. There is not one or default direction for your incarnation. You are experiencing a few potentialities simultaneously; despite your conscious mind having you believe otherwise. Think of an ex. There are at least a few parallel lives your soul is currently experiencing where you are still together. Did you lose a loved one? There is a parallel life out there where that person is still alive.

The reason these principles are important to consider is that they expand your perception. The truth is that this life and everything in it is exceptionally malleable. Remember: your soul's primary interest is to experience as many things as possible, and the multiverse represents just the toolbox to make it happen. Because of this multiverse reality, there is a version of you somewhere that already received what you are currently trying to manifest. There can be no other way— there is a version of you somewhere in the vast consciousness of the multiverse that "made it." And because this version exists, it can be amplified. The following exercises will show you exactly how to do it.

PRACTICE: THE GREAT MERGING EXERCISE

This is a powerful exercise that will free up your energy so you can funnel it toward manifesting the life you want.

1. Get into a comfortable position and close your eyes. Use slow, deliberate breaths to quiet your mind. Notice how with each breath you feel more and more at peace. Allow yourself to notice the power oozing from your body. You are power. You are infinity. You are Universal energy. You are in control of your life. This multiverse exists for you—it was created as a tool for your personal evolution. And because it was created to serve you, you are its master.
2. Notice that you are standing in the center of a circle. Just like the rays of the Sun, multiple paths emanate from the circle in all possible directions. These paths are different; each of them is beautiful in its own way.
3. One of these paths is calling your name. It is lit with the most beautiful etheric glow. Examine this path and notice that what makes it different is that at the end of the path, there is an object or event you desire so much. This is the path that leads you to manifesting what you want. This path feels right. It feels good to you in a way that the other paths don't.
4. Working with the multiverse is like working with modeling clay. It is extremely flexible and can take any shape you'd like. As you are standing in the center of the circle—a crossroads of sorts—notice that all the other paths don't lead you to your desired outcome. Remember that each of these paths is currently chipping away at your energy stream. From this place of power, from this place of being fully in charge, order the rest of the paths to collapse into one—watch as they get glued together and merge to become whole. The distance between them disappears, and as they become one, you notice that the process frees up a great amount of energy.
5. Notice how this energy starts to form itself into a sphere at the top of your head.
6. Now you see only two paths—the one where you have manifested all you could possibly want in this life, and the other path, a merge of all the undesired paths.

Take the two paths and merge them together once more—making sure the version you desire ends up on the top. It feels like placing one sheet of white paper over the other—picture how the two paths are merging and how the seams of them become one.

7. Now you are standing in front of the only path available to you—you have condensed your multiverse and have declared one path as your desired future. Focus on the sphere of your energy at the top of your head and allow that energy to power your desired path further—allow it to illuminate and solidify this path. See yourself taking the first step on this path and know in your heart of hearts that today you made that first step. Know that this journey must end with you getting what your heart desires. There is literally **no other way**.

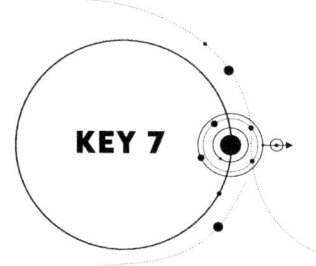

KEY 7

THE POWER OF NOTHING

> *"I begin with nothingness. Nothingness is the same as fullness. In infinity, full is no better than empty. Nothingness is both empty and full."*
>
> —Seven Sermons to the Dead, Basilides/Carl Jung

Everything that ever existed in the Universe came as a convergence of two core energies—the feminine and the masculine. The world as we know it wouldn't exist without either of these energies.

The Great Masculine is the energy of action, achievement, matter, growth, the great conquering, and the great taking. The material world is impossible without the miracle of masculinity. In manifestation, masculine energies are paramount; they are the building blocks to creating a life you want and deserve. The Great Masculine takes the uncharged energy of potentiality and turns it into something tangible that you can enjoy. So far, in all the previous chapters, we have been working with the masculine energies—the energies that take. Where does the Great Feminine fit into this picture?

The Great Feminine energies are those of pure potential. They are the great everything (ether) and the great nothing (*nihil*). The feminine energies exist before the energy of form and factor—both micro and macro. All things are possible and impossible through the Great Mother womb of our Universe. In cosmology, they call it "the void" or the "black hole," but on the energetic level, it is the feminine source of life that is always available to you. Just like you need masculine energies to bring something into existence and give it direction, you need feminine energies to remove any resistance that might be in the way. The mysterious feminine is the masterful remover of obstacles.

So what is in the way of your achieving what you want? There is always specific energy that stands between you and your desired outcome. For the sake of clarity, let's call it "counter energy." It may take different form factors— fear, doubt, worry, helplessness, and the like. The end result is the same—it prevents you from moving quickly or from moving at all. Counter energy is a test, and it's testing the strength of your resolve. You might start out excited about manifesting the life of your dreams, but as time goes by, counter energies take over, and you start procrastinating, doubting, and worrying your way out of achieving what you want. The counter energies are real, and they are the number one reason for not getting what you want. Many choose to fight counter energies with bravado. People spend their time downplaying the impact of these counter forces until they feel completely overwhelmed by them, enough so that they just give up and settle for the status quo. Many of the counterproductive energies described above are ruled by fire. When you are pouring more force (read: fire) into trying to overcome them, in essence you are attempting to cure fire with fire—which creates a complete state of desolation and a barren terrain. The energies of resistance need to be addressed with water—and that is the prerogative of the Great Feminine.

The best remedy against counter energies is the energy of nothing. You heard me right. The energy of nothing is the absolute and complete zeroing out of all energy streams. It is the descent into the dark Great Mother womb where nothing matters, yet everything does. And there is no better cure for your doubt, fear, and worry—the biggest assassins of human dreams. The following two exercises will help you overcome your personal counter energies and move toward seamless and barrier-free manifestation.

PRACTICE: THE GAME OF ABSOLUTE ZERO

Despite knowing that fears and worries are irrational, no amount of physical convincing could cancel them out. Remember, they come from the great subconscious and thus don't take well to the gibberish of the active conscious mind. Whenever you feel taken over by the fear of failing or not getting what you want, practice going to the state of zero. Here's how it works.

1. Close your eyes. Breathe in and breathe out freely, without controlling any aspect of your breathing. Don't constrain your breath—this wondrous lifeforce given to you by the Universe.

2. Imagine standing at the intersection of ley lines (power lines of the matrix). Below your feet are vertical and horizontal lines of light stretching as far as your eyes can see. You are located amidst the sea of energy lines and intersections.

3. Allow yourself to feel the negative emotions that may be in the way of your achieving what you want. These emotions have a frequency—unbeknownst to you, they have taken you to this particular intersection of power lines. This location has a unique set of coordinates, and chances are, you have been here before. Chances are, there have been many instances in your life when fear or doubt stopped you from getting what you want and paralyzed you in this exact spot. You know this place—everything about it is familiar, like a deep, dark, suffocating den, both recognizable and off-putting.

4. Make a note of how this place feels, but don't allow yourself to stick around here. Instead, imagine an invisible wind lifting your body up into the air and carrying you away from this place. This wind is powerful, and yet it feels safe to be completely taken over by it. And so this wind takes you to a place far, far away. As you approach this place, you know that it is a point of zero. A point of nothing—no emotion, no feeling, and no counter force. This is the Great Zero of our Universe. Allow the wind to plant you firmly here, with your feet on the ground.

5. You have arrived at the Great Nothing—a place that transcends all fear. The energy of zero is exceptionally liberating—both cooling and warming all at once. Let it stream up your limbs and penetrate your body. Let it replace any other energy that was there before. Cement this feeling into your bones, in your muscles, in every organ, and in every cell in your body. Give your body permission to hold on to these energies for as long as possible. Feel free to repeat this practice as often as necessary.

6. To ground fully after the practice, allow yourself to take a few deep breaths. Wiggle your fingers and toes and only then open your eyes.

Any time you get paralyzed by fear or stopped by doubt, you can come here for the gift of a great cleanse. Here you can be nothing, a nobody. From a place of complete zero, you can finally find the strength to be someone, to be you. Bring this feeling to mind, or even create a word—a shortcut of sorts—that will quickly take you to this spot any time you need it. Feel and savor the bliss of *nihil*, and may it become one of your greatest guides on this path to your perfect manifestation.

PRACTICE: SIMPLE CHAKRA ALIGNMENT FOR MANIFESTATION

If you want to amplify the state of complete zero and thus complete liberation, try this simple chakra practice. You can perform it by itself or in combination with the previous exercise.

1. In a meditative state, with your eyes closed, notice the vertical axis that runs through your whole body alongside your spine. This axis is your personal center, where your personal power is concentrated. Think of this axis as your zero state—a state without any distortions inside your energy field.
2. Picture yourself having seven horizontal lines running through your body—each going through one of your major chakras (see Figure 2).

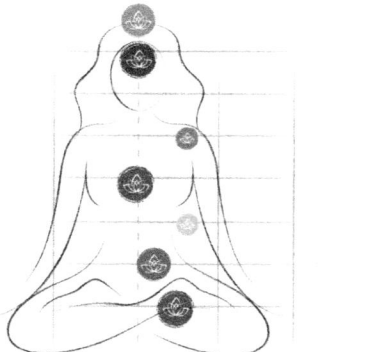 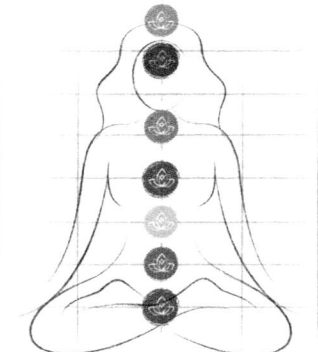

FIGURE 2: CHAKRA ALIGNMENT

3. Start with your root chakra at the base of your spine. Notice where it is located in relation to your spinal cord. Is it to the right, to the left, or right in the center? The correct zeroed-out, healthy chakra state should be aligned with your spine—right in the center. If your chakra is located slightly to the left or right, it is out of alignment. Don't worry: simply move the chakra toward the center of your body and toward the point of zero coordinates for this chakra—a point of release of all the pressure within this chakra.

4. Repeat this process with each of your chakras in turn, finishing with your crown chakra at the top of your head. You may notice that some chakras are more out of alignment than others. This is completely normal and might change for you day to day. The beauty of this practice is you don't have to understand why a particular chakra is out of alignment—you can just simply bring it back into equilibrium.

Upon completing this exercise, you may notice that the energy is flowing differently in your body. It may start flowing freely, in a completely unrestricted way. This is your most powerful and healthiest state. Your manifestation from this place of alignment will have special power and momentum. Enjoy!

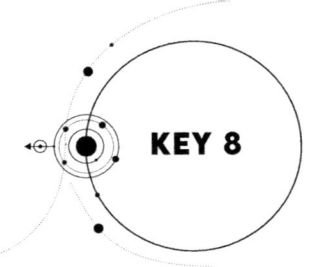

KEY 8

THE LAW OF THREE

In the grand scheme of life, there are only three things that matter for impactful manifestation. If you get them right, you will never need to pick up a book on manifestation ever again. Drumroll, please. The three things are:

- △ Clarity.
- △ Energy.
- △ Faith.

It's that simple. The devil, as always, is in the details. Let's examine each of these aspects separately.

CLARITY

I mean EXTREME clarity of what you want. Forget approximations and rounding errors. The Universe is a complex mathematical system that operates with the precision of a Swiss watch. Unless you are surgically specific, you might spend years manifesting a house in Arkansas instead of Hawaii. So indeed, be careful what you wish for—in more ways than one. The Universe might not fill in the gaps in your favor. If you start with a vague idea of what you want, you may get a poor and imprecise imitation of your desired outcome. What's even worse: it may take you years to realize this. So yeah—"more money" could just mean $1,000 more, just as "a pretty house" might mean a new set of floral wallpapers in your old home, or "more free time" might mean spending a month in a hospital bed with all the time in the world to spare. With manifestation, you must be specific. However, getting clarity might be harder than you think. As part of getting clarity, challenge yourself to write at least a couple pages of specifications that describe every aspect of what you'd like to manifest. If there is an image of what you want, make sure to include that in your spec.

Example: "I would like my business to grow by 100 employees and $50M in annual revenue. I would like my office to look like [*insert specific details*] and have custom vegan leather furniture with fluffy pink pillows. I would like us to have over 10,000 happy customers that use our products every day. I would love for us to have offices in New York, Texas, and Florida. I want articles written about us in *Forbes* and *Business Insider*."

You get the idea—you want to be extremely specific. No detail is too small. As you are painting a picture of exactly what you want for yourself, the Universe gets a front row seat into how you are thinking and can hone in on the exact aspects of what you want. This is step one.

ENERGY

This is where things generally go sideways. By the time we reach adulthood, we are often weighed down by a slew of expectations, responsibilities, and disappointments that collectively limit our creative energy. Think of your energy as your bank account that has a balance. Without any savings in reserve, it is hard to put a down payment on a new house. Energy is the primary currency of the Universe, and before you can attract what you want, know that you will have to pay for it with your energy.

Energy is a complex subject, and by using the practices in the previous chapters, you have started recouping yours. The more energy you have, the faster you can move toward achieving your goals. However, your energy needs to be targeted toward achieving a specific thing, or it will get dispersed and scattered. Later in the book, I will give you the tools to direct your energy and fully align with what you are trying to achieve. We will also free your energy from any spots where it may be stuck and unable to serve you.

FAITH

Alas, this one would require true mastery. Our logical brains are wired to only believe things that we can find the physical proof of. But manifestation works in reverse—first, you have to believe, then you can receive. The challenge here doesn't lie in having faith once; it requires you to maintain faith for a prolonged amount of time, like a slow-burning candle that cannot go out. Later I share the cultivating habits and mental constructs that will help you maintain high levels of faith despite outside circumstances.

PRACTICE: THE KEY OF ASCESIS

Most of you will choose to bypass this practice as it is indeed not easy. And yet it is one of the most ancient and potent practices that can enable you to liberate massive amounts of your energy. An *ascesis* is a discipline that you adopt willingly, and it consists of giving something up. Usually, this something is an activity, a pastime, or a substance that you really like (or are even potentially addicted to). As you give up a thing or activity you enjoy or do regularly, you enter a ninja mode where you become a true energy alchemist. If you feel tired, experience a lack of energy, or find it hard to find motivation but you are dead set on manifesting the life of your dreams, adopting an *ascesis* is a perfect place to start.

Some examples of the things you could give up: coffee, alcohol, red meat, smoking, sugar, gluten, gossip, social media, or watching TV before bed. Please don't drop any habits that actually serve you—for instance, don't stop working out or drinking plenty of water. Generally, the energy is freed up when you give up something you have known you should give up anyway. Every so-called vice claims massive amounts of your energy, which, when released, can significantly speed up your manifestation process.

As you select an *ascesis*, make it count. You want to commit to it for a prolonged amount of time, ideally 90 days. The more you are attached to the object/activity you are giving up, the better. This level of attachment is completely correlated to the amount of trapped energy you can free up. For instance, if you somewhat like chocolate but are crazy about fizzy drinks, give up the fizzy drinks. You will thank me later.

Once you adopt an *ascesis*, make a pact with the Universe that whatever energy is liberated in the process must go toward fueling your manifestation. Then watch what happens—you are bound to notice rewards from the Universe if you stick to your *ascesis*. You might get an unexpected gift or a piece of great news. *Ascesis* really makes magic happen, and it starts working within days.

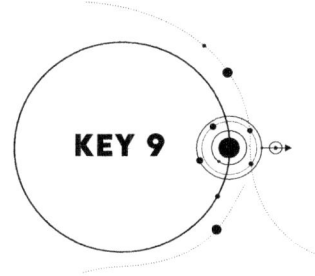

KEY 9

THE QUANTUM LEAP

One of the greatest impediments to success is time. You see, humanity as a species is not very patient. Yet, from early childhood, it is ingrained in our brain that "good things take time." But do they?

Anyone who is anyone in the field of spirituality will tell you that time is an illusion. Time doesn't exist. Yet it feels real. Not only that, but we seem to have ample evidence that time not only exists, but also governs our lives. We never have enough of it, we are worried about being late, and frankly, we feel we can only take so much of it for things we actually enjoy (just think about the fact the weekend is only two days long). In the world we live in, time is perpetually in charge—and we are mere followers. And yet, what *IS* time?

Time is a construct of a material world. For many of you, the idea that we live in the matrix will not be new. From a higher perspective, worlds like ours are flat—they are almost too rigid, so the construct of time exists as an artificial additive to make a rigid reality more fluid. If you could see this world for what it truly is, you would see a very low resolution computer simulation. Worlds like ours are hard to maintain as they require plenty of rudimentary and uninspiring mathematical equations to upkeep. Here black is black and white is white. You see, higher forces that created this world do not enjoy this type of duality. They are above that, so they actually left many gaping holes in the programming code of our world. And to make it less visible to us, the participants, they have invented time—a construct that helps everything flow better and hides any inconsistencies.

What if I told you that your manifestation happened in an instant? That it doesn't require a thing called "time" to materialize? Your Higher Self is not used to waiting for what it wants—once the desire has been formulated and clarity has been achieved, it can get what it wants immediately. When you desire something, a version of it is instantly created in a collector cell—a random section of the matrix that tracks newly created objects or phenomena. As a player in this grand computer game, you were given the right to create what you see fit—for yourself and others. Manifestation, even in this third-dimensional world, is instant. What takes "time" is matching up your set of coordinates with a set of coordinates of the object you have manifested. Sometimes the two are very far removed indeed. The manifestation process is a gradual movement from sector A—where you are today—to sector X—a matrix cell containing what you have just manifested.

And so we come full circle. What takes time is not the act of manifestation, but the act of moving from one sector of the matrix to another, believing that you can indeed have what you want. For instance, if you wanted to manifest a single white rose for yourself, it would take you less "time" to do than manifesting $1 billion. Do you know why? Because your logical brain finds the rose an easier target and thus easier to believe in. Time, in its turn, is just a variable that reflects the strength and quality of your faith.

To recap: "time" is an artificial construct. There is nothing real about it. It is simply a form factor that helps our otherwise clunky reality feel more seamless and logical. Since time is artificial, we can choose to collapse chunks of it when it serves us. Through the use of portals, we can collapse the construct of time and artificially speed things up. All we need is to have the right tools and to believe that we are in charge of this game called life.

PRACTICE: THE QUANTUM PORTAL TECHNIQUE

Portals are the keys to the matrix. Some portals open doors; others can take you into higher dimensions or lead to hidden knowledge. Then there are very special portals that can help erase whole sections of the matrix. Today we will be working with exactly that kind of portal. The end goal is to minimize the distance between you and what you want.

1. Close your eyes and imagine that you are standing on a small island amidst a vast ocean.
2. Look around and notice that this ocean is full of many islands—some empty and others containing different objects. Every object is someone's desire. As you examine the different islands, you notice that one of them has your heart's desire—the exact object or event you are trying to manifest. The island is far away from where you currently are, and you feel like it might take you a lot of time to reach it.

3. Notice that there are about ten different islands that separate you and the island that contains your desire. Imagine that there is a white sphere of energy in the sky. This sphere is quite large and has a mirror-like surface, and you can see the ocean and all the islands reflected in it.
4. Notice how the sphere is starting to open up, like the petals of a flower, forming an opening in the very center of itself. You can feel a very special kind of power emanating from this sphere. "The world eater," they call it, "the great eraser of matter." Yet it doesn't feel scary. Just like vultures exist to cleanse the earth from sick and dead animals, this portal removes obstacles and obsolete matrix sectors.
5. Feel a great power starting to emanate from the portal and watch as it sucks a whole sector of the matrix into itself: the ten islands that separated you and the island with your heart's desire are quickly absorbed into the hungry belly of the portal. In their place, there is nothing—just empty white space.
6. Notice how the ocean closes in on itself, bringing the island with your heart's desire closer to you, through time and space. Now you are just a step away from what you want—you have never been this close. It is so close that you can almost stretch out your arm and touch it.
7. Jump onto the island and walk up to the thing you desire. Observe it carefully. Feel it becoming yours. Feel a thread of light connecting you to what you want. Notice how the thread is becoming stronger. See how you are powering it with your energy and how nothing can keep you apart from it any longer. Notice time and space disappear; know that nothing is separating you from the object of your desire. Time is an illusion and has always been. You have already manifested your heart's desire. Now it must be yours—there is no other way.

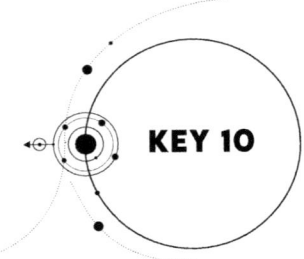

KEY 10

FINDING YOUR ORIGINAL SOUND

Each of us has a unique code—a sound, a vibration, that makes us not only special but also completely indispensable in the grand quantum plan of existence. No two people sound (read: vibrate) exactly the same. Your personal sound vibration is innate—you come into this body and into this world already possessing it. It is like a vibratory thread that mimics the vibrations of your Higher Self, the "true you," in this much denser world.

Through conditioning and trauma, you learn to bury your personal sound vibration under a thick layer of sediment that masks who you truly are. When masked, your original sound vibrations lose their potency and power, in essence becoming obsolete. This creates two potential issues.

First, everything in nature is created to recognize and respond to you based on your personal sound. If your vibration is true, nature can be your greatest ally—it can heal, restore, and guide. But when you mask your vibration, nature cannot provide for you in a way that would fully meet your needs. You may receive healing at face value instead of getting what you actually need—like a perfectly healthy actor being treated for cancer because their character is sick with it.

Second, your vibration is meant to point you to your true north—it is a built-in compass and a powerful navigation tool. So when it is broken, you pursue the wrong ideals and goals. Worse still, you are convinced you're on the path because it takes time, sometimes many years, for the masked frequency to reveal itself and start course-correcting.

Finding your personal sound is not unlike finding your voice. Only while speaking is an act of will, vibrating at your own sound frequency is completely effortless. Unfortunately, too many have forsaken their unique sound to fit in. Too many have adopted the sound of the collective—the bland, uninspiring frequency of the grand average—in an attempt to be accepted. Yet, the collective sound cannot (and does not) define you. It cannot fill you up or make you feel like you are on your path. When you are not vibrating at your own frequency—the frequency that is in harmony with your

Higher Self—you are OFF the path. And someone who is off their own path struggles with manifesting even the simplest things in the material world.

True power is knowing your personal sound and being able to use it in your daily life.

PRACTICE: FINDING YOUR ORIGINAL SOUND

Finding your own innate vibration or your original sound can be incredibly impactful in enabling you to live the life you want.

1. Close your eyes and focus on your breathing. Let the breaths flow in and out smoothly, without effort.
2. Imagine you are surrounded by ether—the great everything. It feels like being in a vacuum, like floating in a transparent viscose substance. Ether is a great truth serum—it enables your innate vibrations to come through without any obstacles.
3. Notice that your body is becoming transparent, and you can observe it from a distance, like a silent onlooker.
4. What comes through now is your personal matrix—a blueprint of your body, the way it currently stands. The matrix is silver in color and forms an outline of your body with its thin thread. Looking at yourself this way is like looking at a version of you made entirely of silver light. This is your current essence in this lifetime.
5. Now, if you focus hard enough, you should hear a sound that your body matrix emanates. It might be a single note repeated in perpetuity or a complete song. Tune into that sound. Listen to your current vibration. Do you like this sound? Is it pleasant to your ear? Does it feel right?
6. Now look around and notice another version of you close by—not dissimilar, but woven by a golden thread instead. This version of you is the original blueprint. The one that your Higher Self intended for you to have in this lifetime. This version of you hasn't gone through any negative conditioning or trauma. This pure version of you also has a sound. Can you hear it? Is it different from the sound your body currently emanates? Take a few moments to be present to this sound, to feel it reverberating inside your body.

7. Your original vibration, your true sound, always points you in the direction of your greatest abundance—your true personal north. If you prefer the sound of your original blueprint, you now have a chance to tune your current sound to match its original vibration. All you need to do is take the golden blueprint of your body and lay it over your silver blueprint, placing one frequency on top of the other. Notice how your true sound becomes your *only* sound. Notice how the two aspects of you intertwine and form one integral whole—one mind, one body, and one soul. Remember your true Divine sound—the song of your soul.

Anytime you feel unsure about the direction you should take or worry about making a bad decision, return to this place, to this sound, and it will show you the way.

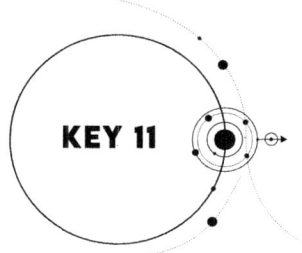

KEY 11

THE STACKING PRINCIPLE

> *"THE ALL is MIND; The Universe is Mental."*
>
> —The Kybalion

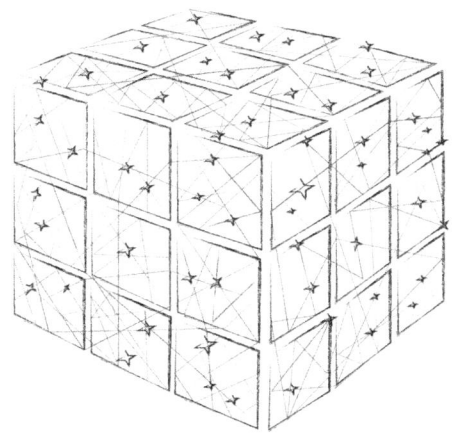

FIGURE 3: THE RUBIK'S CUBE OF THE MATRIX

The matrix is like a giant Rubik's Cube consisting of multiple cube-like sectors differentiated by the level of their collective energy emanations. Simply put, it consists of sectors that are arranged in a particular order with lower dimensions located at the bottom of the cube and higher dimensions at the top (see Figure 3). The matrix operates according to a set of programmatic rules—not unlike a supercomputer. Everything that ever existed in the matrix was at one point programmed by a System Architect. Thus, every aspect of the Universe—from how the leaves grow on a tree to how the planets revolve around the Sun—operates according to a set of precise mathematical equations. While a bit complicated to understand, knowing this simple truth is instrumental in manifestation. Here is why: everything that was at one point programmed can be rewritten. And being the one in charge of your personal sector of the matrix—your personal cube—you have just the set of keys to make it happen.

Everything in the Universe is Divinely geometrical. Every phenomenon can be reduced to a single number or mathematical sequence. Every angle, every surface, and every vector is intentional, precisely cut, and planned to a tee. It is at the intersection of complete chaos and perfect geometric symmetry that we exist. Due to the mathematical precision of the world, it becomes infinitely moldable if we use the same tools that went into creating it in the first place.

Welcome to the Stacking Principle—your new favorite life hack and the shortcut that works. Every. Single. Time. The Stacking Principle is about compartmentalizing. Once you compartmentalize something, energetically, you literally put it in a box (or a cube inside the matrix). You define and separate it from the rest of existence. Once you do that, you can easily replace it with another cube, completely erase the cube from existence, or duplicate it as you see fit. This is like a very adult game of Legos—and in this game, you always win.

PRACTICE: REMOLDING EXISTENCE

Today we'll be working with the different sectors or cubes within the matrix. Remember: these instructions are very precise. Follow them as closely as you can to ensure the best results.

1. Visualize your current circumstances around the situation you'd like to change and place them inside the black cube (see Figure 4). Make sure that all of your emotions around your current circumstances are placed inside of this cube. This is your current cell of the matrix, or what you commonly refer to as "the present." Remember, "the present" is no more "real" to the matrix than the imaginary sector you'll envision in the next step. It is only more "real" from a limited human perspective.

CURRENT REALITY  **DESIRED REALITY**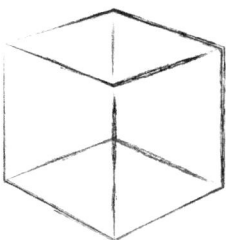

FIGURE 4: CURRENT AND DESIRED REALITY CUBES

2. Imagine your desired reality or outcome and place it inside a large transparent cube (refer to Figure 4 above). Get very specific about what you want to bring forth. Are you dreaming of a new apartment? Get specific about what kind of apartment it is—how many rooms, does it have a view, does it get sunlight, do the windows face south? You want to spend a significant amount of time designing this new reality. Imagine the sounds and the smells of the new place. Picture how it would make you feel. Now, in your mind's eye, imagine that you are inside of this apartment. That you are walking around and sitting down in a comfortable armchair. Know that you are at home. Notice how it feels to live there. It is very important to "write yourself" into this new storyline. Try to get as many tactile feelings out of this experience as you can. Are the walls smooth or textured? How does the fabric of the curtains feel to your fingers? Again, get as specific as you can. Cultivate the feeling of confidence that this place is already yours. That you have just created a version of reality that will quickly replace your current slide. Know that it is simply a matter of time that this new reality is materialized.

3. Define the timeframe. The matrix is very precise. Unless you define the timeframe, it will take its sweet time executing your heart's desire. Write the time out on a piece of paper—this solidifies the intention and amplifies the power of the practice.

4. Stack the new reality on top of the old reality (see Figure 5 on the next page). Notice how the old cube is being completely submerged inside of the new cube. Notice how the cubes are merging into each other, creating a whole new sector of the matrix. This would, in essence, be the third cube in your visualization.

5. Take a blank piece of paper and draw the three cubes (see Figure 6). Put down the desired date for manifestation. Place this drawing next to your bed or your work desk. Come back to this drawing as a reminder for the next ten days. Every time take special care to remember the new reality that you are trying to manifest. Allow the energy of the two Suns to power your new reality by sending streams of powerful energy from them to your cubes.
6. Watch your reality transform completely.

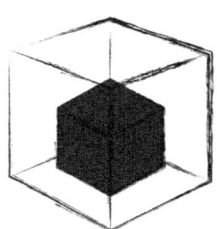

FIGURE 5: STACKED (CORRECTED) REALITY

Date _____

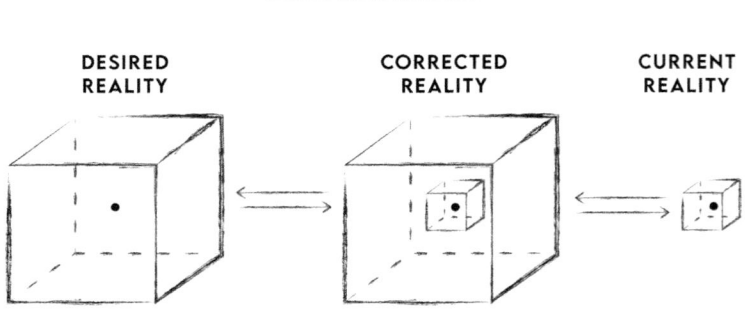

FIGURE 6: REPROGRAMMING YOUR REALITY – A BLUEPRINT

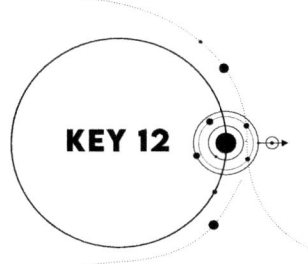

KEY 12

THE BLACK SUN ACTIVATION

Now that you are familiar with the two Suns and have started cultivating a relationship with them (see Keys 3 and 4, pages 30 and 34), you are ready for stage two: amplifying that connection and working with the suns as your greatest allies in manifestation.

Let's start with the Black Sun—the master of your subconscious and your emotions. The Black Sun is extremely potent—its energy is dense and viscous, more powerful than the force of a trillion atomic bombs, and wild, untamed, and impossible to contain. On a physical plane, the Black Sun represents the force of **universal magnetism** with the power to attract or repel other objects as it sees fit—and no force can match it in that ability. The world's most powerful magnet, the Black Sun is ancient magic incarnate. Very few things are quite as integral to manifestation as the magic of magnetism (and thus the magic of the Black Sun). Most of you have heard about the Law of Attraction—like attracts like. The Black Sun takes that concept to a whole new level. Not only will the Black Sun ensure this world reflects your own personal vibration back to you, but it can and will be instrumental in getting you that which you most desire. The Black Sun is thus the Master of Desire.

By virtue of your existence on Earth, you have already formed your own personal sector of reality—a world that is unique to you. From this perspective, every object in your Universe only exists in relation to you. Following this logic, you have your own version of the White Sun and your own version of the Black Sun—the twin guides who make sure you are on the path to getting everything you came to this planet to get.

Here is the trick: unless you take the time to tune both of the Suns into exactly what you want, you are leaving things not only to chance, but also to a default setting. The default setting works as follows.

Throughout your life, you collect experiences that are stored in the great memory of the Black and White Suns. All of your trauma, joy, and everything in between is automatically uploaded to these two great databases. But not only does it get stored inside of the memories of the two suns, but also it forms a default program that governs your logic and your intuition, and therefore, your life.

The main purpose of the Suns is to keep you safe and generally keep you on track toward your purpose. So at any point in time, the two Suns are doing a balancing act. On the one hand, they constantly scan your surroundings for danger to help keep you alive. On the other hand, they try to stay true to your personal north and communicate if you are off track. Unfortunately, often actions that would ensure you are pursuing your true north are the very same actions that could get you in trouble from the Suns' perspectives (think: risk taking). Ironically, this becomes the reason why a lot of people don't live self-actualized lives and never pursue their dreams.

By default, most of our lives are lived on autopilot; we go through the motions, and at any point, we are guided by one of our two suns—logic and habit (White Sun) or emotion and intuition (Black Sun). Living on autopilot, while generally safe, prevents us from achieving our full potential. It will certainly not help you manifest the life you want. In fact, the two Suns, when left to their own devices, will give you more of the same—a life where the future is a complete spitting image of the past. If you are serious about making changes in your life, you will need to get the two Suns to follow the plan you create and not the other way around. And not only that, but you will also need to work with both of these energies, regardless of how different they are, as one approach certainly doesn't fit all.

PRACTICE: BLACK SUN ACTIVATION

Use this practice any time you are calling something big into your life. At any point in time, you can leverage the power of the Black Sun to help you manifest up to three major things. Working with the Black Sun is essentially working with the energy of magnetism. Enjoy!

1. Get in a comfortable position and close your eyes. Take a few deep inhales, breathing out into your lower belly.
2. Imagine a beautiful star-studded sphere the color of the night sky and located in the center of your belly. With every breath, feel the sphere growing and expanding. Notice how it grows large enough to leave the confines of your body—large enough even to enclose your body completely. Feel the warmth and bask in the ethereal glow that emanates from the sphere, your personal Black Sun.

3. Feel the space between your skin and the edges of the sphere disappear as you merge together. At this point, you are one organism with the same past, the same future, and the same set of needs and wants. Notice that you are surrounded by a body of water. You and the Black Sun are floating in it freely with no effort whatsoever.
4. Notice that the tides of the water are responding to you. Notice how the Black Sun is starting to pulsate with the most beautiful magnetic energy, producing a spark of the most otherworldly glow. As it happens, the deep waters carry toward you all manner of objects—seashells and pearls of every kind, as well as treasure troves and jewels floating in the water. Nothing is impossible for the magnetic magic of the Black Sun; magnetism is the most integral part of its nature. And today the Black Sun wants to help you attract what you want to yourself.
5. Look toward the horizon and notice a beautiful boat that carries your heart's greatest desire. Whether it is a material object, an event, or a state of mind, the boat can still hold it. As soon as the Black Sun notices you are looking at the boat, it recognizes your heart's desire. It recognizes the unique vibration of that object or event, and as it does so, the Black Sun starts pulsating even more. It is sending a signal to the boat to come closer. And because all things in the Universe revolve around the Sun, the boat obeys.
6. Watch how the boat is moving toward you. Notice that this movement requires no input from you. This progress is effortless, seamless, and beyond easy. Not all things in life are obtained by conquest. Some objects and events can just as easily be magnetized into your orbit. Watch as the boat approaches you. Step on it and grab the thing that you so desire.
7. Notice how it feels to have it, to hold it in your arms, and to be with it. Let the Black Sun memorize it as well.
8. Let the Black Sun know that from this day forward, the two of you are on a mission to manifest the reality where you can have this object. Ask the Black Sun to assist you with the full might of its magnetic power. Notice how the energy of the Sun changes in response to your request. Now, it has a mission—a task to complete and a job to do. So when you go to sleep every night, it will be working hard to attract the life you want toward you.

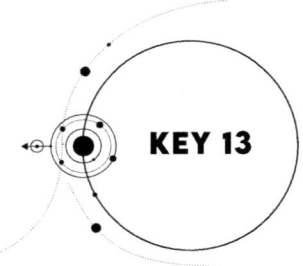

KEY 13

THE WHITE SUN ACTIVATION

Whereas the Black Sun is magnetism, the White Sun is electricity. It guards all movement, direction, activity, and achievement on the physical plane. The energy of the White Sun can best work with you when you don't sit still. The White Sun is a natural companion of active souls—the ones that thrive in movement and are always in a rush to experience life. The White Sun is a master of applying your physical energy toward achieving your goals. The energy of the White Sun is incredibly potent, eternal, and all-encompassing. Quite literally, it makes the world go round. The tricky thing about this energy is, unless properly directed, it can create a lot of work for the sake of work and movement for the sake of movement. So the White Sun needs to be synced to what you want, less it sends you on a fool's errand of busy work without getting you to your preferred final destination.

The energy of the White Sun counteracts the frequencies of doubt and worry. That's why if you are worried about the future or are in doubt whether you can manifest what you want, you are NOT aligned with the energies of the White Sun. On the contrary, when you are in the midst of action related to your goals, you generally don't experience worry. Remember, you are a human vessel that, at any point in time, can only be filled with one dominating frequency. The choice is yours: it is either to be worried or to be confident in the uninterrupted movement toward the life you want. If you catch yourself in a moment of doubt, close your eyes and take some time to reconnect with your great electric parent—the White Sun. And remember that taking action always moves you closer to your goal.

Electricity is the heartbeat of the Universe. It is a force that grants life to inanimate objects, taking them from slumber to overdrive in seconds. At the inception point, electricity animated the White Sun—the first domino that jump-started the chain reaction called a living ecosystem. Since then, everything in this world has been moving in a constant dance of light and shadow—an evergreen process of evolution and involution. And in this process, the White Sun is a rightful King, ruling with much vigor and authority over the Universe where everything, down to the tiniest fractal, is movement.

One of the best ways to stay in tune with this energy—the driving energy of the White Sun—is physical exercise. Get that body moving! And not just because "it's healthy." Do it to amplify the power of your manifestation. Fifteen minutes of cardio a day is one of the best recipes for swift manifestation. On the contrary, spending your life in a seated position (hello, computer screens) could drag out the process of your manifestation into decades.

Nothing kills the potent fertile energy of the White Sun like procrastination and excessive planning. More than a fair share of human dreams have been crushed by hesitation and desire to have everything planned down to the last detail. The White Sun favors the brave, the reckless, and the impatient. So if you want the help of the White Sun, err on the side of taking action and just going for it. This is the energy that the White Sun can easily understand and amplify to help you find the right path.

PRACTICE: WHITE SUN ACTIVATION

This is a standing meditative practice to help you cultivate and amplify your White Sun energy. Use this exercise any time you feel low on energy or experience the counter forces of fear, doubt, or lack of confidence.

1. Stand with your feet hip-width apart and firmly planted on the ground.
2. Imagine that your body is covered with a grid of vertical and horizontal lines that collectively make up the matrix of your physical body. These pathways have always been here—these are the pathways through which your energy flows.
3. Imagine that yellow-gold light is starting to circulate through this network of lines. It starts in your heart like a stream of potent yellow-gold energy and travels throughout your body—your arms, your feet, and all of your internal organs. This is *prana*—your lifeforce, the electric force behind every action that you take.
4. Imagine that there is a small sun located in the center of your belly area. This sun is pulsating with electric charges. Now imagine that you are actually standing inside a large White Sun, fully engulfed by it. The surface of the sun is scorching and potent. Imagine that this sun is sending a massive electric impulse straight to the center of your belly—right where the small sun dwells. And as

this happens, your inner sun becomes fully activated. It starts pulsating like a mini star within you, causing your body to expand.

5. Watch as the pulse from the mini sun inside spreads throughout your body, making you feel hot and tingly all over. Know that the energy of the White Sun is always available to you—any time you are in doubt, any time you require a pick-me-up, and any time you experience fear. Know that you can stretch out your arm and receive another portion of the white-hot electricity to power your manifestation.

6. Finish this practice with connective Sun breath. Take a breath in and, on the out breath, expand your mini sun to the size of the master sun—the larger sun that envelops your whole body. Hold for a count of three. On the out breath, allow your mini sun to retract to its original size. Repeat three to five times to be fully saturated with the potent action-prone energy of the White Sun.

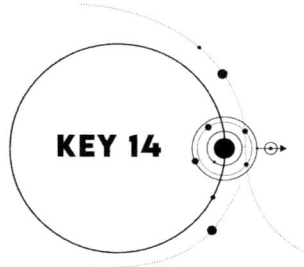

KEY 14

GETTING RID OF CLUTTER

Mental and emotional clutter is much less visible than physical clutter. Which is why it often remains untouched. Yet it still takes up space and resources away from being focused on manifesting your dreams. Today we'll examine a few types of clutter that you need to clear up before moving toward a life you love.

OLD GOALS

Do you remember that thing you really wanted in high school but didn't get? It is still holding a portion of your energy hostage. Ironically, that amount of energy could be all the difference you need to help you manifest a better life. It is very important to create a list of all the things you wanted as a child/teenager and cross them out from your wish list. Take the time to remember all the toys, trophies, relationships, or trips you wanted at one point but never got—from childhood to today. All of this invisible mental clutter gets heavier and heavier over time, taking a toll on your abundance stream. If it is helpful, feel free to burn the piece of paper with your list and mentally let them go, removing the mental hooks you once attached to all of those objects. Let them go freely—better things will come to fill their place. Get really good at letting go.

OUTDATED RELATIONSHIPS

Every person we have a relationship with takes a portion of our soul energy. Some of these relationships last a lifetime, but more often than not, we grow out of them. Think of all of your former friends, exes, and even enemies. Dreamed of any of them lately? This is a sign that you still have an energetic cord that connects you two. Often, these cords are a way of subconscious energy exchange. This means that the girl you hated in high school could still be sucking away your energy. Cord-cutting is one of the best self-care habits you could possibly establish. When cutting a cord with an old acquaintance, close your eyes and examine the energetic aspect of that relationship. There can be one or many cords connecting you to the other person. The connection tends to be established at the chakra level (see also diagram, Key 7, page 47). For your reference, below are some of the common meanings of the different chakra connections.

- Red (root) chakra connection: relationships based on survival, money, and security.
- Orange (sacral) chakra connection: sexual connection; deep emotional bond.
- Yellow (solar plexus) chakra connection: relationships that help you form or maintain your identity (think power couples), status-based relationships, and relationships that give confidence.
- Green (heart) chakra connection: relationships centered around love, compassion, and nurturing one another.
- Blue (throat) chakra connection: relationships based on meaningful conversation and perfect communication; also karmic relationships (student/teacher, creator/muse).
- Violet (third eye) chakra connection: spiritual relationships based on helping each other grow.
- White (crown) chakra connection: deep soul connection; common for soulmates and souls with a common (collective) planetary mission.

Whatever your connection is to an old acquaintance, it could be holding you back. When you sever that connection, your energy comes back to you—and the other person's energy goes back to them.

OLD VOWS

Vows are strong, emotionally charged promises that you give to yourself and others. Vows are extremely powerful—enough so that an unfulfilled vow may follow you across incarnations. Vows are tricky since many of them live in the subconscious—you set them and forget them, but they never forget you. That is why curses are so powerful: a curse is a negatively charged vow, after all.

What were the things you promised yourself as a child? What promises did you give your parents? Was there something you intended to do "when you grew up"? Your body still remembers every single promise you made. What about your New Year resolutions? Your body remembers those also. Some unfulfilled vows can create an inexplicable sense of dissatisfaction despite things going well at face value. A cord of the vow is a bookmark of sorts—it always pulls you back toward what you once promised. It is a distant reminder that you still "owe" something on the energetic level.

To remedy this predicament, make a list of the old vows and promises you once gave but no longer intend to keep. Burn that list and let them go. Alternatively, you could get rid of the old vows through a meditative state. Imagine multiple energetic cords coming out of your body in multiple directions, each one representing a vow you forgot you made. Take the time to cut each of these cords with a mighty sword of light. Set yourself free from all these promises that have been weighing you down.

OLD HABITS

Last but not least, declutter and do away with any outdated habits. This relates to both the bad habits you have wanted to give up and the empty rituals that used to bring you joy but no longer do so. Habits are hard to rewire, so most people don't bother. And yet they hold a lot of our energy hostage and could be one of the culprits preventing you from manifesting what you want. And I am not just talking about giving up smoking or drinking. Grab a piece of paper and write down what your typical day looks like—every ritual that goes into your day. Examine it closely. Are you noticing anything that shouldn't be there? Anything that is merely occupying space? If the answer is yes, take the liberty of rewriting that list. After all, you call the shots, so you get to recreate your days as you see fit instead of just going through the motions.

Today's practice consists of two parts: a right-brain activity followed by a left-brain activity, both of which will help you reset your goals, vows, relationships, and habits to align perfectly with your desired future.

LEFT-BRAIN PRACTICE: RECORDING NEW GOALS, VOWS, RELATIONSHIPS, AND HABITS

Now that you have created all of this empty space, you are ready to put it to good use—toward manifesting the life you want. You'll need to work on having each of the four areas (goals, vows, relationships, habits) assist you with manifestation.

1. Take a blank page and divide it into four sections; title them "Goals, Vows, Relationships, Habits." Take 10–15 minutes to fill in each section with NEW things you can establish for yourself to help you manifest what you want.
2. *Goals:* Write down three specific and measurable goals that describe what success looks like. In trying to achieve what you want, how will you know that you are succeeding? What metrics could help you get there?
3. *Vows:* Disclaimer: this part is VERY powerful, so proceed with caution. Generally, one good vow is enough to propel you toward achieving your goals. Vows might range from "I promise to do anything possible to achieve my goal" to "I promise to do my best in achieving the life I want."
4. *Relationships:* Write down what kind of relationships you need to attract into your life to help manifest what you want. Be specific about the kind of people you need and what these relationships should look like.
5. *Habits:* List one to three new habits that you can establish to help you achieve what you want. Commit to following through on these.

RIGHT-BRAIN PRACTICE: VISUALIZING NEW GOALS, VOWS, RELATIONSHIPS, AND HABITS

Following on from the previous practice, you are now ready to visualize all the new things you want to bring to your life.

1. In a meditative state, imagine that you are standing in a spacious room. In the middle of the room, picture a golden sphere of light representing your desire already fulfilled. This is an energetic imprint of what you are trying to manifest.
2. Notice how the sphere divides itself into four equal parts—one for each of the key areas we'll be visualizing – goals, vows, relationships and habits.

3. Allow each of the four spheres to become saturated with the goals, vows, relationships and habits that you defined in the previous practice, allowing them to become a vibrational match to what you want.
4. Notice the four cabinets lining the walls of the room. The first cabinet is titled "Goals." Take the corresponding globe of light and place it inside this cabinet. Allow the Universe to assist you on your journey. Trust that it will do so no matter what since your goals are now known to it.
5. The second cabinet is titled "Vows." Place another gold sphere of light inside of this cabinet. Watch as the Universe absorbs it. Trust that the Universe has heard your vow and will assist you in fulfilling it.
6. The third cabinet is called "Relationships." Place your third sphere of light inside it. Now that the Universe has received your support request, it will start working to attract the right set of people to your life. Trust that these people are already on their way to you.
7. The last Cabinet is called "Habits." Place the last sphere of light inside it. Ask the Universe for assistance with changing your habits. The Universe is wise and here to help you.

Rest assured that this visualization will align people, circumstances, and events to help you get what you truly desire.

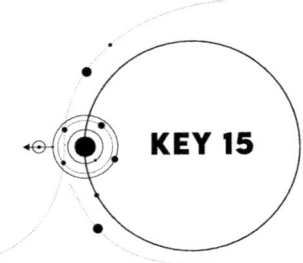

KEY 15

SUN BREATHING

Sun energy is the strongest creative energy available on planet Earth. Anything created in the material world was powered by the energy of the Sun in one way or another. By learning to integrate the energy of the Sun into everything you do, you can multiply your personal power and speed up any and all material transformation. Our ancestors were well connected to the energy of the Sun. They knew that a simple habit of waking up at dawn and greeting the Sun was an indispensable ritual for unlocking abundance. The Sun always provides for its children, especially when they are in alignment with it.

There are a few simple ways to stay connected to the Sun in your daily life. One of them is Sun Breathing. To understand how Sun Breathing works, you first need to dive into the concept of *prana*, which I've mentioned before (see Key 3, page 30). *Prana*—or lifeforce energy—is all around us. It is a thread that connects potential and manifested reality. *Prana* is everywhere and is closely related to the element of air in our physical world. Concentrated *prana* is white, but it can come in a rainbow of colors depending on its source. Sun *prana* is golden in color and represents a high vibrational frequency that makes the world go round. Sun *prana* is a great chameleon and can amplify any vibration it comes in close contact with. This is why you can use the Sun energy to manifest anything you want—from rent money to peace on Earth.

When your breathing is automatic, you're inhaling whatever *prana* is in the vicinity. In essence, teaching your body not to be selective. Although these breaths are certainly keeping you alive, it is not a strategic way to live. Not all *prana* is created equal. And even worse, you might be starving for a particular kind of *prana* and not even know it. Golden Sun *prana* is a creative force—it takes whatever building blocks are necessary and helps create your dream reality. You need golden *prana* to manifest. You need golden *prana* to make big changes in your life. You need golden *prana* to fully be on your path. Bottom line: you NEED golden *prana*. Period.

The Sun *prana* is about as potent as an energy stream gets on this planet. It has the power to transform your body from within. As the Sun *prana* enters your body, it upgrades everything inside at the cellular level, raising your vibrations and preparing you for the upcoming synchronicities. This is the closest you can get to experiencing and sharing space with your mighty Celestial Father here on Earth.

PRACTICE: SUN BREATHING

Any time you start a new project, I recommend you do a session of *pranic* breathing to charge your new project with the energy of the Sun. For any ongoing project, repeat Sun Breathing once every few weeks or on an as-needed basis. Sun energy is also extremely potent if you feel tired or have lost motivation to keep going. The following meditation is best done in the morning or the afternoon. Doing it in the evening may disrupt your natural sleep cycle.

1. Settle into a comfortable seated position and close your eyes. Start with some light breaths as you center into your body and quiet down your internal dialogue.
2. Imagine the beautiful bright Sun shining overhead. Take a moment to greet the Sun and thank it for its willingness to fuel your dreams.
3. As the Sun stretches its rays toward you, notice a stream of beautiful golden energy emanating from it. This energy is warm and comforting—glowing and gleaming with its rich splendor. Take a deep breath and invite this beautiful golden energy into your lower belly. Allow the Sun *prana* to go as deep within you as possible and hold your breath for a second.
4. See how this splendid creative energy is spreading through every organ of your body, getting into your bloodstream, powering your strong heart and muscles and penetrating your bones.
5. As you breathe out, send the breath through the middle of your forehead (your third eye area), and then follow it through toward the center of the Sun. Use force and intention on the out-breath. This is an energetic exchange between you and the Sun—the more you give in this instance, the more you will receive.
6. Draw your next breath right from the very center, very core of the Sun—the spot with the purest, most concentrated form of Sun *prana*. Breathe it in deeply, hold your breath for the count of eight, and notice how the Sun's energy is upgrading your body at the cellular level, giving each cell a membrane of pure, shimmering gold—your great protection and your great power source.

7. Breathe out with force and intention through the center of your forehead. Notice how your third eye becomes activated. It may start pulsating, feeling warm, or tingling lightly. At this moment, know that it is building alignment between you and the Universe—between you and your true potential. In this state, you may get downloads or messages from Spirit. Whatever they are, you may want to jot them down quickly before going back to your breathing exercise. These messages are great for contemplating later.
8. Repeat this breathing technique twelve times to saturate your body with all the Sun energy you might need for manifestation.

This is a very powerful practice, especially if you have never experienced it before.

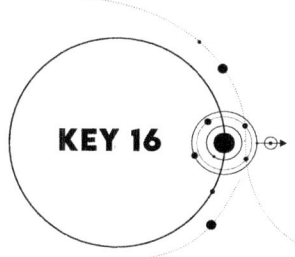

KEY 16

THE GESTATION PRINCIPLE

> *"Everything flows, out and in; everything has its tides; all things rise and fall; the pendulum-swing manifests in everything; the measure of the swing to the right is the measure of the swing to the left; rhythm compensates."*
>
> —Three Initiates, Kybalion: A Study of the Hermetic Philosophy of Ancient Egypt and Greece

The evolution of the soul is the process of moving from lower vibrational worlds to higher vibrational worlds while learning to master the process of creation in each of them. The rules of manifestation (read: creation) vary from one dimension to the next, arguably becoming progressively easier with each layer.

Your Higher Self, for instance, can manifest things instantaneously, without much effort at all. At the same time, most humans on planet Earth will struggle to manifest the simplest things over decades. Manifestation is one of the more complex lessons to learn in third-dimensional reality. The reason why is that some things in the process of manifestation don't seem terribly logical. Firstly, there is very little outward confirmation that you are moving in the right direction, at least initially. Secondly, there is generally a whole chain of setbacks and impediments on the way that often lead you off the path completely. Enough so that most people stop playing the game and settle for what they have.

There are a great many misconceptions about what manifesting truly feels like. Most people believe it is an ever-present feeling of becoming successful and things generally going as planned. Yet, manifestation is VERY far from being so linear. In reality, the energy of manifestation is not a straight line connecting the two dots of where you are today and where you'd like to be. In fact, it is more of a stepladder, where you must climb step-by-step, only rarely skipping levels. With manifestation, you often might experience a period of rapid movement that feels exhilarating, followed by an often much longer period of stagnation and a visible absence of any progress.

During the latter, most people get off course, believing that nothing is going according to plan. The truth is, you are NEVER more on your path than when you are feeling stuck. Let us get one thing really clear. Nothing in nature gives fruit all year. Everything in nature (including you) goes through a process of ebbs and flows that collectively align into a perfect path. And yet today's society is forcing us to be in constant go mode, praising the state of overdrive and condemning any periods of low productivity or low yield. If it weren't for those false ideas of constantly overachieving, humanity would understand that the period of feeling empty is just as critical for creation as the period of feeling full.

So let's set your expectations straight. On your journey to manifesting the life you want; you are meant to experience off days and even weeks. On the energetic level, it is simply a gestation period—something that must happen once you plant the seeds. It takes time for the sprouts to take root and grow. Your manifestation path will lead through many cycles of rapid growth and then apparent lack of movement. If you ever watched a wild cat hunt (think: lion), you may have noticed that the animal goes through a cycle of being quiet and fully focused before going for the kill. At that moment, the animal is accumulating its energy and gathering its strength.

Know that when nothing in your life serves as proof that you are on track, you are going through a period of collecting your energy and gathering your strength before a major upgrade. During that time, allow yourself moments of stillness and calm, and let your body and mind regroup without applying pressure or complaining. Know that you are still very much on the path, and this stillness is a VERY natural process for manifesting something in a third (or even fifth) dimensional world.

PRACTICE: PLANTING SEEDS

Let's take some time to plant and nurture the seeds of your ideal future today.

1. Get into a comfortable position, close your eyes, and allow your breaths to enter and leave your body freely.

2. In your mind's eye, imagine that you are standing in a beautiful vast field, and the soil beneath your feet is perfect for growing anything. It is supple, full of nutrients, and hungry for any seeds you might choose to plant there.
3. Place your hand inside your pocket and take out a few of the seeds you carry around with you. Imagine that these seeds are the seeds of your manifestation. Know that with their help, you can grow a new life for yourself—a better life. Each seed is custom-made for you by the Universe, and it is perfect.
4. Plant the seeds in the field, wherever it feels right. Water the seeds so they can sprout. Picture the Sun warming up the soil around the seeds with its loving, life-giving light. Start sensing the movement inside the seeds that you just planted.
5. On the surface, it doesn't seem like anything has changed. The field, the trees, and the birds are the same as they have always been. There is no visible movement, and yet, inside the seeds, there is all the movement that you could possibly need. Zoom in and enter one of your seeds to watch all the inner workings from the inside. Picture the nutrients and the water coursing through the seed, making it supple, waking it up from the deep slumber. Notice all the inner work the seed needs to go through to grow even a tiny root.
6. Watch as your seed grows beautiful roots. Picture it taking hold in the soil and anchoring itself with force and intention. And yet, as you zoom out, notice that there is still seemingly nothing happening at surface level—nothing to let you know that your seeds are alive and thriving.
7. Watch as days later your seeds grow their very first gentle sprouts—the first visible evidence that one day they will mature into healthy, luscious plants. From this moment on, remember never to force nature and never to force the Universe. Just like the seeds, your new life needs to gestate and grow roots first. The roots always come before the sprouts. Don't shame your seeds for taking their time to ground themselves and establish a solid foundation. Allow yourself and your creations to move at their own pace; it is Divinely guided.
8. Watch your seeds grow into beautiful sunflowers. Notice how the sunflowers open their hearts to everything around them—the wind, the sky, and most importantly, the Sun, their greatest ally. Allow the Sun to nurture the sunflowers, and thus nurture you as you create your best life. Watch as a few sunflowers become a field of sunflowers. This world is abundant, and it is always on your side—if only you give it some time to grow.

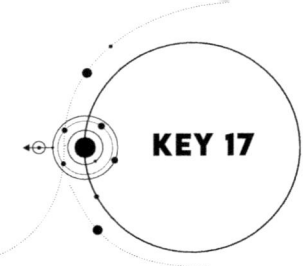

KEY 17

MATTER AND ANTIMATTER

> *"But today, everything we see from the smallest life forms on Earth to the largest stellar objects is made almost entirely of matter. Comparatively, there is not much antimatter to be found."*
>
> —CERN

Scientists believe that at the inception of the Universe, equal amounts of matter and antimatter existed. What we are experiencing today is quite different: there is significantly more matter than antimatter in the observable Universe. What exactly does this skew mean?

Matter and antimatter are building blocks of the cosmos that represent energy in its rawest, elementary form. Matter is the materialized aspect of the Universe—the part that has already taken shape and locked into a particular frequency. Antimatter, on the other hand, represents the potentiality of everything in the Universe—that which comes before form and factor and will, arguably, come after. Antimatter is pure potential in its most untamed form—a state from which anything is possible. On the physical level, matter and antimatter are represented by particles with the opposite charge and spin, like two sides of the same coin.

Earth is located on the outskirts of the Universe—the great periphery. While we still get some amounts of antimatter courtesy of cosmic rays, we are far removed from its source. Thus, we are constantly experiencing a lack of antimatter, which significantly diminishes our creative potential and slows down the process of manifestation. There are simply not enough building blocks to go about—our potential feels limited. This inhibition is simply a byproduct of matter/antimatter distribution in our immediate vicinity.

The world as we know it—the material world—represents the masculine aspect of existence. It has form, factor, direction, amplitude, and weight. Antimatter, on the other hand, is the feminine aspect of the Universe—the dark womb made of volatile particles that can be incubated and gestated so that new material objects can be born.

There is a myth of scarcity on this planet. We are conditioned to single out the various examples of scarcity in their immediate surroundings and the world. No matter where you look, you see evidence of just how limited the material world is—we have only so many fossil fuels, only so many animal species, only so much wealth to go around. And on some level, it's true. Matter is finite, which means things that have already made it to the material world are exhaustible. And yet, the Universe at large has an unlimited supply of antimatter that can bring forth anything into existence. In other words, if you only look to the material world, you might not find the resources you need to manifest a better life for yourself. Truly, if the observable Universe has limits, it must mean that to get access to the things you want, you have to take them away from someone else. Welcome to the prison of the zero-sum game: for me to win, someone else has to lose. And yet, if you play this game and subscribe to these rules, you will never experience abundance. True unrestricted abundance is the realm of the Great Feminine—the realm of antimatter.

PRACTICE: UNLOCKING THE REALM OF ANTIMATTER

This practice will teach you how to harvest the unrestricted abundance of antimatter to benefit your manifestation. Make sure you are well rested before attempting this practice.

FIGURE 7: COSMIC WOMB – THE SEAT OF ANTIMATTER

1. Close your eyes and slow down your breathing. Inhale on a count of three through your nose, and exhale on a count of three through your mouth.
2. In your mind's eye, imagine the great cosmic womb—a large vortex of energy rotating faster than the speed of light (see Figure 7 on the previous page). Woven from the fabric of cosmos itself, it is spectacular, with vast streaks of stardust mixed with a lot of gooey, viscous darkness. As the vortex rotates, its spiral movement spews out particles large and small, expanding the Universe as you know it.
3. As you observe this great miracle of creation, notice that the crux of the action is in the vortex's center. You can feel massive amounts of energy entering and exiting through it—the birth canal of the great womb. As the birthplace of stars, planets, and asteroids, the womb is hard at work.
4. As you rise above this surreal scenery, notice an opening in the core of the womb; it's large enough for you to pass through. Allow yourself to move down, flying through the vortex's center.
5. The inside of the womb is no less spectacular. It is gleaming with the most ethereal glow, more majestic than an ocean of stars. The great womb is no ordinary place—it is the key to all manifestation. Picture yourself surrounded by small particles that look like stardust. These particles are plentiful and float up and down in a somewhat haphazard fashion. This is antimatter—the stuff the dreams are made of. This is one of the rarest substances at the outskirts of the Universe, but yet it is plentiful here.
6. As you stretch your palms out, notice that the particles of antimatter are arranging themselves around your hands, reacting to your energy. They want to be helpful with whatever project you have. It is their destiny and their role in the Universe.
7. Take a moment to focus on what you would like to manifest. Think of every aspect and every facet of your desired future. When you're ready, allow this version of the future to be encapsulated by a golden sphere of light—a protective shell that will incubate it for the time being.
8. To take form, your desire requires antimatter. Antimatter is not unlike water for your unmanifested dreams. Now that the particles of antimatter have arranged themselves around your palm, you can control them and their creative expression. Reach your palm toward the membrane of the golden sphere and touch it.

9. Now, with the full force of your intention, send the antimatter particles inside of the golden sphere. Command them to fuel and nurture your desired future, helping it materialize in your world as quickly as possible. Establish a constant stream of antimatter flowing into this golden capsule so your creation has as much support as it requires.
10. Thank the Great Mother womb for her generous gift and for working with you today. When you are ready, focus on your breath and return back.

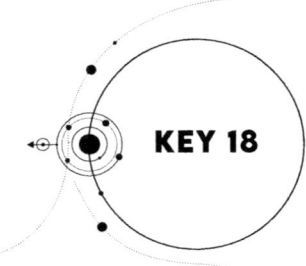

KEY 18

THE AMPLIFICATION PRINCIPLE

There are essentially two types of energy streams in existence—concentrated and dispersed. Concentrated energy streams carry a lot of momentum and weight. All the things that you see manifested in the physical reality are concentrated energy streams. You cannot be physically incarnated unless you carry enough of a concentrated energy stream within your body. From this perspective, human beings are concentrated energy forms, while dreams are not. Another example of a concentrated energy stream is your core belief system. By virtue of your wholeheartedly believing in something, you create density around it—that is how a dispersed energy form becomes concentrated. Once a thought-form turns concentrated, it immediately starts co-creating your reality. One more example of a dense energy form is persistent feelings—the ones you experience repeatedly. Depression and anxiety are examples of a concentrated emotional stream, and therefore, they tend to influence your reality. Bottom line: Anything that is a concentrated stream of energy impacts the physical. It has enough charge and momentum to alter your life.

Dispersed energy streams, on the other hand, are lighter, more volatile energies. They can be nascent, subconscious, or higher spectrum vibrations that haven't grown a foothold in the physical yet. These energies tend to belong to the "invisible" realms. You could say that they carry less dense and less potent energies compared to visible things. Your dreams, wishes, worries, random thoughts, and emotions you get throughout the day are all examples of dispersed energy streams. Ghosts are another example of a dispersed energy stream. While largely invisible, they can become visible if the entity of a ghost puts enough effort into focusing their energy stream. But even when this is accomplished in the moment, it is hard to maintain over time.

The trick to manifestation is taking a wish (a dispersed energy stream) and turning it into an intention (a concentrated energy stream). A concentrated energy stream always manifests in the physical—it is the law.

So what helps transform an energy stream from dispersed to concentrated?

- △ **Good old repetition:** The more you repeat a thought or an image in your head, the more concentrated its energy stream becomes. This is the reason that visualizations and vision boards are helpful with manifestation.
- △ **Writing things down:** Writing a thought down automatically turns a dispersed (non-physical) thought into physical words on a page. That is why it is extremely important to document all aspects of the world you are trying to manifest for yourself. Even spoken words are a concentrated energy form; they are incredibly powerful in manifestation.
- △ **Belief:** Believing something is true or possible increases the focus of an energy stream, especially if you keep that belief at the forefront of mind. On the other hand, believing something is impossible disperses the energy stream and makes the manifestation of that belief highly unlikely.
- △ **Telling other people:** People have the power to feed concepts and ideas with their energy. When multiple individuals lend their energy to a particular concept, it grows and materializes. That is why sharing your vision with others could help it materialize faster.

PRACTICE: THE HALL OF MIRRORS

If you are reading this book, chances are there is at least one thing that you want and don't yet have. This means you are currently experiencing a dispersed energy stream as it relates to that concept. Today you'll be working on turning this stream into a more focused substance.

This meditative practice uses the physical property of mirrors (reflective surfaces) to amplify and condense light. This property of mirrors is widely used today in everything from industrial lasers to solar panels.

1. Take a few deep breaths, close your eyes and center into your body. Quiet down your internal dialogue as much as possible. Today you'll be visiting the Hall of Mirrors—a place of wonder and opportunity. In your mind's eye, imagine a long corridor lined with large floor-length mirrors. The mirrors look timeless—both modern and ancient at once—and they line both walls of this unusual corridor. This corridor is located in a place not constrained by dimension—somewhere lost in time and space. This unconstrained environment is one of the great

secrets that you will become privy to. Being here is an honor and a one-of-a-kind opportunity.

2. Look toward the end of the corridor. There, at the very end, is your dream—encapsulated in a golden membrane and frozen like a snapshot in space. It is right in the middle of its gestation period and waits for the time when it can be fully manifested in the physical.

3. Picture standing at the opposite side of this corridor, some distance away from your encapsulated dream. Watch as a stream of golden light enters the corridor. This light belongs to the Sun—your great Celestial Father—and is exactly the kind of fuel you need to make your dream a reality. The only catch is that the energy of the Sun is dispersed—it is unfocused and thus is of limited use to you.

4. Imagine that you can control this fertile energy stream, its directions, and its intention. Direct the sunlight stream toward the closest mirror on the left wall (see Figure 8).

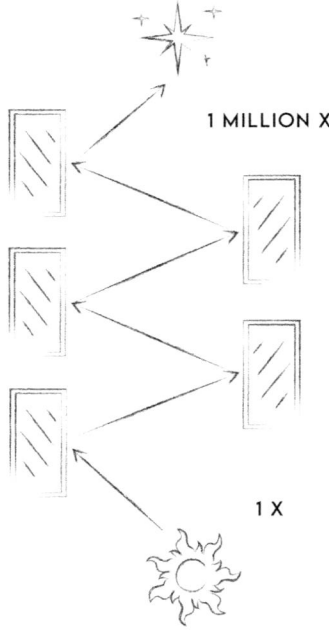

FIGURE 8: HALL OF MIRRORS

5. Watch as the mirror reflects the light and sends it across the corridor to the mirror directly opposite it on the right wall. As that happens, the power of this energy stream is multiplied tenfold. Mirrors are natural light reflectors: they cannot hold on to or absorb it; they can only amplify and reflect it.
6. Watch as the steam of energy is reflected off of a second mirror, multiplying it ten times in the process. Let it travel across the corridor to the opposite wall, toward a third mirror.
7. Picture the original stream traveling from one mirror to the next, bouncing off each mirror, all the while moving toward the end of the corridor and your encapsulated dream.
8. Allow the stream to bounce off at least ten mirrors, each time increasing its power tenfold. Witness the stream become pointed like a laser beam and turn stronger than a dozen atomic bombs. Watch as this majestic energy stream enters through the porous membrane surrounding the gestating seed of your dream—of your future reality.
9. Notice that your dream is now powered with a mighty electric Sun force—amplified and enhanced through the Hall of Mirrors. Know that it now has all the electricity it could possibly need to be manifested in the physical. Let the seeds of your dream bask in this newly found focused energy stream and finally start to take physical form.

Repeat the practice if needed after a few weeks.

PRACTICE: DISPERSED TO CONCENTRATED WRITING EXERCISE

You can practice turning a dispersed energy stream into a concentrated stream with the help of writing. Respond to the following list of questions in writing. Save your answers for your future reference.

- △ What is it that you want to manifest?
- △ Why do you want it?
- △ How will you know that your dream is coming true? What will you start seeing in the outside reality?

- How would it feel waking up in the morning if you had what you want? Be specific.
- How would people start reacting to you?
- How would your day-to-day change?
- What will that dream enable in your life?

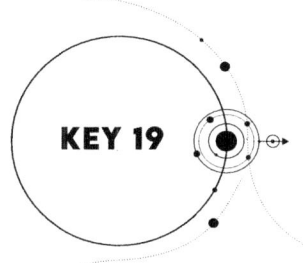

KEY 19

SOLAR WIND RISING

Everything you observe in the surrounding cosmos is, by definition, Heliosphere—the ecosystem created and ruled by the Sun. We are alive thanks to the Sun's plasma—an extremely dynamic substance that serves as the backbone of all material creation. Every human on Earth today is partially made of the Sun's plasma. Each Sun particle within us is multifaceted: it represents the body, the heart, and the soul of the great Celestial Father. Yet for most of us, that energy lies dormant—nothing more than a distant memory of our grand design.

We are Sun's emissaries here on Earth, and through our daily activities, we are either living up to that title or failing to do so. As Sun children, we are meant to do much more than connect with our Father. We are meant to resemble him and reflect his energy back into the world. More importantly, we are meant to become master creators and master manifestors. This is our greatest gift and our greatest challenge. And one way we get there is by understanding and integrating the energy of the solar wind.

The solar wind is the breath of the Sun. It is how the Sun communicates with its surroundings and shares its energy with other aspects of the Universe. The solar wind is the connective tissue of the Heliosphere, and it ensures that we all stay connected to one another and our celestial brothers and sisters. It ensures we all live as one ecosystem—one big Sun family. The solar wind is an outward moving essence of the Sun: it travels at a million miles per hour in all directions and spans vast distances in a blink of an eye. Through the movement of the solar wind, the Sun gets to upload its desired codes and frequencies into all of its creation. At this point in time, all of the Heliosphere is going through a massive upgrade. Through a new turn of the spiral of evolution, the Sun is awakening to its true purpose and mission, and so are we as humanity. We are finally ready to face who we truly are and just how much power we wield.

There is a unique manifestation code created by the Sun for you, patiently awaiting its unpacking. You see, there is nothing random in the Universe. And you reading this book is no coincidence. It means the Sun recognizes you as one of its magical children and has a set of codes for you to unpack. Your Celestial Parent has been awaiting your arrival, and he is so glad you made it to this point.

PRACTICE: INTEGRATING SOLAR WIND ENERGIES AND AWAKENING YOUR SOLAR POWER

Claiming your celestial nature starts with integrating solar wind particles within your own body and unlocking your unique Sun code so you can get the assistance you crave on your way toward becoming a master manifestor.

1. Find a comfortable place to sit or lie down. Close your eyes and start with a few full-bodied, deep breaths. Breathe in the energy from your surroundings. On the out-breath, send the energy toward the soles of your feet. Watch as the soles of your feet are awakened by your breath. Feel the energy start to course through them. Repeat this breathing technique a few times until the soles of your feet become saturated with life energy and are ready for the next step.
2. Picture in front of you the magical fiery Sun, emanating its beautiful, potent solar wind energy in every possible direction. Recognize this energy for what it is— proof of how much the Sun loves its children, enough so that it wants to share parts of itself unselfishly with its creations and expects nothing in return.
3. Notice how a significant stream of solar wind is carrying something toward you. It looks like a double helix made entirely of golden light, not dissimilar to the DNA molecule, only much, much larger in size.
4. Watch as the solar wind gently lays the double helix right next to your feet. This object contains the wisdom of the Universe but also a very unique set of codes that are meant specifically for you. The golden helix is an upgrade—it works at the DNA level and can only be unlocked by you and the range of your personal vibration.
5. Watch as the double helix separates into two separate strands right in front of your eyes. Each individual helix is moving straight under each of the soles of your feet—one helix per foot.
6. Allow the solar wind to move one of the helices up your left leg in an upward spiral fashion. Allow this new DNA material to fill the whole left side of your body. Experience the power of the solar wind rising. This power is transformative—one of a kind.
7. Watch as the solar wind works to move the second helix up your right leg in the same sweeping upward spiral motion.

8. Picture the two helices combining again in your heart center. The solar wind rising is like the good old *Kundalini* rising, but times a thousand. Watch as the golden double helix gets fully integrated into your heart muscle as well as the energetic field of your strong heart, merging with all that you are.
9. Notice how this beautiful golden energy floats upward and forms a magical golden star at the very top of your head—your new center of manifestation. Feel a slight tingling at your crown as this integration is happening. Know that from this day onward, you can rely on this new energy center of your body to assist you with all things creation and manifestation.
10. In future chapters, you'll learn how to work with this solar wind energy.

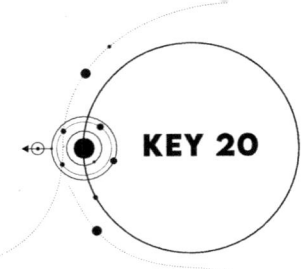

THE SUN HAS A CROWN

> *"Astronomers have been trying to solve this mystery for a long time. The corona is in the outer layer of the Sun's atmosphere—far from its surface. Yet the corona is hundreds of times hotter than the Sun's surface."*
>
> —NASA

FIGURE 9: SOLAR CROWN

Did you know that the Sun has a crown (see Figure 9)? Despite only being observable by humans during the solar eclipse, the crown is one of the most integral aspects of the Sun.

Solar Corona (or crown) is the Sun's most potent creative energy field. Located at the outer edge of the Sun's surface, Corona encircles the Sun, serving as the pinnacle of its outward-facing energy stream. While the Sun's life-giving energies originate from its very center, it is through Corona that this power becomes amplified and targeted. The Sun's energy cannot make it to the crown area until it is in its most potent, action-ready state. Also called the halo of the Sun, Corona is the amalgamation of all the best energies the Sun has to offer.

Before the Sun energies can achieve their purest, most elevated state, they have to go through the arc—an internal sequence or process of energy purification. The arc of the Sun starts at the very center of the Sun (the Sun's personal solar plexus chakra) and ends at the outer rim of the Sun's atmosphere—the Corona, the Sun's crown chakra. Like every celestial body, the Sun has its karma. By going through the process of the arc, that karma is being cleansed and renewed, and the Sun's energy becomes ready for distribution in its most nurturing, loving, and healing state.

As above, so below. The arc of the Sun exists within the human body as well (see Figure 10). It symbolizes the energy of the Sun ascending through a human body. Starting in the solar plexus area and ending in the crown chakra, the energy of the Sun morphs from the self-serving, low-vibrating yellow spectrum to the omnipotent, high-frequency white light. This is the arc of personal evolution that all souls must go through. The crown chakra is the most potent creative space within the human body: it's the center of your Divine manifestation and your creative fortress as well as the part of your body most cherished by the Sun. In truth, you can manifest from either the solar plexus chakra or the crown chakra—both energies are quite potent. But true Divine abundance can only come from the Corona space, and it comes from a place of unity and alignment with the Higher aspects of the Sun.

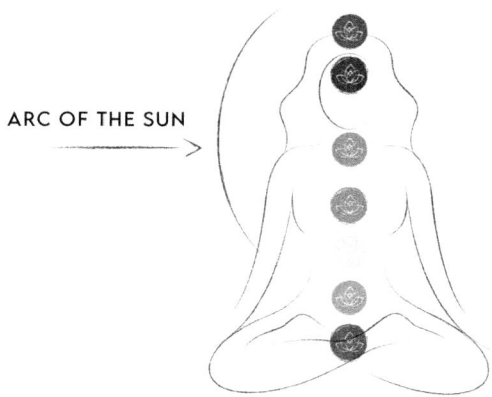

FIGURE 10: THE SOLAR ARC WITHIN THE HUMAN BODY

THE SUN HAS A CROWN

The crown chakra is one of the lesser understood human energy centers. And yet, when that center gets activated by the purest Sun energies, it can be a true asset to humans: it connects them to everything in the greater Universe and turns them into master manifestors.

PRACTICE: INTERNAL SUN ENERGIES

In this exercise, you'll work on upgrading your internal Sun energies and on using the newly minted energies for manifesting the life you want.

1. Find a comfortable place to sit or lie down. Focus on your breathing: breathe in through your nose for a count of three. Breathe out through your mouth for a count of three. Allow the negativity and stress to leave your body with each out-breath.
2. Focus on the center of your belly, right around your belly button—the location of your solar plexus chakra. Imagine it as a pulsating yellow sphere full of potent life-giving force. Rotate this sphere in a clockwise direction, giving it momentum and pushing the energy inside it to start moving faster.
3. Picture an arc not unlike that of a rainbow that connects your solar plexus and your crown chakras. This arc is tubular with a hollow center, yet perfectly crystalline in its nature. Watch as your energy stream flows from the rotating yellow center, through this beautiful arc, and toward the crown center. And as it enters the crown center, picture it as it assembles into a sphere that starts rotating in a clockwise direction and pulsating with the most beautiful white light.
4. Stay here for a few moments. Watch as both of your centers are now perfectly activated and notice how more and more streams of yellow energy get transformed into the purest form of white light as they travel up this arc.
5. Picture how the pure white light gives you a halo—yes, exactly the kind that the angels have. The angels are master manifestors, and they create using the same white light that you now have access to. This light can purify the aura of your body and your surroundings. But most importantly, this light is pure creative energy.

6. Watch as this light becomes focused on your heart's desire—on the kind of life you would like to manifest for yourself. You see how the white light cocoons the image of your future reality: it is picture-perfect—exactly how you want it.
7. Notice that the white light makes that picture more pronounced, adding its own details and making it more real than ever.
8. Watch as the white light creates a miniature copy of that reality and places it within a small opening within your crown center. From this day forward, this vision of your future is the jewel of your Corona—your crown jewel. And not only will it serve as a reminder of what you want, but also it will bring what you want to you in accordance with the Law of Attraction. After all, right now you have an exact replica of the vibration you seek as part of your energetic body.

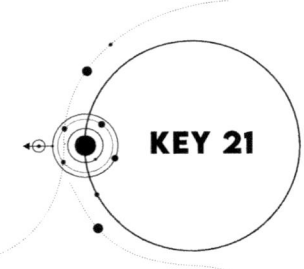

KEY 21

THE PATH OF AN ALCHEMIST

The road of manifestation is just as much about overcoming obstacles as it is staying in the flow. Since you have spent some serious time exploring the different celestial bodies that aid manifestation, it's time to address those that don't. Probably the biggest culprit on this list is good old Saturn.

Saturn is symbolic of many great things like structure, authority, and hard work, but it also imposes restrictions and sets limitations upon human activity and undertaking. Saturn favors slow and steady movement, loves law and order, and supports the measured flow of things. Think about the physical aspect of this massive planet. Saturn is famous for its system of rings—the most extensive set of rings (read: constrictions) in our Solar System, and one of the most elaborate in the entire Milky Way. Saturn hates all things fast and hasty; it doesn't tolerate shortcuts and, on some level, frowns upon all kinds of magic (manifestation included). Saturn is the great equalizer and is responsible for the wheel of karmic payback. Saturn likes things that take their sweet time in being earned and things that come with plenty of blood, sweat, and tears. Arguably, Saturn's preference goes against all you would like to accomplish through manifesting—a swift, impediment-free movement toward what you want.

Any time you're fired up and ready to manifest, you are powered by the active forward-moving energy of the Sun. But as you proceed toward execution, more often than not, you'll be slowed down by the inert energy of Saturn that wants you to "earn" things.

Let's take a deep dive into the ancient science of alchemy since it contains a few profound lessons in transcending the energies of Saturn. If you are familiar with alchemy, you know that the alchemists were obsessed with the idea of turning base metals into precious metals—specifically lead into gold. The science of alchemy was closely related to astronomy. In fact, true alchemists were obsessed with both chemistry and astronomy and studied both the elements and the celestial bodies. It was at that time that the connection between planets and metals was established. The alchemists actually used the same symbol to signify both a planet and its corresponding metal (see Figure 11). As you can see from the chart, the Sun was closely linked with gold while Saturn was associated with lead. Bottom line: The science of alchemy is about the mastery of turning Saturnian (lead) energies into Solar (gold) energies, both figuratively and literally.

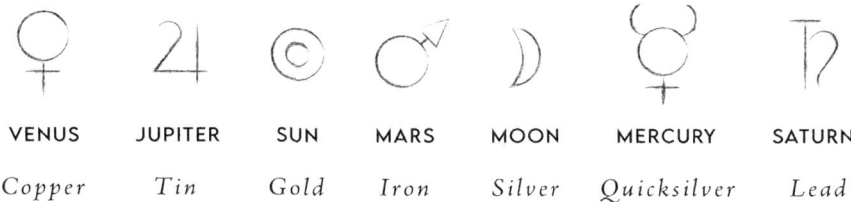

FIGURE 11: ALCHEMICAL SCIENCE: PLANETS AND THEIR METAL CORRESPONDENCES

Let's quickly explore this duality. The Sun is symbolic of lifeforce abound. Saturn is symbolic of lifeforce restriction. The Sun is about expansion—finding and exploring new territories. Saturn is about preserving and containing already-conquered territories. The Sun is about just going for it. Saturn is about earning it. The Sun is about passion (heart) and outward movement. Saturn is about intellect and circular movement inside a predefined orbit. So how does one turn lead into gold and Saturn energies into Sun energies?

Glad you asked. Because today's practice session is all about that.

PRACTICE: TRANSMUTING SATURN'S ENERGIES

A word of caution. Saturn is one of the greatest teachers of our Solar System. Beyond anything else, it exists to help you achieve true mastery. The kind of mastery that can penetrate your every cell and imprint deep within your light DNA structures. The kind of mastery that transcends incarnations. When manifesting something, we will be asking Saturn for a free pass—the end result without some of the hard work. And while Saturn is on board with this pass, it wants you to know that true mastery is a valuable gift, and certain things are worth the wait and the hard work.

With this message from Saturn out of the way, let's move forward to the practice.

1. Close your eyes and sit or lie down in a comfortable place. Start out with a few slow and deep breaths; each inhale and exhale should last for about ten seconds.
2. Imagine that you are floating in a vast, starry cosmos. Feel the sense of calm and expansion that being here brings. Remember that you have always been a part of this eternal celestial terrain, and you belong here, fully.
3. Notice that as you are floating, an invisible force carries you closer to the mighty, magnificent Saturn.
4. As you approach the planet, observe its famous set of powerful rings (see Figure 12). It looks like there are seven from afar, but as you move closer, you can see that the rings are much more plentiful than that. Saturn has thousands of concentric rings circling around its core and entangling the planet in their loyal, steady embrace. The rings of Saturn are the great guards of their ancient master. Before anything can get through to the gaseous giant's heart, it needs to pass this intricate system of trials and tribulations.

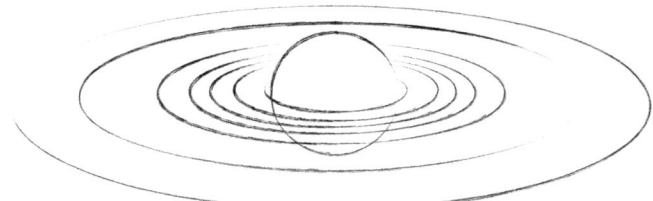

FIGURE 12: THE RINGS OF SATURN

5. Focus on the outermost ring of Saturn—the utmost layer of the ring system. It is light yellow in color and quite hard to distinguish from the surrounding atmosphere, but it is there, nonetheless.
6. Now think of your heart's desire: for a moment, focus on the life you are working to manifest. Imagine it's being encapsulated in an orb of golden light. This is the imprint of your intention that we will be working with today. Place the golden orb of light on the outermost ring.
7. Greet your great celestial teacher, Saturn. Ask Saturn for permission for this free ride—for permission to manifest things quickly without taking the long and hard route. If you are willing, you can even imagine the human aspect of Saturn—a wise, old man with a long beard and a cloak. The human version of Saturn has a set of concentric rings on his neck and waist. If you are curious,

you can ask Saturn for a message for yourself. As a great teacher, he probably has something that needs to be communicated.

8. Trust the message you get—whether it is a word, a feeling, or a sudden urge to do something. If the message doesn't come right away, be patient. You will receive it in the coming days. As you ask Saturn for permission to bypass his defense system, ask for his agreement. If he is in alignment with your request, you will know it.

9. Now that you have permission to move forward without obstacles, allow the golden orb of light to move clockwise toward the planet's center (see Figure 13). This movement is in accordance with the great spiral of life—the energy behind the golden ratio and the Divine wisdom of transformation.

10. Witness how your orb is passing each ring of Saturn one by one, moving swiftly, and encountering no obstacles. Watch the orb accelerate and start moving faster and faster, passing one ring, then ten, then a hundred, until there is only one ring left to go through—the innermost inner ring of Saturn, and the last guard on your path to Saturn's heart.

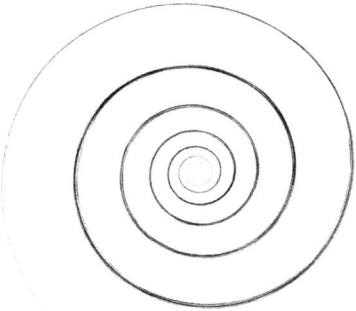

FIGURE 13: THE SPIRAL OF LIFE

11. Watch your golden orb slow down and come to a complete stop next to a small opening—a door that leads into the very core of the planet.

12. Watch Saturn himself invite you in. Know that from this day forward, you are Divinely guided and supported by this wonderful teacher. Know that he is now on your side and that he is fully aligned with the vibrations of your new life and will be assisting you on the path.

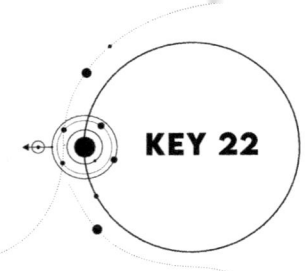

KEY 22

BENDING TIME

> *"People like us, who believe in physics, know that the distinction between past, present and future is only a stubbornly persistent illusion."*
>
> —Albert Einstein

Time is one of the greatest fallacies of our reality (also see Key 9, page 55). Even though we measure our lives as a journey between two points—our birth and our death, with time being a major consideration in between—time is far from linear.

Bending time is the ability to accelerate and decelerate time in accordance with your needs. The absolute prerequisite to obtaining that ability is understanding that time is not "real." Time is merely an anchor that creates an illusion of continuity. It gives humanity the sense of control and sanity that comes with recurring phenomena—days flowing into nights, and seasons changing with an enviable level of regularity.

The truth is: time is infinitely malleable in its nature. The only reason that time on Earth feels consistent and predictable is that most physical aspects of our planet are quite static: its mass, speed, and gravity remain virtually unchanged day to day. If this weren't the case, the illusory notion of time would become immediately apparent. It is a commonly known fact, for example, that astronauts age more slowly because time flows differently for them when they are in space. In fact, the faster an object moves, the slower the time passes in relation to it. From this perspective, time is nothing if not relative. That means there is no one unified time, but rather there is a time as it appears to one person and a time as it appears to another person. Neither one is more valid than the other.

Now that we established each of us has our own frame of reference as it relates to time (and thus our own time continuum), we should learn how to use this fact to our advantage.

CONTAINING TIME

Time loves being contained and operates like water. It will fill whatever container you give it to fill since it can take any shape and stretch itself into infinity if needed. Yet it loves itself a good boundary. Time loves being defined. The way you define time is through establishing timeframes and deadlines. Time is incredibly viscous. Like a good chameleon, it can adjust to anything. One of the bigger mistakes to make with manifestation is to give the Universe carte blanche as far as the "when" you want things to happen. Establish the timeframe for your manifestation, ideally down to a month and a year. Write it down and hang the poster on your wall. Establishing a realistic but aggressive timeline is a good balance. Give the world too much time, and you might lose momentum; not enough time, and you create too much pressure and stifle the flow.

So does the future you want already exist?

Yes and no. You are probably used to the notion that your past affects you. But so does your desired future. Once you create a future vision you are excited about and feed it with enough energy, you create an energetic pull between present and future you. This energetic pull could alter your whole life—your habits, your circle of friends, and your interests long before you fully align with that future. Remember, there is always a default version of the future you are moving into. And your current habits are a dead giveaway for the version of the future you are moving toward. The good news? You can always align with the most optimal "future you" and ask for advice and feedback. Some of the most insightful messages could come from these types of exercises.

FIND YOUR PACE

Alarm clocks, strict schedules, and predetermined days for work and leisure are the culprits behind your messed-up relationship with time. For every correct notion about time, there are at least a dozen myths. Have you, for instance, heard that most successful people wake up really early? How about that they work 80 hours per week and hardly ever take vacations? Have you perhaps heard that successful people don't take the weekends off? All of these myths are perpetuating our obsession with creating pressure in our own lives. And yet, pressure is the absolute absence of flow. Take control of your time. And no—that doesn't mean bullying yourself into waking up with the dawn. Learn to listen to your body. How well do you know yourself? What time does your body like waking up? Are you most productive in the morning or in the evening? There are no right answers.

Some people can create more in one hour than others in a whole week. Give yourself permission to find and stick to your own pace—to move as fast or as slow as you prefer. Start belonging to yourself fully—from the moment you wake up to when you go to bed.

EXPERIENCE THE FLOW

The flow is surrender in action. To experience the flow, you need to make amends with your personal timeline and your personal timekeepers. You need to allow yourself to be in agreement with the way things are. Yet you need to keep moving. Flow is not static or an absence of action. Flow is the most powerful force that there is. Flow is your personal intersection point with the larger Universe; it is a point of equilibrium. Flow is moving through the fabric of the Universe in the direction that you have chosen with plenty of speed and momentum, but without causing negative ripple effects.

PRACTICE: BENDING THE TIME-SPACE CONTINUUM

Today you'll be working with the matrix structure that makes up your personal reality (for more on the matrix, see Keys 9 and 11, pages 000 and 000). Visually, the matrix is a system of vertical and horizontal intersecting lines that make up a grid of light (see Figure 14). Every object in the observable Universe is nestled in a particular area of this grid—everything in the Universe has its predetermined and fixed place within the matrix. The matrix doesn't discriminate between things future and things past. That is why everything exists in the matrix simultaneously, albeit in very different areas of the greater whole.

FIGURE 14: THE MATRIX AND BENDING TIME

1. Close your eyes and relax. Take a few deep breaths and settle into your body. Take a few moments to quiet your internal dialogue.
2. First, find the exact location of the object of your desire within the matrix. If you have given the object or the event some thought, it MUST exist in the matrix, simply because your thoughts are instantly material. The imprint of that object was likely created in a remote location of the matrix, so aligning with it will take real effort.
3. Now zoom into the location of your desired object. It will appear inside of a golden bubble at the intersection of a few cells of the matrix. Chances are that this bubble is light and airy. Most new desires are—they are as light as a feather. This is 100 percent normal: the initial imprint of a physical object is meant to be no more than a whisper. Objects that are already manifested in the physical have a lot more weight to them. Feel free to compare by imagining a large object you know from real life—perhaps the building of your local church or your own house—whatever you know to be 100 percent real in the physical world. This object also has a location within the matrix. Please find that location and zoom into it. Notice how this object seems to have plenty of heft to itself. It seems that this object is very well anchored into the fabric of the matrix—it is not going anywhere. This is what you would like to achieve with your dream bubble.
4. Take a moment to refocus on the bubble with your desired object inside. Imagine the bubble becoming heavier and heavier. Imagine it's starting to sink

into the matrix due to its newly found weight and momentum. See it anchoring deeper and deeper into the matrix.

5. Watch the density of your bubble increase, turning into a sphere made of solid gold. Watch as your golden orb sinks deeper into the matrix and creates a ripple effect in it. Your orb now carries so much weight; it is so heavy that it is starting to distort the matrix structure around it, in turn creating a curvature in a shape of a crater around itself. Please know that the more weight your golden orb has, the better your chances of manifesting your desire in the physical. Feel free to come back to this meditation as many times as it feels right and increase the weight of your golden orb.

6. Before you go, locate your own place within the matrix—in the here and now. Notice that there is plenty of "distance" between your current location and your desired object. What separates you is what Einstein called "space-time continuum." But since you know that time is incredibly relative, you'll proceed with bending it today.

7. Imagine that you can bend this matrix grid like a piece of paper (refer to Figure 14 above). Fold it in half so that your location and the location of your desired object are now perfectly aligned, and one is directly on top of the other.

8. Now create a stream of energy connecting the two points—your location and that of your desire. Feel a torrent of golden light stream from one point to the other, connecting them through space and time. Now these two points are closer than they have ever been before.

9. Declare a strong intention to cut the time it would take for you to get to your desired outcome by ten times. Or 100 times—whatever feels right. Take some time for this intention to be solidified.

10. Whenever you are ready, come back to daily life.

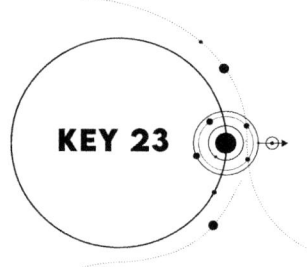

KEY 23

CLAIMING TERRITORY

As you learned in the previous chapter, the matrix is a highly complex, intricate structure. While being a logical system, it is dynamic enough to enable as much creative freedom as possible. At any point in time, you might, unbeknownst to you, be creating completely new sections of the matrix. You might even create them as you sleep (yes, the creative process doesn't stop when your physical body is resting). Often these new worlds are located in faraway locations, so upon completing the creation of a segment of the matrix, you may never return to it again. There are vast territories within the matrix that are being created from scratch or erased into nothing daily. If the matrix isn't seeing activity in a sector, it may choose to delete it to free up space for more things to be created.

Claiming territory is an essential concept within the matrix. It is a process of letting the matrix know that you not only intend to create a whole new sector of it conceptually, but also materialize it and enjoy the fruits of your labor. The claimed segment of the matrix cannot be erased without consequence, especially not while the claimant is still incarnated. Claiming your territory within the matrix is an absolute must for successful manifestation, especially if you aim to achieve something sizable. Claiming is a sacred act that lets the matrix know what you want—and that you are 100 percent serious about it.

There are three major ways to claim your territory within the matrix—intellectual, emotional, and energetic. Collectively, these three aspects give you the power of fully aligned intention.

INTELLECTUAL CLAIM

This claim relates to your Mental Body—your subtle body responsible for your thoughts and overall belief system. Believing that you CAN and WILL get what you want is the first building block of manifesting. For many of you, it would involve reflecting on your realm of possibility and even reassessing what it means to be good or bad. This process would also entail releasing old, limiting beliefs that don't align with your new direction.

EMOTIONAL CLAIM

This claim relates to your Emotional (Astral) Body—the subtle body that governs your feelings and emotions. The feeling in your bones that goes deep into every cell of your body is your emotional claim. Until you align with your desired outcome emotionally, you truly haven't claimed that territory and will be dragging your feet on the way there.

ENERGETIC CLAIM

This claim relates to your Energetic (Etheric) Body—the subtle body responsible for your flow of energy. It includes things like chakras, the flow of *kundalini*, the energetic cords to your ancestors, and your connection to Mother Nature. Your energetic body needs to be fully aligned with your desired outcome to help you attract things that align with your new path and help you avoid things that do not. It also needs to know how to distribute your energy daily. This distribution can be a big puzzle—at any given time, your Etheric Body is deciding whether to allocate your energy to long-term or short-term needs. When you claim something energetically, a portion of your energy stream will automatically be allocated to helping achieve that goal until it becomes a reality.

PRACTICE: CLAIMING TERRITORY—INTELLECTUALLY, EMOTIONALLY, ENERGETICALLY

In this practice, you will be claiming your territory in all the ways that matter for manifestation—intellectually, emotionally, and energetically.

1. Make sure you are lying down or are seated in a comfortable position. Close your eyes and relax. Settle into your body and take a few deep breaths. Take some time to quiet your mind.

2. Imagine that you are standing in the middle of a valley—your safe place within the matrix. The valley may be unfamiliar to you, but it is extremely beautiful, and you feel very safe here, as if you truly belong.
3. For a moment, concentrate on your desired outcome—the subject of your manifestation. Think of the day in the future when you achieve what you want. How would you know that you "made it"? What specific indicators would serve as proof? Think of ALL the quantifiable information that would signify that you made it. Is it a certain amount of money in your bank account? Or perhaps a certain number of followers, a particular number of books sold, or dollars raised for a cause that is dear to you? Think of every number that would denote your success.
4. When you are done, ALLOW yourself to have that number. Claim that number intellectually with all you have. Claim it as already yours. Once you claim something, it is the law that it must be yours. There should be no doubt left in your mind. The number you want is already yours. When you are ready to claim this number, take a metal staff and, with as much force as you can master, drop the staff into the ground where you stand. Notice how the ground around you is cracking due to the power of the staff and the force of your intention. This is the first claiming—the intellectual kind.
5. Now return to thinking about having your desired outcome. What emotions would it give you? Allow yourself to dive deep into those feelings, and allow them to consume you. Become fully aligned with that feeling from now on—after all, you are already on the path. When ready, lower the metal staff to the ground and plant it into the soil with much force, marking this new emotional territory as yours. Allow the Universe to bring you more of this feeling today and every day. This is the second claiming—the emotional kind.
6. Lastly, focus on your energetic body—the part of you that is pure lifeforce, alive with a million different colors. Watch as three energy streams enter your body. The first one comes from the top; it is a thread that connects you to your Higher Self and your Spirit energy, and it's the highest vibration that you have access to. Watch as it enters the crown of your head and descends toward your solar plexus chakra in a downward spiral motion.
7. Picture another energy stream entering the sole of your left foot: this is the energy of your mother's ancestral lineage – abundant and gentle. Watch as this

beautiful energy spirals up your left leg and your lower chakras, starting at the base of your spine and culminating in the solar plexus.

8. Finally, the third energy stream is entering the sole of your right foot: this is the energy of your father's ancestors—brave and true. Watch this beautiful energy spiral up your right leg and move from the root chakra through the sacral chakra and culminating in the solar plexus.
9. Watch as the three mighty energy streams form a triple helix of glimmering etheric light. Feel your solar plexus area becoming warm and starting to pulsate with this endless, strong energy. Know that this energy is yours for the taking; it wants to help you build a better life for yourself.
10. Allow this magnificent energy stream to pour out of your belly and into a golden orb of light—an orb that contains an imprint of your heart's desire. Allow the orb to take as much energy and as much sustenance as it needs.
11. Now, take your magical metal stake and repeat: " I declare that I want my energy, the energy of my Higher Self, and the energy of my ancestors to power and feed my intention. I commit to allocating whatever energy necessary to the manifestation of my desired outcome."
12. With these words, place the metal stake in the ground with as much force as you can. Watch the ground shake beneath your feet and notice the cracks below becoming wider. Know that this is your territory now and that you have absolutely nothing to worry about. It is merely a matter of time before you see your desire manifested in the physical.

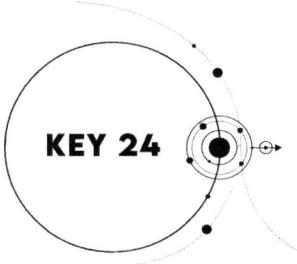

KEY 24

THE PRINCIPLE OF REPETITION

Nothing is quite as powerful as the power of attention. Whatever you "pay" attention to inevitably becomes your life. One of the bigger mistakes around manifestation is to set and forget. Claiming the territory is paramount, but nurturing and taking care of that territory is perhaps more important in the long run. We have planted the seeds; now it is time to start tending to the garden. Your newly manifested reality is your energetic child. You quite literally birthed it, and it feeds on your energy. That is why it is incredibly hard to manifest many big-ticket items at the same time: there are only so many times you can split your energy stream and remain effective. However, below we'll look at just a few ways to keep your manifestation alive and strengthen it every day without exerting too much effort. Being systematic and doing one small thing daily is more important than sporadic, in-depth effort.

REFRESH YOUR INTENTION

It is important to take the time to write down your intention—the details of the world you are trying to create for yourself. Feel free to print the page with your intention and place it somewhere you can see it daily. Every time your eyes fall on that piece of paper, you will inadvertently send a new portion of your energy to fortify your original intention. Set one day of the week to be your "refresher" day. All you would need to do is reread and re-commit to the vision you wrote down. Try to find something new and exciting about your vision so your brain doesn't perceive this as a boring exercise. Your goal is to keep the fire burning.

THE RITUAL OF GRATITUDE

Remember to feel grateful every day. Feel gratitude for receiving that which you want. Gratitude is the great multiplier. It can be helpful to set a gratitude calendar and mark each day that you express your gratitude with a check box. This is a powerful ritual that will start bringing true abundance to your life, above and beyond what you originally intended.

CREATE A "SPELL"

The spoken and the written word are two incredibly impactful tools in our manifestation kit. A word is an embodiment of an energetic frequency and the precursor to material objects. Before an object becomes material, it comes in the form of a word or a sentence. Thus our language and how we use it is the first step in manifesting. Create a meaningful sentence around your manifestation that will call it into existence. Speak that sentence out loud a few times a week.

Example: "Every day I get closer and closer to achieving the outcome." or "Every day my Universe is bringing me more and more abundance." or "The Universe is always flowing in my favor, bringing me closer to my dream."

ESTABLISH A "SIGN"

The material world is inert, and it takes time to change your circumstances in a meaningful way. Don't get discouraged—this is a natural and healthy part of the process. One of the challenges around manifestation is that, at times, the outside circumstances don't seem to match what our version of a positive sequence of events is. When that happens, it is easy to get derailed and start emitting a contradictory frequency—the frequency that could get you further away from your desired outcome instead of closer. Because of that, you have a right to create an agreement with the Universe. Establish an object or a word that would serve as a symbol for you. Any time you see or hear it out in the world, it would mean that you are on the right track, and everything is flowing exactly as it is supposed to. Ask the Universe to put this object in your path as a reminder. Examples of objects are:

- △ a black (or white) cat
- △ an eagle
- △ any combination of numbers (1111, 777, or 0000)

△ a particular crystal or flower that you like—it can be anything

You want to pick something hard to come by, but not impossible. Every time you see the sign—acknowledge it and smile at the Universe. Know that it is on your side and will always be.

FIND A TALISMAN

Another great way to nurture your intention is to find an object that will co-manifest alongside you. The best talismans are natural objects—crystals, feathers, wood, shells, etc. These objects are alive because they come from the mineral, plant, or animal kingdom and thus carry the primordial vibrations of creation. Select an object that you feel best aligns with your vision and has a similar vibration. Trust your heart with this—it can never go wrong. Once the object is determined, take some time to align with and charge it. Simply hold it close to your heart and fill it up to the brim with your heart energy. Connect to the core of this talisman and ask it for assistance with manifesting your perfect outcome. Keep this talisman on your writing desk or close to your bed, so it is never too far away from you. The power of a well-charged talisman is hard to overestimate. This object will help align the energies of nature and the Universe to help accelerate your manifestation process.

PRACTICE: MULTIPLYING THE ENERGY OF YOUR MANIFESTATION

In today's practice, you'll work on amplifying the energy of your manifestation using this meditative visualization.

1. Close your eyes and settle into your breath. Allow your thoughts to come and go without paying much attention to them.
2. Focus on your desired outcome—on the one thing you are trying to manifest. Imagine it symbolically. If you were to condense it to a simple object, what object would it be? Try to see that object in your mind's eye. What shape

does it have? Is it big or small? Does it have a color? Does it have a sound? Try to imagine every little aspect of this object. Rotate it to examine it from different angles.

3. Having observed the object, create an exact copy of it in your mind's eye. Watch as both objects rotate at the exact same angle—complete duplicates of one another. Multiply the original object a few more times, creating exact copies of it. See how all the space around you is filled with identical copies of your desired outcome. Feel free to keep multiplying the object until it feels sufficient.

4. Now that you are surrounded by the many copies of your desire, start stacking them on top of each other so that one is absorbed into the other. As two objects align with one another, they become one and the same but double the potential, double the energy, and double the power. Keep stacking the objects on top of each other and see their collective power multiply. Continue this practice until there is only one object left—the same exact object you started with, but with much more momentum and pure lifeforce.

5. Place both palms of your hands over the unified object. Feel the warmth and energy emanating from your amplified creation. Feel how the two of you are on the same wavelength—mere extensions of each other.

6. Drawing energy from the Sun, send that energy through the palms of your hands into the object. Watch the object becoming larger and stronger than before.

7. Allow this cycle of energy to carry on even once you are done with this meditation. Allow the energy of the Sun to feed and nurture your desired outcome day in and day out.

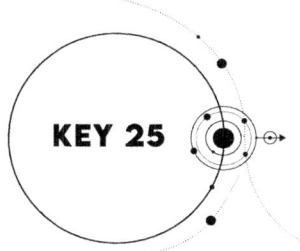

KEY 25

THE THREE STATES OF ENERGY

To manifest, you require a focused energy stream. Energy streams come in all shapes and sizes. Naturally, you know that every person has an aura—which already implies that your energy is unique to you. Your aura is the sum total of all energy streams that are inherent within you. There are three types of energy present within your body—focused, dispersed, and stuck (also see Key 18, page 86).

Stuck energy (also blocked energy) represents all the trauma and negative emotions that took root inside of your energy field. Stuck energy is very condensed; it is heavy. That is why people who have experienced a lot of trauma in their life feel heavy and sad when you meet them.

Dispersed energy resembles a cloud—this is your unfocused creative energy that exists in its untapped state. This is your reserve—your inner pool of energy that is largely dormant. Your dispersed energy is waiting to be ignited and called into action. Another use for this kind of energy is inner healing and replenishment of your resource state. This energy travels around your body, seeking ways to heal you and restore you to your state of perfect health and balance. Dispersed energy is your inner healer—wise and true, it is always the first to come to your aid when you are in pain, physical or otherwise.

Focused energy is the active state of energy. It is a deliberate stream, a perfectly directed flow, and a spear on its way to finding the target. Only about ten percent of your energy exists in its focused state, which is a shame compared to about 30 percent that exists in the blocked state. Arguably, this balance is correlated to the overall level of happiness and wellbeing, especially in the West. Yes, we live in a largely unhappy (and tired) society trying to distract itself with whatever means possible from what truly matters—why we came to this planet in the first place.

DREAMS AND INTENTIONS

Now, armed with this information, let's explore two concepts core to the art of manifestation—a dream versus an intention.

More often than not, we engage in the practice of dreaming and not intending. Of all the fatal manifestation errors, this by far is the most critical. This practice may be exactly WHY your manifestation hasn't worked in the past. A dream as an energy structure belongs to the dispersed energy cluster and thus doesn't represent an actionable state. The purpose of a dream is to heal your body. That is why you may get a warm fuzzy feeling inside when you are daydreaming—this is the healing process at its finest. A dream is not meant to spur you into action—it is an energy that is contained within itself, and its purpose is to balance your emotional state or fill up your inner well when it lacks in something. An intention, on the other hand, is focused energy. The energy of intention moves mountains. Anyone that has ever succeeded in manifesting has tapped into the power of intention and not the power of daydreaming.

ENERGY FLOW FOR MANIFESTATION

Your intention resides in your throat center/chakra (*Vishuddha*). That is exactly where this powerful force is born and where it goes to rest once its mission is complete. Your throat is connected to self-expression, vows, and commitments. The power and integrity of your word, therefore, play a critical role in the creative process. In fact, all Divinely inspired creations take shape in this powerful energy center. As far as manifestation is concerned, the throat chakra is a heavily underused and underappreciated center.

The energy of daydreaming could reside in any of the chakras (see also diagram, Key 7, page 47) depending on what is being healed right now, and it also tends to move around, just like a cloud. This energy is hard to pin down or fix in one place. Therefore, the energy of a daydream is much less reliable than the energy of intention.

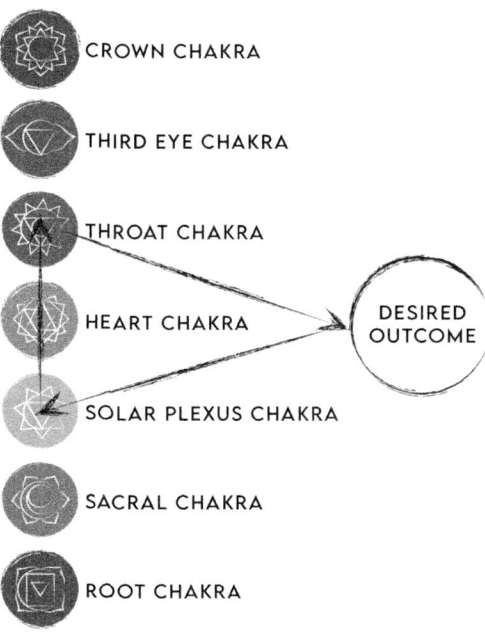

FIGURE 15: TRIANGULAR FLOW FOR MANIFESTATION

Outside of your throat chakra, the other critical energy center is your solar plexus—your inner Sun, the powerhouse within—that both manufactures and distributes your lifeforce throughout your body. This is where your manifestation begins: it's the first step, the inception point, and the genesis of your present, past, and future.

There is an energy flow within your body that is most helpful with manifestation. This flow resembles a triangle (see Figure 15). It starts off in your solar plexus—powered by the energy of the Sun and light. This is the force of your will. It then moves with intention toward your throat area, where it connects with the force of your commitment and creative power. At this moment, if this energy receives the support and blessing of the throat center, true momentum is created, enough so that it can move outside of your body and start working in the outer world. When this happens, the combined force of your will and your intention start moving energy around to reach your desired outcome. That intended and desired outcome gets manifested as a potential future, which propels the energy forward to close the triangle. The process is repeated as long as there is enough energy in the solar plexus and the throat chakras to keep the momentum going. After a few cycles of such triangulated energy movement, your desired outcome becomes manifested.

PRACTICE: INTENTIONAL THINKING

To ensure that the energy of your dreams becomes the energy of your intentions, you can use a simple exercise as an anchoring practice. To benefit from it fully, make sure you are well rested.

1. With your eyes closed or open, whichever feels better, focus on your intended outcome.
2. When your desired outcome becomes vivid in front of our eyes, imagine it as a ball of energy. It will be of a particular color, depending on what it represents.
3. In your mind's eye, move that ball of energy towards the middle of your throat.
4. From here, commit to making this desired outcome a reality for you. When you truly commit, without reservation, you will notice that the ball of energy just dissolves inside of your throat chakra, co-mingling with the other energies that already reside there.

Congratulations—you have just anchored your desired outcome in your center of creativity. You have also turned that outcome into an intention.

PRACTICE: JUMPSTART YOUR TRIANGLE

This practice can strengthen your connection to your desired outcome.

1. Focus on your belly area; feel free to keep your eyes closed or open—whatever feels right.
2. Imagine that there is an inner Sun—strong and powerful—in the center of your belly. Allow yourself to feel that force deeply and breathe more Sun energy into your body until you feel your body get warmer or start experiencing a slight tingling sensation. Then send that energy into your throat area.

3. Picture your throat area as a sphere of effervescent blue light that expands with every breath you take.
4. Focus on your desired outcome. Watch how your throat area reacts to it. There may be some discomfort regarding your goals; allow this feeling to come and go. Nothing prevents you from having what you want—nothing as long as you are willing to commit to that vision. Stay here for a few moments and breathe in and out.
5. With each breath, allow your throat center to claim that vision as your own—unequivocally and irrevocably. Know in your heart of hearts that it CAN and WILL be yours.
6. Feel your throat center continue to expand and take in the new energy with every breath you take.
7. Expand this center until you feel ready and willing to go for what you want.
8. You will notice this integration creates a focused energy stream that travels into your possible future—the one where you have what you want, and a point in time that you desire greatly. This connects you with and aligns you to that future.
9. Imagine that future as a point in time and one of the points of the triangle you are creating. Once that point is established, allow your energy to saturate that point fully and then, when ready, to come back into the center of the belly—the first point of the triangle.
10. Repeat this practice when you want to continue strengthening this connection.

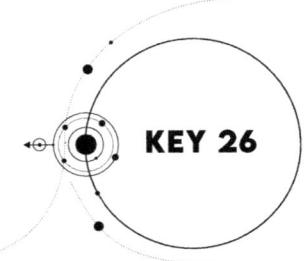

KEY 26

THE MANY ASPECTS OF MATTER

Did you know that there is a natural energy force that is already aligned with your best outcome? Let's call this energy your sponsor, or more specifically, the sponsor of your manifestation. Frequently, this energy belongs to one of the founding energies of matter—fire, earth, water, or air. This energy has already selected you. Moreover, it has probably already been helping you behind the scenes. Aligning with this energy can help you harness its power to a higher degree while preserving your own resources. This is the great borrowing of energy—a phenomenon that allows you to achieve your outcome with the help of something much bigger than yourself. Your own energy is finite, and powering your manifestation takes a lot of energy, perhaps much more than you have. The most successful manifestors know how to tap into large pools of energy and work with them over time to bring things to fruition.

So, let's examine the main elemental energies and how they can aid with manifestation.

FIRE

Working with fire energies is not for the faint of heart. Fire is the ultimate masculine force—full of action, passion, and a sense of urgency. If you enlist the energy of fire to be your sponsor, you better prepare for a wild ride. Fire energies are the opposite of tame. Fire is a risk-taker. It is the type of energy that likes to dive in headfirst. It likes rapid movement and fast progress and will always push you outside of your comfort zone. Fire energies favor the brave. They also like the ones who are pursuing big, bold dreams and outcomes. Fire energies like the conquest and are incredible allies for those who dare to challenge the status quo.

- △ **Magma/Lava:** The original fire energy, magma is both the revolutionary and the heartbeat of this planet. It is pure potential. It is the great molder of mountains and the precursor of continents. There is nothing that magma energy cannot take on. Word of caution: magma is not the most patient of energies. It requires complete commitment. It would expect you to work tirelessly if it were to join your cause.

- △ **Flame/Torch:** This fire energy is much more contained—perfect for creative and innovative projects, as well as projects that require a spark of inspiration to be fully birthed. This fire, while powerful, is easier to control and won't require reckless sacrifices from you. On the other hand, it won't give you as much momentum as the original magma energy.
- △ **Star Fire:** Star fire is the cosmic fire of the Divine Masculine. This energy is perfect for fueling societal change or planetary-level projects. If the sky's the limit and you aim to achieve something bigger than yourself, star fire energies might be exactly what you need. The challenge? These energies are picky beyond measure, and they would only select you if you are pure of heart and won't misuse your Divine gifts.

EARTH

Earth energies are extremely diverse, just like our planet. They are generally very pleasant to work with. They are patient—a bit slow-moving, but steady, and they always get the job done. They are also some of the easiest to work with—flexible, nurturing, and incredibly symbiotic. They will work with your natural rhythm and limitations. They are quite forgiving. Earth energies are challenging to align initially, but once they are aligned, they require very little upkeep, which makes them very simple to maintain.

- △ **Mineral Kingdom (Crystals):** Minerals are incredible amplifiers of your natural energies. So if your success depends on amplifying your existing energies, you will find great allies in crystals. Crystals are amazing protector spirits, and they are also master attractors, as plenty of them have magnetic properties.
- △ **Mountains:** If you need help strengthening your resolve and dreaming big, mountain energies are your best bet. The energy of the mountain is solid, stable, and steady. It is supportive and grounding. Mountains can also provide a vantage point and help you avoid getting lost in the maze. Mountain energies

are perfect if you want to manifest the mastery of something—a craft or a skill—since they can ensure you have the resources and the resolve to keep going.

- △ **Wood (Plant Kingdom):** Woods can be helpful if you require a more fluid, intuitive approach to manifestation. Wood is a great equalizer: it is a harbinger of balance and, on some level, justice. For gentle, loving souls who understand that to receive, you first need to give, wood energies can be incredibly lucrative. They will ensure good karma doesn't keep you waiting.
- △ **Animal Kingdom:** Harnessing the energy of any animal—real or fictitious—can be a great aid on a path to manifestation. The dragon's energy is forceful and full of magic, the lion is royal and brave, and the eagle is powerful and far-reaching. There are plenty of energies and skillsets to select from in the animal kingdom if you are called to it.
- △ **Soil:** Nurturing mother energies are ever-present in the earthly soil. If you expect to grow a little seed into a beautiful garden and are ready to work for it, soil energies are an amazing sponsor for you. If you experience joy from taking something small and growing it over time, nurturing soil energies could be exactly what you need. These energies will help maintain and multiply abundance long after you reach your goals. These energies are your partners for life.
- △ **Metal:** Beautiful in their resistant qualities, metal energies are perfect if you need stamina and the ability to go the distance. They are also perfect for people who tend to be too noncommittal or tend to give up easily. Metal can strengthen your resolve and allow you to keep going where others stray off the path.

WATER

The ultimate feminine domain, water is lifeforce incarnate. There is nothing that water cannot achieve if given enough time. Yes, it even sharpens stone. Water is one of the most abundant energies on this planet and can be an all-sweeping force if properly directed. Water is moldable and forgiving energy, so if you are new to manifestation, water might be the best place to start.

- △ **Ocean:** The ocean works in mysterious ways. It is moody, deep, and has a mind of its own. It moves according to the tides, so the energy it brings, while powerful, has its ebbs and flows. And yet the power it brings is majestic. The ocean could be your greatest ally on a path of knowledge and discovering your own true potential, as well as discovering the mysteries of this Universe.

- △ **River:** Commanding the power of flow and the natural electromagnetism of this planet, rivers are the perfect energy for people who thrive on a fast pace and dynamic movement. The energy of the river brings results and a sense of true adventure. The river energy will remove obstacles from your path and will ensure as smooth of a ride as possible.
- △ **Waterfall:** The master energy of rapid change, waterfall energy is the great remover of obstacles and the great agent of clearing, cleansing, and healing. If you intend to manifest health and wellness, the energies of the waterfall could be some of the best energies to call to your aid. Waterfalls are also perfect for manifesting abundance and money—yes, let's make it rain.
- △ **Ice:** A unique energy to partner up with, ice is achieved through the absence of flow and is perfect for eradicating something that no longer serves you. If you need something removed to feel happy, ice is your energy. Need to freeze up cancer cells or the energy of your ex that still keeps calling your name? Let's bring the ice out.

AIR

Another masculine energy, the air, is multidimensional and omnipotent. It brings plenty of intention and momentum without the harshness of the fire. Air can meet you where you are—at any level, high or low. It is malleable and flexible. It brings the energy of breath—both the inhale and the exhale, or the new beginning and the welcome relief. The energies of the air are perfect if you require the help of lighter, higher dimensional beings such as angels, as it permeates the fabric of the Universe and can take things from one dimension to another.

- △ **Wind:** Having the advantage of air travel, the wind doesn't believe in obstacles. Paths that can trip up plenty of earthly beings are no impediment to the wind. If you expect to face plenty of obstacles on your way, wind can be a perfect sponsoring energy. It has plenty of force, an undeniable sense of direction, and an ability to get fast, if not instant, results.

- △ **Tornado:** Hold on to your hats: this energy is nothing to mess with. It can bring with it both massive destruction as well as massive change. If you think you can handle the tornado, it certainly has enough power to get you anywhere you are trying to go without wasting a breath. It is scarily effective, but it will require you to be all in. No, you cannot stop this ride halfway. Whatever starts with the help of a tornado must find a resolution.
- △ **Aether:** While not technically an air element, aether is a soup that makes up most of the Universe. It is a viscous substance that connects all the material objects of the Universe. It is also a massive creative force. Are you dreaming of something that very few have achieved or even seen in their lives? It surely exists in the realm of aether, and it can be yours with the help of this ethereal ally.
- △ **Cosmos:** Last but not least, the great cosmos is about as broad as we can go as far as sponsoring energy. This energy is a phenomenal ally in creating something monumental, life-altering, and society-changing. It shuns small-scale and unambitious projects but can be your best choice for things that are awe-inducing.

PRACTICE: ENERGY ALIGNMENT

Now that you have taken a quick tour of the different sponsoring energies, the following practice can help you determine which energy best aligns with your intention.

1. Close your eyes and start by taking a few deep breaths.
2. In your mind's eye, imagine that in front of you, there are four transparent pipes—one for each type of element. The first one belongs to fire, the second one to water, the third to air, and the fourth to earth.
3. Now focus on your desired outcome. Notice that at this point in time, your desire is already powered by one or two of the energy forms. The pipe that is feeding your dream reality will be filled with its corresponding energy while the rest will appear to be empty. What energy is lighting up for you? What energy carries your vision forward and nurtures and fuels it? You should be able to see one (or two) quite clearly.

4. Trust what you see and, once you get clarity, thank your sponsoring energy. Know that any time your manifestation is seemingly getting off track, you can call in this force of nature to assist you. Whatever element naturally comes through for you, rest assured that you can select a sponsoring force from within its range. So if you got the element of air, know that you can work with any sub-air energy you choose—from cosmos to wind. The choice is yours. Simply call that energy in to assist you on your path.

If you feel like you could use another energy to assist you with making your dream a reality, add it to your toolkit by filling an empty pipe with it. Once full, allow the pipe to start feeding the sphere that encapsulates your desired outcome. Voilà—just like that, you got yourself a sponsor.

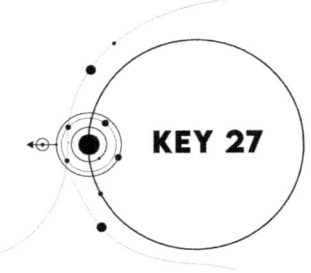

BOND WITH YOUR SPONSORING FORCE

Now that you have determined which natural element is your sponsoring energy (see Key 26, page 120), it is paramount to start building on this relationship. The more you are in touch with your allied power, the easier and faster things will manifest. If you are not getting enough of your sponsoring energy, manifesting may be incredibly painful and slow. Below is an overview of all the sponsoring elements; feel free to focus only on the relevant force(s) for you.

FIRE

Fire energy is fairly volatile and is more challenging to maintain over time since it requires constant nourishment. Fire is passion, drive, and action incarnate. First things first—fire always fuels fire the best. So surround yourself with as much "healthy" fire as you can in your day-to-day life. Keep candles next to your bed or on your desk—wherever you spend a lot of time. If you are fueled by fire, you really need to go overboard by burning candles. Put them in every room if you can, and having a fireplace is even better. If you have one, make sure to spend some quality time next to it at least twice a week. Above all, you need to be in the Sun—the fire that holds this whole Solar System together. Everything from sungazing to sunbathing is your new best friend.

Fire also loves hot liquids—whether it's coffee or tea, especially with a touch of spice and herbs—as they are like inviting a liquid fire to fuel you from within. Fire loves honey, clover, and cinnamon, so add them to your food and drinks any chance that you get. Fire also thrives on taking rapid action. When this energy fuels you, it will compel you to do things fast and often. Try to keep up with the fire's pace—the more you play ball with this energy, the more giving it becomes. But it certainly needs you to work for it. Manifesting with fire is no walk in the park, but it is 100 percent exciting, 100 percent impactful, and 100 percent full of meaning.

EARTH

Manifesting with the earth element is truly working hand in hand with nature and requires you to stay grounded and connected to your roots—or find them in the first place if you haven't done so yet. From a practical perspective, you will need to take at least a couple of minutes every day to connect physically with one of the earth elements. Walking barefoot if the weather allows is a must, as this is one of the quickest ways to strengthen and maintain your bond with Mother Earth.

Alternatively, work with trees and absorb their energy by placing the palms of your hands on the trunk. If you are working with Earth energy, you'll also need to invest in a crystal companion or two. No crystal will fit everyone, so have your heart select one that feels right for you in a specialized shop. The earth's energy is deeply connected to truth and authenticity, so you'll need to be as honest with yourself and others as possible. You cannot fool or cheat your way into strengthening your relationship with Mother Earth. Practicing yoga helps maintain the earth connection fueled by eating root vegetables, stone fruit, cocoa, and hearty soups. Earth energy is a very stable companion—it is patient and true. It provides a very steady stream of support that is 100 percent reliable and always there for you whenever you need a little pick me up.

WATER

Manifesting with water energy is all about keeping up with the flow. Water is patient but often dynamic. It is a master with a thousand faces—at times calm, at times inviting, but incredibly temperamental. It contains within itself the full spectrum of the emotional ebb and flow. Water doesn't like rules; it prefers freedom and learning by doing, by discovering. Working with water is above all about practicing surrender—to this moment and to the path overall. Water is wise, and it is all about the unconventional path. First and foremost, it requires your trust. Trust it has just the right solution, just the right person, and just the right circumstance to help you move toward your goals.

If you don't drink a lot of water (about eight glasses a day), it will be harder for you to stay in its vibration. Water is a bit of a purist at heart, so soda, coffee, and juice don't count. Taking long showers and, ideally, regular baths will help build on your water connection. If you live next to a natural body of water, try swimming in it regularly, or at least dip your hands and feet into it to connect to its spirit. Water energy loves flowers of any kind, especially white ones. Ensure you have potted flowers (orchids, for example) and freshly cut stems in your house if you want to manifest with water energy. Some citruses also carry the yin water energy—think lemons and grapefruits—so eating them or using them in the form of essential oils will strengthen your water connection. Water energy is quite forgiving, and it will give you ample chances to get it right. The harder aspect of mastering this energy is full alignment with it. As soon as that alignment is achieved, manifestation can be incredibly fast.

AIR

Strengthening your connection with air is all about cultivating your personal vantage point—expansion and elevation. It always implies deep personal growth to shed the layers that no longer belong so you can finally soar. Think shadow work, healing relationship trauma, and minimizing negative self-talk. The energy of air is cleansing on many levels—it would expect you to go within and perform some serious spring cleaning. Strengthening your relationship with air energy is all about developing a higher perspective—a different way of looking at things—and becoming more in tune with the world, but in a way where you elevate yourself and those around you—reaching for the stars and getting away with it.

Air requires clean lungs, so habitual smoking is a non-starter. Breathwork as a practice is essential if you are trying to master the air element. And if you're lucky enough to live close to mountains, breathing in mountain air is literally one of the quickest ways to get in tune with the energies of the air element. Air purifiers, as well as air humidifiers, are great gadgets to have in your home, as is anything that improves the air you breathe. As far as food and drinks, air prefers space, which means that it would rather you practice intermittent fasting instead of a five-course meal or all-day snacking. Air also likes being active, so running, cycling, or any other sport gets the air energy going. Air also loves spacious homes and high floors—so the more up in the air you are, the better for cultivating your relationship. It also loves the practice of smudging—so stock up on that sage and *Palo Santo*.

PRACTICE: STRENGTHENING THE BOND WITH YOUR SPONSORING ENTITY

Today's practice will help you strengthen your connection with your elemental energy. Feel free to use this practice anytime you need a little boost or feel out of alignment.

1. Get into a comfortable position and close your eyes. As always, start with a few deep breaths. Let all the worries of your day drift away—they will be here when you are back.
2. Do a quick diagnostic to check your connection with your sponsoring force by imagining that your body is transparent, like an empty vessel. You will see that your body is filled up with the energy of your ally force to a certain degree. Can you tell how strong that connection is in percentage points? The exact percentage may clearly emerge inside your head—you will see it, hear it, or just perceive it to be true. Whatever this number is, you can strengthen this bond today.
3. Stay here and imagine that right above your head, there is a source of your sponsoring energy—the source of all the fire/air/earth/water of the Universe. This source is infinitely abundant, and there is more than enough here for you.
4. Picture the energy from that source flowing to you through a cord—an umbilical cord of sorts. And as the cord connects to your body, the flow of elemental energy is solidified.
5. Watch as your body is filled with this beautiful energy to the very brim. Now it has more than enough, and it always has a means of getting more. Now that the two of you are connected, you will never be lacking in this energy.

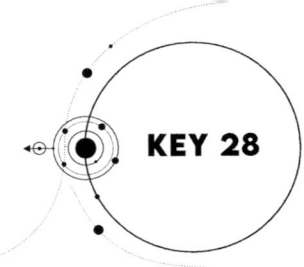

SOURCES OF ENERGY

Your capacity for manifestation is directly proportional to the amount of spare energy you have. Spare energy is the energy that is above and beyond what is required for your daily tasks.

The human body is an open system that enables an exchange of energy—giving and receiving, and transformation from one form to another. Still, it cannot make its own energy from nothing. It needs a source of sustenance—food, nutrients, water, the Sun—to stay alive. Manifesting, however, is more than just staying alive. Manifesting is a creative endeavor that is both gratifying and resource-consuming if done right. Every master manifestor first masters their personal energy, then masters the world—in that order.

ENERGY SOURCES

If you lack energy or are feeling depleted, you can never manifest the life you want, no matter how many hours you spend visualizing it. Master manifestors are not only intuitively (or intentionally) tapping into various external energy sources; they can accumulate and use that energy toward a very specific purpose. They rarely experience apathy or burnout despite often giving their all. Below is a general overview of some of the main energy sources you can tap into. Step one is understanding what energies you could be tapping into. Step two is actually tapping into them.

PLANETS AND STARS

Being the largest observable physical objects, planets of the Solar System are perfect manifestation energy sources. The overall proximity and dimensions of the planet are important in energy exchanges—the closer and larger the planet is, the more energy it exudes and, thus, could share with you. Each planet is unique and carries its own personal imprint. Not every planetary companion is an equally good manifesting partner—it all depends on your intention and the specifics of what you are seeking to manifest.

White Sun

As the strongest star in our immediate vicinity, the White Sun (or simply, the Sun) is your number one energy companion and source. As part of its mission, the Sun has committed to serving every being in its household (the Solar System). A portion of the Sun's energy has been reserved for your needs while you are incarnated here on Earth. Use the energy of the White Sun for general manifestation—nothing is beyond the scope or below the pay-grade of our Celestial Parent. From daily energy boosts to long-term energy support, the Sun is there for you. You need only to ask. (See also Key 3, page 30.)

Black Sun

The darker companion to the White Sun, The Black Sun, contains the power of a trillion atomic bombs. It can assist with massive transformation in your life, and its energies are not for the faint of heart. The energy of the Black Sun is potent, intentional, and forceful. When you require a massive change in your life, refer to the Black Sun. It can move and shake things up rather than preserve the status quo. When looking for a radical shift, you can find no better companion than the Black Sun. The Black Sun is also a great ally when you are extremely emotionally connected to what you are trying to manifest. Being the governing force of all emotion, the Black Sun can turn its natural magnetism into an unstoppable force that will bring you closer to what you want. (See also Key 4, page 34.)

Mars

The master warrior planet Mars means business. Its energy is directed, harsh, and contagious. Powered by fire, Mars is a great ally when you want things to happen faster. The master of blitzkrieg, Mars can amplify your efforts with one massive energy swing. The energy of Mars is especially helpful if you are manifesting things where military prowess could be helpful—for example, creating a business in a competitive market. Mars is a good army general—it gets things done, no matter the cost. Be warned: Mars' energy can be intense and demanding to work with—it will propel you into action whether you like this or not.

Venus
Venusian energies are instrumental in attracting a perfect home or a dream-worthy romantic partner and supporting an artistic venture or anything beauty or design-related. Venus is a powerfully inspirational and harmonizing force. The muse of humankind, Venus offers that spark all creators need at the onset of each project. Venus is a bit of a perfectionist—so if you are truly looking to excel at something, she is a one-of-a-kind ally and exactly the planet that can help you make it happen.

Mercury
A master communicator, Mercury favors the truth-seekers—the writers, the politicians, and the journalists. It can amplify the power of your word and your ability to convince others and assist with becoming an inspirational, visionary leader. In the Solar System, Mercury represents your personal truth and your intended path. Call on the energies of Mercury if you are still seeking your path or if you have already found it and require assistance with staying on the path.

Jupiter
Jupiter is the planet that causes things to expand and grow. It's ambitious, tireless, and optimistic. It is here to create a better world through all matter of things. It loves big picture thinking, drive and innate confidence. If you like operating outside of the box, or if you are manifesting something that is larger than you and is meant for the greater good, Jupiter could be your best ally.

Saturn
Saturn is all about building for the long haul. It favors projects that have the potential to impact large masses of people or exist for generations. Saturn is also a material and an intellect-based planet; you probably shouldn't call on it for heart matters. It is steady, measured, and exceptionally powerful. It contains the energy of a dormant volcano within, and it will donate that energy to the ones brave enough to claim it. Saturn plays big, so if you have great ambition, you may find a worthwhile ally in Saturn.

NATURE

The loving frequency of Gaia, Nature is not only cut from the same cloth as Homo Sapiens; it is the resource that humanity is meant to dip into when it is feeling depleted or lacking. While everything from mountains to rivers to forests can fill you up, each person is unique and thus has a unique natural element that has the highest propensity for filling them up. Notice how you feel next to the different natural features. Listen to your body. What is the particular aspect of nature you enjoy the most? That would tend to be the aspect that gives you the most energy. Tap into that aspect whenever you need a little pick me up. (See also Key 27, page 126.)

ANCESTORS

We are all connected to at least two ancestry pools that we could tap into at any time. This energy is always available to us and is given freely by our ancestors to make our existence easier. Get to know the energy of your ancestry lines—the more you tap into it, the easier it will be to use that in your daily life, for manifestation or otherwise. (See also Key 32, page 146.)

HIGHER SELF

Your Higher Self determines exactly how much energy you need for your incarnation, but you could still borrow from it from time to time. There is always more energy where your original spark came from. As a projection of your Higher Self, you can ask for an energy top-up, even demand it when the going gets tough. The energy of your Higher Self is also trapped in your past lives and parallel lives—they can be a great source to tap into if you have the know-how. (See also Key 71, page 315.)

SOURCE (MALE/FEMALE)

You are a projection of Source energy, and as such, you are always connected to it (or the Universe). The energy pool of the Universe is infinite and never lacking. This is one of the easiest energies to tap into and borrow from; it is always available to you. (See also Keys 34 and 35, pages 156 and 161.)

SPIRIT GUIDES

You always have several spirit guides watching over you. They can be a great source of energy, as each one of them has resources to spare if they deem fit. Getting tangible help from spirit guides, however, is predicated upon actually having a relationship with them, which takes time.

EGREGORES

Egregores are energy structures or thought-forms created subconsciously by a group of people whose thoughts are aligned. Every movement, organization, celebrity, country, and club has an *egregore*. If you are connected to an *egregore* on a deep level, you can tap into its energies—with permission, of course. The *egregore* of your country and your hometown are good examples of *egregores* on your side and, thus, are great energies to tap into when you need energy help.

PRACTICE: TAPPING INTO AN EXTERNAL ENERGY SOURCE

Use this meditation any time you feel depleted or when the going gets tough to remind yourself that there is always more energy available to you,

1. Close your eyes and focus on your breathing.
2. Focus your attention on the external energy source you want to work with today.
3. Imagine this object as a sphere of light brimming with energy. Notice that when you peel off a layer or two, the sphere starts looking like a grid of light with vertical and horizontal lines running it through and through. Like human bodies are filled with blood vessels that carry lifeforce, energy sources are filled with vessels that transport energy particles throughout the "body" of the object.

4. Imagine your body is also full of these pathways of light—a golden grid that powers everything that you are.
5. Now picture a cord of light attaching itself to your light body—somewhere around your solar plexus chakra. Imagine this cord stretching itself out to the external energy source and hooking itself into it, anchoring around one of the main energy pathways of the object.
6. Notice how the object is starting to reroute some of its lifeforce your way. Notice how light is starting to travel from the object's grid to yours and coursing through it with much intention.
7. Stay here and allow your body to be saturated with this energy. Then thank the donor for working with you today. After all, gratitude is the great multiplier, and it enables your source to replenish its energy quickly.
8. To maintain the connection, simply leave the anchor where it is if it feels good.

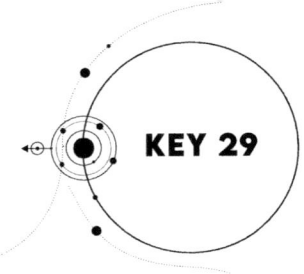

KEY 29

THE MIRROR UNIVERSE

When was the last time you felt inspired by someone?

When you feel inspired by another person, it means they hold more light than you in a particular aspect of their life. Moreover, you find the frequency of their light exceptionally appealing. It is impossible to get inspired by the light frequency if you're indifferent to it. Inspiration is a calling—where like attracts like—as a stream flows from its source into a receptacle. In this Mirror Universe, when you admire someone, you can reflect their light and, through that intricate process, match their vibrations for a period of time.

How do great leaders lead? They lead through the Mirroring Principle. Charismatic leaders possess a concentrated energy stream that, when presented to the world, can be easily reflected by others—their followers. From this perspective, followers tend to reflect the leader's shine, or their unique vibration. Whether we examine Jesus and his disciples or Gandhi and his inner circle, the driving force behind these historic bonds is the Mirroring Principle. According to the Mirroring Principle, everything reflects something else, which is another way of saying that we are all interconnected. And because of that, you choose what aspect of this reality you want to reflect, and therefore become.

Inspired action is a key to all manifestation. Let's rephrase: action taken in a state of reflecting a light bigger than yours is a key to manifestation. This is the opposite of doubt, procrastination, and feeling stuck. When you are reflecting a light that is bigger than your own, you are raising your vibrations. The state of rising vibrations is a state of productive bliss where things happen quickly.

You don't need to have what it takes to get what you want. You merely need to know someone or something that already has what you want and mimic their energy. It's also important to note that by becoming a reflection of someone's light, you are not taking that light away from the source. In fact, the process of mirroring is the process of multiplying, not taking away. Your chosen source will only become richer and more abundant in the process, and so will you. Mirroring someone starts and ends with a vibration and a state. You do not need to start walking and talking like them. You just need to adopt their attitudinal frequency.

This world is an intricate system of mirrors and mirroring behaviors. We copy each other's frequencies and then reflect them into the world so new mirror chains can be created. Everything in your world is either mirroring (copying) or reflecting (reacting to) you. To mirror someone is to imitate someone's vibrations in order to be like them. To reflect someone is to react to their vibrations. We all adjust one way or another to people and circumstances around us. But that is only half the story. Circumstances and all living beings are adjusting to us in the same way. At the very same time, we both impact the Universe and are impacted by it. The weather, for instance, is collectively manifested by the thoughts and feelings of the people in a particular geographical location. And then those people are impacted by the weather they, unbeknownst to themselves, created. This is the great cycle of the mirrors of existence.

You are a sum total of everything you choose to mirror. We tend to start our lives by mirroring the opinions and reactions of our parents. Then we mimic our friends, teachers, and significant others. So how come you still don't have what you want? Because you have been mirroring the wrong sources all along. Both reflecting and mirroring are largely unconscious processes, but they don't have to be. Apart from human beings, you could choose to mirror natural phenomena, planets, constellations, and pretty much anything else in the material Universe.

PRACTICE: MIRRORING THE VIBRATIONS OF AN INSPIRATIONAL SOURCE

You can be proactive and intentional regarding whom you choose to mirror, and this intentionality is where this practice can be helpful. Feel free to repeat this practice as many times as necessary; the energy imprints are fleeting. Initially, they may only last a few minutes. Make sure to take action in this state, and you will notice that it always gets you results.

1. Close your eyes and imagine the person (or source) that inspires you most in front of you. Try to focus on their essence—on who they are, truly. This essence is beyond what they look like and what they sound like. What is the feeling they

give you? How does their energy feel to you? Is it warm and inviting, or strong and unapologetic? Try defining it for yourself.
2. Imagine their body is made entirely of white light—pure energy. Watch as this energy starts pulsating—always dynamic, always flowing, and never static.
3. Imagine a floor-length mirror right next to that person (or source). In the mirror, you can see the blueprint of their body of light being reflected and projected onto you.
4. Try on this new energy frequency as if it was a new coat or sweater. How does it feel? Do you feel any different? Don't worry if the feeling is very subtle—it works regardless.

The more times you practice this mirroring, the stronger this new vibration will become within you and the easier it will be to maintain it. However, change in vibration always brings about change in the outside world, so all the mirrors around you will have to be retuned. Keep at it, and you are bound to start noticing the difference.

PRACTICE: MIRRORING THE POWER OF THE STARS

Think of this practice as a precursor to inspired action. The energy of the stars is one of the most potent energies in the material Universe. It is Divinely vibrational, charged, comparatively infinite, and in essence, pure light. Regardless of what you are manifesting, you cannot go wrong with adopting the energy of a star.

1. Close your eyes and focus on your breathing. Let the breaths in and out freely. Inhale for four counts, exhale for four counts, and hold your breath for four counts. Repeat a few times.
2. Visualize a star in front of you—bright and shimmery in all its splendor. There are many stars in the Universe, and it is no coincidence that this star chose you specifically. There is much that this star can contribute to your journey, and it wants to do so willingly.
3. As you get closer to the star, notice all the movement of light around its glowing surface—an intricate dance of light particles.

4. Picture a large mirror suspended in a cosmic void. See how the star's light is reflected in that mirror. Now picture the star's bursting into a billion smaller stars, each a tiny carbon copy of the original Mother Star.
5. Watch as the myriad of stars are projected into your own body. Feel the energy of the star get evenly distributed within your own light body: each cell now houses a small version of the projected star.
6. Allow this etheric energy to light you up fully from within—cell by cell, organ by organ, and tissue by tissue. Know that in the next hour or so, you will be emanating the power of the star in everything you do. Make it count!

Feel free to come back to this practice any time you are working on an ambitious project, in need of more confidence or inspiration to embark on a new journey, or are simply looking to align more closely with your full potential.

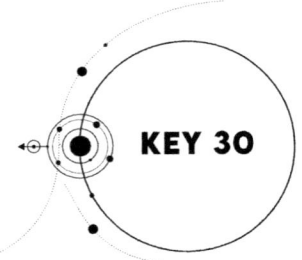

KEY 30

CYCLES OF MANIFESTATION: LUNAR, SOLAR, AND EARTHLY

In life, timing is everything, and manifestation is no exception. While we should "always be manifesting," some periods are optimal and others just average. Since we are exploring the full toolbox of tricks to help you manifest effectively, don't bypass the critical topic of timing.

First things first, the best time to manifest is when you are inspired to do so. Feeling inspired serves as an energetic indicator of Spirit and is never random. The second-best time to manifest? Glad you asked. For that, you will need to follow the natural ebbs and flows of the three celestial bodies—the Moon, the Sun, and Mother Earth. Below we'll explore each of them individually.

LUNAR CYCLE

The Moon cycle governs the state of liquids inside our bodies and our planet. As such, it is largely responsible for the state of flow within each of us, as well as in society. Any time we choose to align our personal lives with the phases of the Moon, we are harnessing its true majestic power and are enabling it to work with us, not against us. Manifestation is an energy-intensive process, so any time you can leverage tailwinds to help you move faster and with more momentum, you should do so.

The best time for manifesting is the Waxing Moon phase because it is a period of growth, expansion, and active transformation. A Waxing Moon is a perfect companion for calling forth abundance, starting new projects, and embarking on new adventures. Contrary to popular belief, the New Moon is a less optimal time for the act of manifesting. The Moon can't create its own light—it can only borrow it from the Sun. Therefore, how active the Moon is depends on how much of its surface is illuminated by the Sun. The New Moon phase is essentially a dormant period for the satellite. It is a state of hibernation, momentary stillness, and the deep and finite reset of what once was. This is the time when the Moon's energy is at its lowest. This is a great time for rest and planning, and perhaps some planting of the seeds but not for intense energy work geared towards rapid growth.

SOLAR CYCLE

While the Lunar Cycle is generally well known, the Solar Cycle is less familiar, despite its being one of the greatest resources for manifestation. The Sun is our 24/7 support system, so technically, it is never dormant, but just like every other living being, it has its cycles.

The Solar Cycle spans eleven years. It starts with a point of low Sun activity (Solar Minimum) characterized by the absence of sunspots on the star's surface. The Solar Cycle culminates in the Solar Maximum—the peak Sun activity—characterized by the maximum number of sunspots. The most optimal time for manifesting with the Sun is mid-cycle, starting about two years before the Solar Maximum and ending about two years after. During this lucrative period, the Sun is working overtime by emitting maximum levels of high-frequency electromagnetic radiation, which directly impacts Earth's magnetism and, thus, our ability to manifest. NASA measures the Solar Cycle, so you can always refer to their data. December 2019 marked the start of the new Solar Cycle, which means we'll reach the Solar Maximum sometime between November 2024 and March 2026. If you decide to manifest during low Sun activity, don't despair—it will still work, but you will just need to apply a bit more effort.

EARTHLY CYCLE

The Earth's cycle is a path consisting of two solstices and two equinoxes. The point of lowest activity in the Northern Hemisphere is the Winter Solstice (December)—it represents the longest night of the year and is a great period to recharge and lay low. The point of highest activity is the Summer Solstice (June)—the longest day of the year and the harbinger of the coming harvest and positive change. This is probably the single best day to perform any type of manifestation practices and energy work. If we take a broader approach, the six months starting with the Spring Equinox (March) and ending with the Fall Equinox (September) are overall a great time to manifest. The energies are definitely in your favor during this period.

On the flip side, December is a very poor time to set massive new goals. Both your body and the planet are going through the process of renewal and are internally focused. That's why most New Year's resolutions don't last—they just don't have enough "charge" and momentum to carry them forward because of the low activity period they were birthed in. Make your New Year's resolutions in March, and you might see a very different outcome.

PRACTICE: LUNAR, SOLAR, AND EARTHLY MANIFESTATION RITUALS

Set up some recurring reminders in your calendar for the best days to manifest based on the information in this chapter. Play into the ebbs and the flows. Don't push yourself too hard during less opportune times, and double down during optimal times. This is what "going with the flow" means. The flow, after all, is the natural order of things.

Remember: there is always one force or another that is on your side. You do not need all the stars to align, as long as some of them do. Remember: the cup is always half full. Check all three cycles to find optimal times for manifestation.

Set up personal manifestation rituals for each of the cycles. You can select your favorite meditations from this book and determine which ones you want to do when. Use specific objects to amplify each of the cycles.

- △ For Earth, you can use wooden objects and minerals.
- △ For the Moon, you can use the lotus flower and moonstone.
- △ For the Sun, use amber, citrine, and beeswax candles.

Happy Manifesting!

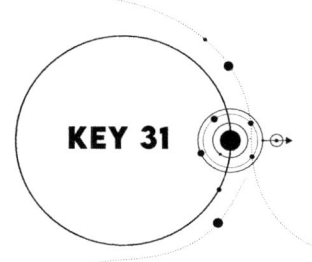

KEY 31

ETERNAL NIGHT OF THE BLACK SUN

There is power in the night. We crave it, we relish it, and we fear it. When the world is enveloped in charred, healing darkness, it is a great time of surrender and letting go.

How do you feel about the night? Do you love it or loathe it? Perhaps you are indifferent? Are you afraid of the dark?

Your relationship with the hours after dusk and before dawn is closely correlated to your relationship with the Black Sun. All of us are Sun children—children of the two mighty Sun twins. But only one of the Suns is even remotely understood. The second Sun—the Sun of the night—is unknown at best and feared at worst. And yet in it lies a mystery we should consider. Before solid, inspired action, there should come a period of inspired restoration, replenishment, and rest. One cannot exist without the other. Manifestation is energy work, and if your personal resource is depleted, you can only go so far. Most books on manifestation stress the active aspects of manifestation, but manifesting your best life is a marathon, not a sprint. And it requires you to get phenomenal at both the "go" time and the "release" time.

What is inspired restoration? It is a period of intentional rest and resetting of the body, mind, and soul. And no, sleep doesn't even remotely cover it. Ask anyone who woke up depleted after eight hours of sleep. If you are burned out, have a hard time falling asleep, or can't consistently get a full eight hours of sleep, this section is especially important for you.

The Black Sun is the guardian of sleep, relaxation, and the deepest states of your subconscious. If you learn to surrender to it, you can experience the deepest state of rest and instant healing. Remember: magnetism makes little sense if all you are attracting to yourself is more of the same. Shedding layers of what no longer serves you should become a habit. Renewal is a constant, ever-evolving process. There is always more to let go of, to release, since most of us make new karma every day. Working with the Black Sun to attain a deep state of relaxation is not dissimilar to a healing bath but is perhaps more critical to your overall wellbeing and success.

PRACTICE: SLEEP RITUAL—THE BLACK SUN SURRENDER

Turning active and inspired relaxation into a practice that you repeat at least every other week can do wonders for your manifestation. It cleans your plate from anything that doesn't belong there or doesn't match your newly found vibrations, so you can experience as little interruption and delay on your journey as possible. This practice is best performed about 30 minutes before going to bed. You can even do it in bed if that feels good. Feel free to fall asleep right after.

1. Imagine that every cell in your body contains a mini Black Sun. Scan your body and examine your cells. Zoom in and see how the healing, deep purple, starry energy of the Black Sun is illuminating your cells from within.
2. Start off by focusing on the cells in your head—the cells in your brain, face, jaw, ears, eyes, and mouth. Relax these areas of your body with the assistance of the healing, nurturing energy of the Black Sun.
3. Move down to your neck. Watch as the Black Sun's energy heals and relaxes the cells here—your neck vertebrae, throat, thyroid, and all the skin and muscles in this area. Imagine this area being enveloped in healing deep purple light.
4. Move down your body toward your chest. Allow the energy of the Black Sun to penetrate your heart and your lungs, the full length of your spinal cord, and your veins and arteries. Allow these areas to heal whatever needs to be healed here, and allow them to relax fully, without reservation.
5. Notice how a true shift is taking place in your body. Watch as your blood is enhanced by this healing, deep purple light, the magma of the Black Sun. Watch as this energy starts to course through your body and remove all the toxins it encounters on its way. Allow the blood to run its full cycle around your body, touching every organ and major system and transforming. This new bloodstream carries with it complete and deep relaxation. There is nowhere that you need to be. There is nothing more important than this.
6. Start moving down from your chest to your abdominal area. See how all the cells in this area also contain a mini Black Sun that generously shares its energy with them. Watch your liver, stomach, kidneys, and intestines transform in front of your eyes. Allow the deep purple energy to heal any cracks, dissolve any dark spots within these organs, and leave them fully restored to 100 percent

health and ability. Notice how this healing happens in the gentlest ways; it is soothing, calming, and patient.

7. Next, allow the healing energy to come up to your arms and hands—every joint, every muscle, and every finger. Let the energy of the Black Sun remove any toxins and erase any stress, hurt, or other stuck energies. Feel your hands and arms relax.

8. Finally, allow the energy of the Black Sun to enter your legs and your feet. Feel a slight tingling sensation in these areas as they are going through their healing experience. This area may be holding on to toxins and stuck emotions. Allow the things that don't belong to you to be easily eliminated. Allow the power of the Black Sun to help remove them from your body.

9. Now zoom in on one of your cells and examine the Black Sun within. Watch as it comes alive with the glow of a billion stars. It is alive with the energy of the night, of mystery, and of healing. The Black Sun is now ready for step two of this ritual. Watch as a crack appears on its surface and the purple starry magma—viscous and liquid—pours out of it. And as it does, it fills the whole cell with its healing, beautiful energy.

10. Watch as the rest of your body's cells go through the same process. This is the ultimate letting go—the ultimate relief.

11. Now imagine this starry magma enveloping your body in a thick, dark blanket, and you are cocooned inside it like a baby. Feel how a force much larger than you starts rocking you back and forth as if you were in the cradle. The truth is: you have always been a beloved child of this Universe, and it has been taking care of you. Surrender your fears, your dreams, and your aspirations to this grand force. It has your back—it always did. Allow this force to rock you gently to sleep, Child of Infinity.

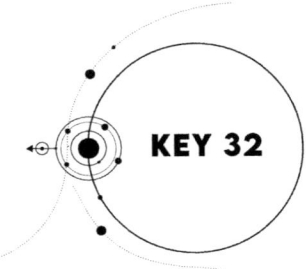

KEY 32

ANCESTRAL MAGIC

The Power of the Ancestors is one of the most majestic and most underutilized resources available to us. You can fall back on the power of your ancestors in all things, from healing to finding answers to your most pressing questions, and manifestation is no exception. Both of your ancestral lines are easily accessible and attuned to your needs. Below is a quick list of practices you could use to receive assistance from those who came before you.

PRACTICE: SOLICIT HELP

This is a planet of free will. So even if your ancestors see you struggling, they cannot engage beyond their usual involvement unless you make a specific request. Making a request is not dissimilar to a prayer—it is a plea for help and should always come from the heart. Prayer is heartfelt communication; it is thus an authentic stream of your consciousness.

The best prayers are unscripted, spur-of-the-moment statements. I recommend saying a separate prayer for each of your ancestry lines— one for each of your parents. Take time to connect with your lineage before making a request—start by thinking of the people's faces on a particular side of your family and connect with their energy. And then tell them what it is you are working on and what you would like help with. It is that simple. If you are unfamiliar with the people in your lineage, you can still connect to them energetically. Simply imagine them as beings of light ready to help you with your request.

PRACTICE: ENERGY RE-UP

We are all assigned a certain amount of energy at birth. This is the resource bank that we can tap into for everything from our daily initiatives to mission-based tasks. Your resource bank is a sum total of the energy allotted to you by your Higher Self and by your ancestors. Manifestation is an energy-intensive process and can consume many personal resources, especially if you have audacious goals. Either way, everyone benefits from an energy re-up.

To achieve it, you will need to connect with one (or both) of your familial lineages through meditation. Each ancestral line has two co-founders—the forefather and foremother of the line. Whenever a request of this nature is made, it will be up to them to grant or deny it.

1. Take a moment to connect to your lineage's founding couple; if you can see their faces and bodies, you are doing amazingly. But even if you cannot see them at all, know they are there to hear your request.
2. Explain that to achieve what you want, you need all the help you can get, and you would really appreciate it if they could allocate more energy to your current incarnation.
3. Now, whether your request is granted or not, be grateful. Your ancestors always know best, and they can see exactly what you are capable of. So even if your request is denied, know that it might be because your ancestors see enough power in you to accomplish what you set out to do with your current energy reserve.

PRACTICE: ANCESTRAL POWER CORDS

Whether you were given additional energy or not, you can amplify what you have to work with. The energy from your ancestors that is most applicable for manifestation enters your body through the spinal cord. There are 33 incoming energy streams—one for each vertebra. The multiple tailbone vertebrae are fused, so this is the largest concentration of your ancestral incoming energy since multiple streams are joined together.

To ensure you receive all the energy allotted to you in a meditative state, perform an audit of your spinal cord. Make sure to remove any energetic constrictions. Imagine 33 streams of light entering your body through the length of your spine. If one of the streams is blocked, you should see no light entering through that gateway. Cleanse it with a stream of water, and you will see that the energy is starting to pour in.

PRACTICE: ANCESTRAL CIRCLE

Ancestral Circle is a practice that allows you to amplify your intention and speed up its materialization.

1. In a meditative state, concentrate on your intention.
2. Imagine standing with both arms outstretched. Call in your ancestors to come and join you. Feel free to invite members from both of your lineages. As the ancestors join you, start forming a circle.
3. When the circle is sufficiently big, everyone should hold hands.
4. State your intention one more time as you face the center of the circle. See it reverberating, as if it were creating a palpable ripple effect in the air in the center of the circle.
5. Now ask your ancestors to repeat the intention with you. Listen to the sound of a thousand voices repeating your intention—amplifying it. And as the power of this collective declaration reaches the center of the circle, watch as a large upward stream of white light is formed.
6. See as the light carries this intention, amplifying it further and sending it to the Universe. Now the collective power of your ancestors is helping you manifest that intention.

PRACTICE: BATHTUB RITUAL

One of the quickest ways to absorb ancestral energy and gifts is through water. Water passes through dimensions and time, and it carries ancestral memories.

1. Fill your bathtub with some water—enough to cover your ankles. Stand in the bathtub and close your eyes (if you are physically unable to do this, sitting in a bathtub works also).
2. Connect to your ancestors. Ask them to give you qualities and traits, as well as their wisdom, to help you achieve your goals.
3. With your eyes closed, imagine your ancestors surrounding you. Each of them holds a little tube filled with liquid.

4. One by one, they start approaching the tub and pouring in the liquid from their tubes. As they do, the water in your tub becomes charged with your ancestors' gifts. Soak it up through the soles of your feet.

You can also ask your ancestors for something specific—like courage or good spirits—and if they have that in their arsenal, it will be given to you.

PRACTICE: CHARGED DRINKING WATER

The water you drink can change your entire state. Charging your water is a common practice among the spiritual community. However, you can also charge your water for manifestation.

1. Place your hands around a water container.
2. Close your eyes and imagine your ancestors' placing their palms over your hands, thus amplifying your intention.
3. Focus on your intention and your desired outcome. Imagine how it would feel to have what you want. For example: "Every drop of this water is bringing me closer to [*fill in the blank*]." You can also tweak this intention as you see fit.
4. Ask your ancestors to amplify this statement and bring about its fruition through your drinking water.

PRACTICE: MANIFESTATION TALISMAN

At this point, your ancestors know exactly what you are trying to accomplish. But there is still more they can do for you.

1. Close your eyes and connect with your mother's lineage. As you do so, take deep, measured breaths. You would generally be connecting with the founding couple of the lineage. Ask your foremother and forefather for a talisman—an object that can amplify your manifestation and bring you closer to your goal.
2. Watch what they bring out for you. Sometimes this object will come with an explanation; other times, without.

3. Receive the object with gratitude and place it somewhere around your body. From this day forward, rest assured that this object will go with you wherever you go. You may also start noticing changes in your energy or how you can handle certain situations—talismans work in mysterious ways.

Repeat this exercise with your father's side of the family for a total of two talismans. Generally ancestors will encapsulate their best resources, intentions, and wisdom into an object they share with you at such a specific request. Cherish the love and support of your ancestors. And know that you are never alone in this quest called life.

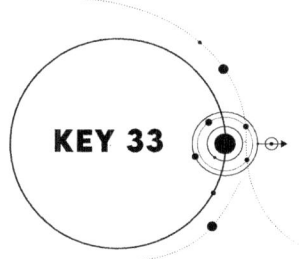

KEY 33

CHAKRAS OF ABUNDANCE

Mastering manifestation has everything to do with cultivating abundance. True abundance in the physical starts with abundance in the etheric—or our energy body. The chakras are just one example of energy vessels that can enhance our relationship with prosperity and help call it into our lives. Below we'll review the seven main chakras and their relationship to abundance. (See also diagram, Key 7, page 47.)

ROOT CHAKRA

Located at the base of the spine, the root chakra is the first major chakra to receive material abundance. Energies move through the Earth and enter our bodies through the soles of our feet. As the energy of material abundance travels upward, it accumulates in the root chakra—the first gate of our spinal energy centers. This is also where any trauma accumulates (including ancestral) related to money, shelter, and food or the lack of thereof. This sort of trauma may cause inflammation in the surrounding tissues and cause various energetic distortions. Clearing away the blocks in your root chakra is a must if you want to move past worrying about rent money and putting food on the table. While this is not true abundance yet, this chakra is the first building block, and your work should start here.

SACRAL CHAKRA

Creative expression dwells in the sacral chakra, which is located in the lower abdomen. More often than not, the road to abundance is via unleashing creativity. Many truly wealthy people did so by tapping into their creative resources. Giving yourself permission to be creative is one of the best things you can do for your sacral chakra. Allowing yourself to be creative in your own unique way brings about true confidence that emanates from within. Over time, following your creative path brings about true abundance—material, emotional, mental, and spiritual.

SOLAR PLEXUS CHAKRA

Located at the center of the belly, the solar plexus chakra is responsible for our ability to set and achieve goals. Charged and pointed, this masculine energy center is about massive action in the present. The solar plexus is your inner overachiever, conqueror, and provider, and it withers away in hesitation and doubt. Nurture your solar plexus by giving it a mission and a purpose. This chakra likes direction and movement and represents the force of electricity in our body. No true abundance in the physical is possible with a weak or malnourished solar plexus. Take time to charge and replenish your action center with ample Sun energy—from sun baths to consuming yellow foods to wearing yellow clothing.

HEART CHAKRA

The heart energy center is responsible for your ability to magnetize things to you. When people study manifestation, they tend to focus on **attracting** the life they want from the place of alignment and flow—the domain of the Divine Feminine. This type of magic—the magic of true feminine magnetism happens in the heart chakra. Alas, this center is only one of the many centers within your body, and to experience true alignment, they all need to work in unison. And yet, if you align with your heart's desire, this center will help put the right people, circumstances, and events on your path so you can achieve the desired outcome. This is the proverbial path of least resistance. The common pitfall, however, is expecting your feminine to do all the work while the action-oriented side of you is dormant. That is why some people spend years visualizing their ideal future while making absolutely no progress toward its materialization. Your heart is a powerful magnet. Allow it to work for you, not against you.

To nurture your heart center, go gentle on yourself and the people around you. Allow yourself small indulgences—from dessert to an impromptu weekend getaway to nurturing meaningful, heart-centered relationships with others. The heart center likes flowers, essential oils, baths, and anything else you might perceive as a "treat."

THROAT CHAKRA

Manifestation is, first and foremost, an intention to materialize something. And that intention starts with formulating the words of what you want. Words are powerful energy forms. They provide structure, purpose, and weight to the otherwise chaotic and somewhat random energy flow. Think of your words as the banks of the river. The river is only powerful because it is contained within its banks. If the river didn't have banks, it couldn't flow.

When you form your intention into words, you are taking the first step on the path of a creator. You thus acknowledge your creative power and your Divine essence. After all, the Universe was created by the great power of Logos—the energy behind the Creator's word. Such is the power of your words—they can create and demolish worlds. Our words and our self-expression belong to the throat chakra realm. Expression is somewhat synonymous with manifestation. Your surroundings are your expression manifested in the physical. Recognize the power of your throat center by always keeping the promises you give to yourself and others. This is how the Universe recognizes your purity as a creator. The Universe doesn't take the abuse of the power of the word lightly. Keep your commitments (yes, this includes New Year's resolutions), and if you know you cannot keep the commitment, don't make it in the first place. Your words are your sacred power and one of your strongest weapons. Treat them as such.

THIRD EYE CHAKRA

Another feminine energy center, the third eye chakra, brings complete awareness of your surroundings. This comes in handy every time you venture into the unknown. The seat of intuition, the third eye, can help you find the shortcuts toward achieving your dreams. However, these gifts don't always come easily.

This chakra requires your full trust and surrender to the great Divine Feminine energy. This is not a chakra where you can easily impose your will or get your way, so the best thing you can do is activate it and then trust you can do the work. Surrender is not a concept that comes easily to us. As a species, we are removed from nature and its intuitive healing energies, so it is hard for us to replenish this chakra naturally. I could write a full book just on opening this energy center. Let's just say that it loves meditation, yoga, introspection, periods of silence, and quiet. You can also place a crystal in your third eye center when you are meditating—this is a quick way of focusing the energy stream and can help awaken this center. Slightly tapping the area of your third eye (between the brows) can be incredibly helpful in reawakening this center.

CROWN CHAKRA

Whereas the solar plexus is about action, the crown chakra is about inspired action. This chakra can unlock a deep force within you that is the closest thing to an act of God you can experience. When tapped into, the energy of this center can be boiled down to a simple mantra: "Go ahead—create with abandon!" Working with this center enables you to create from your Higher Self aspects; it can power up some truly monumental, larger-than-life projects that may be society- and future-altering. Before you can get to this level, however, you have to pass through the rest of the masculine centers—the root, solar plexus, and throat chakras—and learn their lessons. Crown chakra manifestation might require an *ascesis* to be unlocked—an act of giving up the consumption of a particular product (food, drink, social media, etc.) that you have an attachment to. In the process of following an *ascesis*, you will free up a lot of energy that can easily be funneled into manifestation (also see Key 8, page 52).

Lastly, remember, manifestation is not a solo mission when the chakras are concerned. That is why there is no such thing as the "money chakra." Money is just the energy of abundance encapsulated into a three-dimensional shell. And for us to be able to accumulate large amounts of this energy, each of our chakras needs to pull its weight.

PRACTICE: CREATING AN IMPRINT OF YOUR DESIRED OUTCOME

Did you know that the Universe has a blueprint for anything you could possibly want? Do you want to be a billionaire? There is a blueprint for that. Do you want to be famous? There is a blueprint for that. Do you want to make money through your art and live your life on the road? There is a blueprint for that. When I say blueprint, I mean the energetic structure of the body. Imagine there is a great library of every possible abundance path and archetype. So if you could possibly dream it up, rest assured: it exists somewhere in the Universe.

The hardest thing to change is our vibration, and yet, this is exactly the path every manifestor embarks on. Changing your vibrations to align with your desired outcome is paramount; with that, you and your desired outcome start vibrating at the same wavelength.

Today you'll learn how to create an imprint of your desired outcome within your body.

1. Close your eyes and focus on what you are trying to manifest. Imagine there is a human somewhere in this Universe that already has exactly what you want. Imagine they have already walked the path and arrived at the destination. Don't think of an actual person—rather imagine an archetype of sorts.
2. Now focus on the core of the person's energetic blueprint—their chakra system. You will notice that each of their chakras has a slightly different size and speed of rotation. You might also note other interesting or peculiar things about their energy composition—for instance, some chakras can be very vibrant, while others are quite muted.
3. Now place your own energetic body right next to this imaginary person. Notice the difference between the current state of your chakras and those of the blueprint. The good news? Blueprints are Divine shortcuts, and they exist as tools for people like you and me. What you need to do is copy and paste the chakras from the blueprint into your own body. You can also think of the blueprint as a stencil that is infinitely copyable.
4. Depending on your level of sensitivity, you might notice an instant shift in your body.

This practice is an incredibly impactful technique because our vibrations literally create our world. Now unfortunately, until your body gets used to the new level of vibrations, your settings could slip back into the old configuration. To minimize this setback, repeat this exercise three to four times within a couple of weeks to keep realigning your chakras to the desired vibration levels. Your body will adopt them as its own over time.

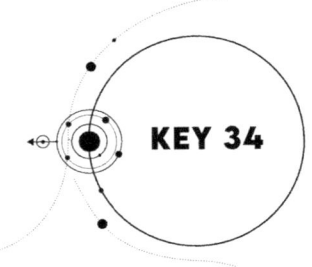

KEY 34

THE MASCULINE CODE

There is more than one way to achieve something. In fact, just believing there is a right and a wrong way of getting somewhere is a limiting perspective. A better one is to learn about all of the tools in your toolbox and master the ones that speak to you the most, and then apply them based on your circumstance.

We are much more androgynous than we give ourselves credit for. As such, we have access to both the masculine and the feminine energy pools of the Universe. Moreover, both of these pools are instantly accessible from within our bodies. Energy is not skin deep. Just being born a certain sex or assigned/presenting as a certain gender doesn't automatically make you a master of those energies. In fact, it means there is more for you to master.

Today you'll learn the intricacies of the masculine energies within your body and how best to harness them for manifestation and creating a better life overall.

THE DIVINE MASCULINE MAGIC

You may not believe in magic. However, what is magic, if not getting what you want by bending some invisible force to your will? Energy is invisible, yet it is every bit as real as your physical body, and perhaps even more so. Being able to bend energy to your will can make all the difference between manifesting the life you want and failing to do so.

Masculine magic is about creating a target and going after it with everything you've got. It is forward-moving energy. Your masculine energy loves direction, thrives when there is something to achieve, and is fueled by strategy. So your masculine magic needs you to give it something to do—new worlds to conquer, great heights to reach, and battles to win. In its higher aspect, the masculine energy within you is a protector force. Its mission is to keep you safe, well-fed, and never lacking. The masculine energy responds well to having a purpose or a calling. It doesn't like just going through the motions. It needs to know that whatever action it takes gets you closer to the Promised

Land—the place of results and glory. That's why when working with your masculine energies, it is important to provide as much definition of what you want as possible.

PRACTICE: NURTURING YOUR MASCULINE

Your masculine energy flow is halted by doubt and fear. If the energy of masculinity is like fire, the energy of fear is like water—which extinguishes that fire. The best antidote to fear is taking action. Fear dissipates with action. Another antidote is courage. And yet, if your masculine energy is depleted, you cannot ask it for courage in the face of adversity. Only a well nurtured and healthy masculine has that sort of ammunition. Are you feeling fear as it relates to creating your future?

To nurture your masculinity, you'll need to:

- **Get active:** Recognize that your masculinity is unique and doesn't subscribe to any standards. Your masculine energy likes staying active, so get your body moving every day. However, release any pressure around having to always be "on." Your masculine energy needs downtime more than your feminine. Your masculine energy is built for short spurts of activity followed by some idle time. Find your own cadence of active and passive activities that feel energizing yet nourishing. Do more things your body loves and less of what drains it. Listen to your body and build a relationship with it. Give yourself permission to fall short of your own expectations and not overachieve all the time. Cut yourself some slack. When you are patient with your masculinity, you allow it to reset and prepare for meaningful action. That state is where you would reap the most benefits from that relationship.
- **Eliminate obligations that no longer serve you:** They are tapping into your masculine energy resource and wasting it. Be ruthless in this exercise—it is important to free up as much trapped energy as possible.
- **Get grounded:** The practice of grounding is not just about feeling rooted in this reality; it brings with it the ability to impact the physical. A practice of grounding is essentially an exercise in committing to this life and your role within it. It makes you an active participant instead of a silent observer. Being grounded allows you to tune up your vibrations and harmonize them with the rest of the planet. A good grounding exercise is to imagine that you are starting

to grow roots from the soles of your feet. However, imagine these roots growing from your belly area—the very center, very core, of you. Allow the roots to grow deep, so deep that they reach the center of planet Earth—the Heart of Gaia. The Heart of Gaia is an emerald-green crystal that symbolizes higher level abundance on the planetary level. Make sure your roots envelop the crystal and center around it. Only then can you fully commit to this incarnation.

- △ **Breathwork**: Working with your breath is one of the better ways to have a healthy relationship with prana or lifeforce. This is a very forgiving yet invigorating practice, freeing any energy that may be stuck in your abdominal and chest area, and enabling you to engage in the physicality of this world with much more power and intention.
- △ **Write a mission statement for yourself**: This act may sound intimidating, but just go for it. You can always change it later if it doesn't feel right. As an ever-evolving being, you get to change your mind as many times as you like, as long as you keep learning. Your mission statement should clarify what you are here for in the next couple of years and where you are going, and it should start with "Right now I'm on a mission to _____."
- △ **Create your vision board**: Make sure to include specific language describing what you want. Your masculinity will relate to it as a set of targets it needs to hit for you. Most dreams die in the murky waters of failing to be defined. No, you cannot get there first and then define where you want to go. It works in absolute reverse. And your masculine energy is hungry for a roadmap, or at the very least, the name of the final destination.

THE MARS CODE

The fearless warrior planet Mars is a major sponsoring energy of masculinity within the Solar System. While Mars' energies are rough around the edges, a strong connection with this planet is a prerequisite to having a healthy relationship with your own masculinity. Mars is all about action, competition, and confidence. As a planetary force, it can come to your aid if you feel weak or unsure of yourself. The energy of Mars is nothing like the energy of the Sun—it doesn't care about being the father figure of all living things. Mars is the energy of a contained explosion: it is feisty, raw, unyielding, and means business. It exists so you can learn to make bold moves; it is here to help you take quantum leaps and massively upgrade as it teaches you always to go for what you want. This is the energy of the God of War. And you should harness it for manifestation, for it has no analogs related to pure passion, achievement, and success.

PRACTICE: AWAKENING THE WARRIOR WITHIN—THE MARS CONNECTION

Mars can become your greatest ally if you take the time to connect to its energies. In addition to the ideas given above, use this practice to tune into your masculinity.

1. Close your eyes and focus on the quiet, ever-present power of your breath. Recognize the work your breath does day in and day out, keeping you alive and well. Send some gratitude to this ancient ally of yours for all of its hard work.
2. Picture yourself standing amidst a desolate terrain of red sand that stretches as far as your eye can see. This terrain seems to be devoid of life—no birds chirping or trees growing. And yet, you can feel the ground underneath your feet is alive. Feel beneath the planet's surface that this unknown place is full of turbulent, raw energies. Recognize they are not Earthly energies—you have been transported to Mars.
3. You can tell that underneath the planet's crust, hidden in the depth of the red sands, run rivers of fire. Those rivers are endless and act as the bloodstream of this unique planet. Welcome to Mars—the land of warriors, the land of battle, the land of victory, and the land of loss. Not everyone is graced with the energies of this primordial warrior fire—they must be earned; they must be claimed. Today you have come to claim these energies for yourself.
4. As you stand tall amidst this foreign terrain, start feeling the soles of your feet warming up. The crust beneath your feet splits open, and you see the primordial fire spill over and make its way to the surface. This fire contains the warrior Spirit of Mars himself. This is the endless resource he taps into before each battle. This is liquid courage, strength, and it holds the promise of future conquests. This energy recognizes you. It knows your immortal soul and your powerful Spirit. Perhaps you met a long time ago. Perhaps it already flows in your veins. In either case, you have always been connected to this power, to

this warrior Spirit within. Today, you have come to reclaim that connection, to strengthen and build upon it.

5. As you stand strong on your own two feet, allow the energy of this fire to enter your body through the soles of your feet. Allow this energy to flow up toward your root chakra—the well of your warrior energies within. Regardless of whether your well is depleted or even completely empty, this energy feels very much at home here. This is a place where it can stay, ready for your next battle. This energy is a gift from the Universe to you.

6. Know that from this day forward, you are connected to the Spirit of Mars—to its courage-inducing power. From now on, you can go the extra mile because you have the strength to take on any challenge. In any moments of hesitation or doubt, you can tap into this inner power, into this ruby-red center, and harness the newly found strength. This power is forever at your service. You cannot run out of it—it will be replenished the minute it starts thinning out.

7. Acknowledge your inner warrior. This part of you that has always been there—the survivor, the fighter, and the conqueror. This part of you has been keeping you safe all these years. Recognize and acknowledge your inner power, for it is a true gift. There is no force strong enough to cut off your ties with your inner warrior.

Cherish and keep building on this connection. Your inner warrior loves fire energies in all of their forms—candles, fireplaces, and fireworks. Every time you encounter the fire element in your daily life, take a moment to stay present in the strength of your inner warrior. Take that time to remind yourself of that connection and to nurture it by simply recognizing it. And use it to lead you to new victories—for you personally and the world at large.

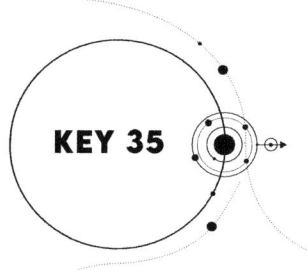

KEY 35

THE FEMININE CODE

Today you are going on a much-revered journey—a journey into the depth of your femininity. It is a place of vulnerability, surrender, and flow that moves in congruence with everything else in the Universe. It is not less than or bigger than—it is simply in harmony with all other living things. It is a place of deep recognition of your value, as well as the value of others. This is a place of deep nurturing and true acceptance; it is a place between worlds. It doesn't belong to any realm but permeates everything, as it forms the fabric of existence itself. It is a place of great forgiveness and even greater compassion—the place of bliss and the place of true knowledge of mysteries. But it is also a place of sharing and a place of giving—for the more you give, the more you have.

THE DIVINE FEMININE MAGIC

Feminine magic is a subtle breeze of drawing things to you. It is devoid of the energy of forceful pursuit. Feminine power is that of magnetism. It starts with setting an intention followed by completely letting go while being rooted in the knowledge that the Universe is wiser than we know. The feminine magic is that of trust and complete surrender—to the path and the journey. The feminine energy knows that there are great powers in the Universe that are happy to "do the work," and sometimes manifesting implies not having to lift a finger. Feminine magic is the ability to wait without a shade of doubt or impatience. It is the knowledge that whatever you desire and whatever you need has already been provided to you. It is infinite patience. And infinite gratitude. The feminine magic is the energy of allowing—allowing yourself to have what you want. Allowing yourself to receive without repercussions and conditions. The magic of the feminine is in drawing things to you and creating pathways so that the flow of abundance into your life becomes permanent.

POSSIBLE LOSS OF POWER

Two things can halt your feminine flow. They are:

- **Pressure:** Nothing stops the feminine flow quite like pressure, boundaries, borders, and rules. Your inner female goddess hates structure of any kind. She operates from a place of deeper Divine wisdom that transcends rules, and, in general, she just knows better.
- **Control:** Being the seat of Universal wisdom, your feminine energy doesn't appreciate being controlled because it signifies a major lack of trust. A controlled femininity is a trapped femininity. And like a caged animal, it cannot live up to its full potential. How have you been controlling your feminine energy? Are you making it give up the foods it loves? Do you let it clothe itself in what feels good? Do you allow it to wake up when it wants and go to bed when it pleases? Did you create room for spontaneity and adventure in your life? Your feminine energy is a free spirit: allow it to run wild.

NURTURING YOUR FEMININE

Your feminine energy doesn't like structure. Being too prescriptive or templated can really put a damper on this energy. Allow your inner female to have some unstructured time—the time outside of your daily routine and automated habits. You need this unscheduled time because your inner female loves to flow. Nothing quite centers her flow like song and dance. Chanting, karaoke, tribal dance, Zumba—she's up for it. Nothing quite communicates unrestricted flow like allowing your body or voice to move freely, clearing out any blocked energies in the process.

Water energies feel like home for your inner femininity. Whether you take long baths and showers, double your water intake for the day, or spend some time by the seashore, your inner female energy will thank you for getting her into her native vibrations. Water is an element of purification, so staying in tune with it will enable your femininity to spread its wings (and fins).

Did you notice that your inner female energy loves the plant kingdom? If not, you haven't been paying attention. From trees to flowers to gardening—nothing speaks to the female energy quite like the realm of plants. Surround yourself with florals and greenery whenever you get a chance. Get house plants, create a small garden for yourself, or spend some time around the trees. Your inner female will thank you.

Your inner femininity loves making art in all of its forms and sizes. Whether that means decorating your living room, painting the walls a new color, or arranging the vegetables on a plate in an artistic way, she thrives on creative expression. If you feel an urge to create something with your hands or get crafty, your inner female energy is calling out to you. Allow her to create what she wants without judgment and a need to be perfect. This self-expression is her way of coming into her power and establishing her flow. Once the flow is established, it will start bringing the things you want toward you.

Your inner female dislikes haste. She is here to savor things and enjoy life and all of its pleasures at her own pace. Allow her that luxury. Give her the time to herself. Making time for pleasure and rest is critical for your inner female energy. Filling your own cup should become a priority, not an afterthought. And just like everything else, this muscle needs to be exercised to become strong.

THE VENUS CODE

Both a goddess and a planet, Venus is a force to be reckoned with. Venus is so much more than the goddess of love, however—her energies are the frequency of pure abundance, luxury, and joie de vivre. Venus doesn't go after the things she desires, yet the Universe has never denied her anything. Abundance comes to her in every shape and size that matters to her. She is fullness incarnate. Any time we meet Venus, whether she is being birthed from the sea foam or reclining on a bed of roses, we know she understands and governs pleasure. She is wholesome and not lacking in anything. You, too, have the energies of Venus flowing through your body. Your inner goddess knows better—she is the one sending you the intuitive hits on your path to manifestation. She is the one with the signs, dreams, and premonitions. She is the one behind your internal awareness that you deserve better. In fact, you deserve anything you desire. There is no treasure too expensive for Venus, no object she cannot get her hands on, and no desire too big. She is a great magnet that prosperity revolves around.

PRACTICE: AWAKENING THE ABUNDANCE WITHIN—THE VENUS CONNECTION

Today you'll be connecting to Venusian energies—the flow of your inner prosperity.

1. Close your eyes and become aware of the pace and rhythm of your breathing.
2. As your breaths come and go lightly, imagine that you are standing by the seashore. Your feet are firmly planted in the warm, white sand. The sea is calm today, and the Sun is playing with the waves, which are the deepest, purest turquoise imaginable. These are the calm seas—the fertile energy of exploration, bliss, and freedom.
3. As you are standing on the shore, feel the waves softly caressing your toes. They feel like a soft kiss—a light touch of the Universe. The waves recognize you as the Divine child, a gift of God who must be cherished and nurtured.
4. As you look into the distance, you see a female figure walking toward you; she is walking on water. Her step is light. Her hair comes down to her feet in soft shimmering waves of gold. Her dress is made entirely of flowers, and she is crowned with an ornament of pearls and seashells. She is accompanied by a pair of dolphins, who are protecting her aura and keeping her company.
5. The female figure approaches you close enough for you to look into her deep eyes, which are the color of the sea. They are full of wisdom and of true understanding. She knows you. She has known you since the day you were born, and perhaps even before that. She nods to you in greeting, and then she smiles. She is stretching out her arms, and you can see that she has brought a gift for you. What is it? This is only for you to discover. Take the object that she is handing you and thank Venus for this beautiful gift.
6. As you connect with the energy of this object, your own inner goddess awakens. What does she look like? What is your true goddess form? There is a mirror on the beach: come over and see for yourself. What is your goddess wearing? What qualities does she have? Can you sense her power? There are many faces of a goddess, and yours is incredibly unique. Your goddess is a key to your own magnetic power.
7. Watch as your inner goddess starts to move in unison with the sound of the waves. Her dance is free and untamed—she is one with this beautiful world; she is an extension of it and a container for all of its abundance. As she continues

to dance, you notice many pathways, almost like little sun rays emanating from your inner goddess. And as she dances, these pathways activate. As the energy starts to flow through them, know that the magnetic principle has begun its work in your life.

From this day forward, your inner abundance is unlocked. So may it be.

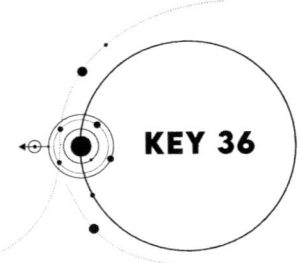

KEY 36

THE CODE OF DIVINE ONENESS

It is through the perfect unity of elements that we discover the power within. The feeling of being complete and whole comes from acknowledging the different forces inside of you and reconciling them in a way that makes each of them stronger. The great unity of your masculine and feminine energies is an ancient code for unlocking your integrated God/Goddess powers. There is nothing random about the composition of your energies. They represent your journey as an individual soul—the exact spectrum of knowledge, wisdom, and skills you need to succeed in this lifetime.

The trick to manifestation is uniting the energies of the heart and the mind—feeling and thought, and the rational and irrational. It is at this intersection that unrestricted magic happens. Yet we live in a society that is decidedly one-sided as far as achievement is concerned. Masculine energies are lauded for their abilities while feminine energies are largely subjugated. And this is exactly how you get a society of tired, burned-out people chasing happiness without ever attaining it.

Your feminine energies are the source of your internal and external abundance. They are the first domino on the path to a better life. And yet the nine-to-five rat race is hardly conducive to awakening and the attunement of those energies. Your feminine energy is that quiet voice that only becomes audible in moments of complete silence, during periods of introspection and rest. You meet your feminine energy on the journey within. Once that connection is established, it can never be severed. It will remain a quiet guide and an inner knowledge of what is, what was, and what shall be. Then and only then can your masculine energy carry the weight of your expectations and start moving you in the right direction. Guided by this deep female energy wisdom and intuition, your masculine energy becomes invincible. Divinely guided masculinity doesn't focus on the busy work—every action is full of intention.

This is what creating from a place of alignment looks like. Alignment is a place of flow where all your parts, all of your elements, are in tune and operate in unison with the Universe. Moving in alignment is moving in accordance with the laws of the Universe and recognizing that you are just one small part of a larger whole. Alignment represents the tailwind and the rising tide—it is the deep knowledge of when to strike and when to retreat. Alignment is a land where no energy is wasted, but is used carefully for the right type of action.

Use the following tips to harmonize your masculine and feminine energies:

- △ Make time every week to tune into your inner state, voice, and world. Meditation is a perfect place to start, but also quality alone time is a great way to accomplish this introspection. Quality time is time without external stimulation, like TV or social media. It is your time to be just with yourself—fully and completely. This is the time to find out what it is you truly like and want from life.
- △ Make it a habit to have frequent rendezvous with nature. Nature is the heart chakra of this reality. It helps you get centered in your own nurturing and healing energies and has all the answers. Get to know yourself on a deeper level. What natural objects fuel you the best? Is it the energy of the mountain, the river, or the forest? Once you establish the answer to this question, seek out alone time with that aspect every chance you get.
- △ Heal your relationship with your femininity. This means your mother, your daughter, the ocean, the night, darkness, chaos, and the energy of water.
- △ Heal your relationship with your masculinity. This means your father, your son, the color yellow, the Sun, and the energy of fire.

THE SHADOW SIDE

Your female and male energies have shadows.

Your inner masculine energy believes it knows better—it is stronger and ultimately can get by independently. It has been taking charge for years while your feminine energy was at best neglected and, at worst, diminished and reduced to the second stage. And yet, as a result, your masculine energy had to carry the weight of the world alone. This would only make sense. If you diminish your partner in crime, your other half, you are left all alone in having to do the "work" for the both of you. To assist with healing this pattern, recognize that there is value to your feminine energy—the wisdom, the nurturing tendencies, the intuition, the love, and the compassion. Invite your feminine energy to co-create with you, to take its rightful place alongside you. Recognize that there is immense strength in what it has to offer. Recognize that if you had such a reliable and strong partner, your weight would be easier to carry, your path would become easier, and your goals would finally be attainable.

Your feminine energy shadow is two-fold. On the one hand, she carries anger and sadness from her power's being stripped away and denied and neglected in every way that counts. On the other hand, this tendency is the complete denial of the calling to support, nurture, and nourish your masculine energy. On some level, your masculine energy is a child that needs tender, loving care day in and day out. Your great mother within is meant to cradle this child part of you; it is supposed to be there when your masculine energy is weak, tired, or lost. Your feminine energy is the inner guiding light meant to show the way for both of your aspects.

Yet, from a place of loss of power, you shine for no one. You have forgotten how to guide and be guided and have rejected this as your strength. You have forgotten that to be supported by the masculine energy, you need to support it first. The flow of energy inside starts with your feminine side—she is the one that gives freely from her endless well of loving, caring energy. Your masculine energy then taps into this great resource and can use it to achieve in the physical. To mend your relationship with the masculine energy, imagine that your inner femininity is finally opening her arms and is welcoming your masculinity in, just the way it is—no judgment and no conditions. Imagine the two coming together and forgiving each other for years and years of a dysfunctional relationship. And as that happens, you can experience something very special for the first time in your life—the sacred partnership between your masculine energy and your feminine energy.

THE SACRED UNION

The Sacred Union within is a state of equilibrium. It is a state of balance—of the giving and receiving. You see, the two parts of you are meant to be a perfect union—where one of them falls short, the other one steps in. It was never meant to be any other way. How do you know that you have achieved the sacred union? When your life fills you up, and every action is inspired and comes from a place of being full and able to give, you know that you have made it. Many of you seek to be completed by a partner outside of yourself, yet to attract that perfect partner, you first need to find and cultivate completion within yourself. You are the sacred partnership in and of yourself. And that makes you more powerful than you know.

PRACTICE: INTEGRATING THE MASCULINE AND FEMININE ENERGIES WITHIN

This practice will enable you to tune into and integrate your feminine and masculine parts.

1. Close your eyes and start breathing deeper, allowing your lungs to be filled with purifying life-giving air.
2. First allow yourself to focus on the feminine energies within you. They dwell in the deepest part of your being and yet are accessible to you in an instant. Imagine your inner femininity. What does she look like? What does she feel like? Whether you can see her clearly, or can hardly make out her energy, don't worry—you are in the right place.
3. Feel deeper into your feminine energy. Imagine she is a vast ocean—endless and deep. Know that she has always been there—from the first day of your existence as an individual part of a greater consciousness, this part of you has been there with you. You were never separate from it, or from its wisdom and its wise council. Imagine that your masculine energy is a little baby that is being caressed by the warm and inviting waters of the deep ocean of your inner mother. Know that your inner child is held by these energies no matter what. This is unconditional love. There is nothing you could do or fail to do to lose this love. It was given to you a long time ago, and it will never be taken away.
4. Imagine your feminine energy's rocking the little baby of your masculine energy back and forth. Imagine that there is a ray of light connecting the body of your mother to the body of the child through what looks like an umbilical cord of light—going from the belly of the mother to the belly of the child.
5. Stay in these energies for as long as it feels good to you. Allow yourself to be nurtured and fortified by them.
6. Watch as this inner child grows and becomes a man in his own right. Watch him standing on his own two feet—confident, strong, unyielding, and unbending. The strength of his mother became his strength, only now it is multiplied

a thousandfold. He is the rock, your sense of stability, and your sense of being in control.

7. Sense this power within you grow and watch as your masculine energy is starting to expand, turning into a tall mountain—your personal inner Everest. Feel the sense of ancient calm and stability emanate from this part of you. There is nothing impossible for this power within.
8. Watch as your feminine energy starts to curl around the mountain as a thin ribbon of colored smoke—it is like a snake that has found its resting place. Watch it settle over the mountain and stay there in its calming, fortifying sanctuary.
9. Stay here for as long as it feels good, soaking up the grandeur of your inner masculine energy.
10. When you are ready, imagine that your body is made entirely of white light. Imagine from the base of your spine, two streams of light starting to curl up—one is yellow (your masculine energy), and the other is blue (your feminine energy). Watch as they curl up your spine like two strands of DNA, intertwining and mixing their energies together.
11. Watch them go through each of your chakras, finally reaching your crown and falling down like a firework of yellow and blue sparks.

Come to this place whenever you require a deep balancing of your two polarities—anytime you feel weak or stressed out. It is through the sacred union of the two that your greatness becomes not only possible but quite inevitable.

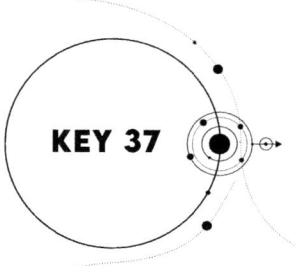

KEY 37

THE SECRET OF THE ANKH

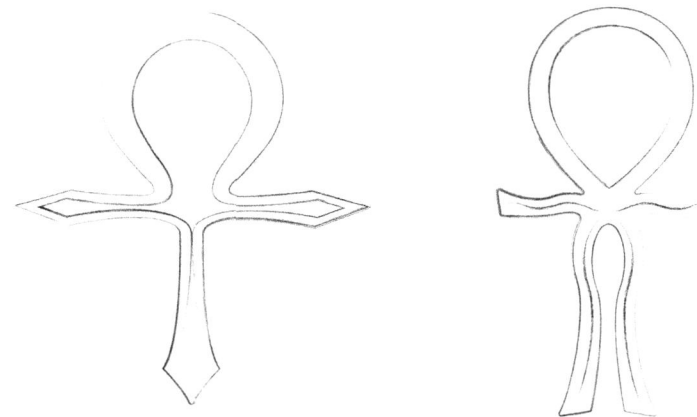

FIGURE 16: TWO REPRESENTATIONS OF THE ANKH

There is much we can learn from the simplicity and the inherent symbology of the Ankh (shown above). While currently associated with the legacy of Ancient Egypt, the Ankh can be traced back to much older civilizations. The Ankh is a legacy of Hyperborea, Lemuria, and Atlantis—the three ancient civilizations that were more developed than today's world. The concept of the Ankh has been reduced to the unity of masculine and feminine aspects of reality, but its true meaning goes far beyond that. Like every rich symbol, the mystery of the Ankh is multifold, and it opens to you, facet by facet, when you're ready to perceive and comprehend it.

Today we'll go beyond the surface meaning of the Ankh. In Egypt, the Ankh was referred to as the Key of Life and believed to belong to the realms of gods and kings. The deeper meaning, however, has always been the realm of the occult—the hidden, the secretive—due to its power to open the door to impactful conscious creation.

The Ankh represents inspired creation through unity, and not just in the very literal sense of procreation. It represents the union of forces within each of us—a particular path of energy, or a key that can unlock our dormant manifesting powers.

Its shape resembles a cross toward the bottom and a loop at the top. The bottom part represents physical life (lifeforce)—all types of physical creation and phenomena you can imagine. The top part represents the domain of mind and spirit (mind force)—the invisible force that spans dimensions and informs what our physicality will become. The message of the Ankh is simple—mind/spirit over matter. That is the key. Mind is the ruler supreme of the process of creation.

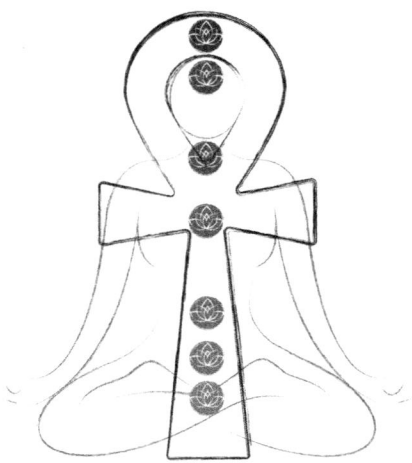

FIGURE 17: ANKH AND THE HUMAN BODY

Now let's explore how the energy of the Ankh fits into the human energy body (see Figure 17). The Ankh symbolizes energy moving through the chakras (see also Key 7, page 47) in a particular way—a way that enables creation.

Before we take a deep dive into exactly what this movement is, let's explore a critical and underrated concept—the Creation Gateway. The Creation Gateway is a spot within the human body that's located along the spine on the back side of your body (see Figure 18). It spans the territory between the base of your neck and the vertebrae located between your shoulder blades. If you imagine a pathway between your heart and throat chakras in the front of your body, this is roughly the area that the Creation Gateway takes up, only it is located on the back side of your body. The Creation Gateway is one of the best-kept secrets. It is powerful in more ways than one and represents a point of connection between you and the matrix of the rest of the Universe. If you have watched *The Matrix* movie, you might remember that to enter the matrix, Neo had to use a metal entryway attached to the back of his neck. While the placement of that object in the movie wasn't exact, it is quite illustrative. The Creation Gateway is a bridge between your personal needs, dreams, and desires and what actually gets manifested in the visible Universe. It was created specifically to simplify and speed up the energy of manifestation and enable humanity to impact the world around us fully. Today in the practice session, we'll learn two very important techniques that can help you manifest anything you want.

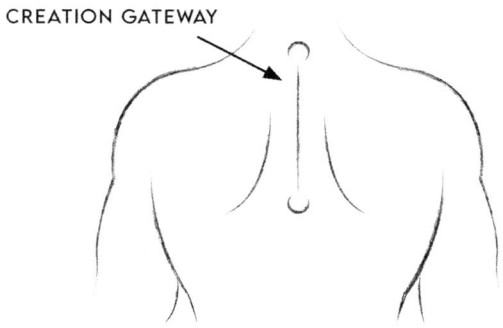

FIGURE 18: THE CREATION GATEWAY

PRACTICE: THE GREAT LOOP OF CREATION

Meet the Great Loop of Creation—the most impactful way to let the matrix know what you want and get the system to comply and assist with your wishes. The Great Loop is merely the path of energy through your body and the Universe (see Figure 19 on the next page). This path has been used by the ancients and the select few who were privy to this knowledge to transform the world around them for millennia. Today you will get a chance to learn it too.

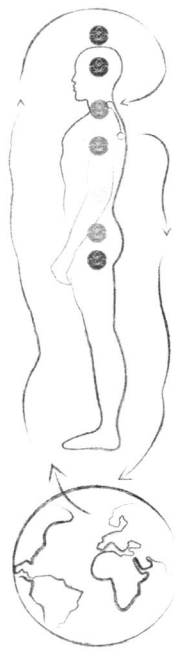

FIGURE 19: THE GREAT LOOP OF CREATION

1. Close your eyes and focus on your breathing.
2. Let's start the loop at the very center of the Earth. Imagine a huge crystal right in the very center—the heart of our planet. This crystal is the clearest emerald green you have ever seen. Feel the energies of this great crystal inside of your own body, filling you up from within, cell by cell.
3. Imagine a stream of energy ascending from the heart of Gaia—this emerald crystal—toward the soles of your feet. Feel how this energy moves up your body, starting at the base of your spine. See this emerald energy moving higher—to your sacral, solar plexus, and heart centers. It stops here just for a beat to recognize the beautiful energy of your strong, powerful, loving heart.
4. Once this connection between your heart and the heart of the planet is honored, let this energy stream move up toward your throat center and then your third eye, allowing the energy to curve as it sees fit.

5. Watch as this energy loops around in your crown center. Take a few deep breaths here. Feel that in this moment, you are one with everything that surrounds you—every object and every living being, on this planet and beyond it.

6. Now, just for a few moments, focus on your heart's desire—the one thing you are working on manifesting. Make the image of that desire crystal clear in your mind. Allow the energy of your crown chakra to fill in the gaps or add its own flavor to your desire to make it even better. Now, for a few moments, shift your focus to the Creation Gateway—the area that starts in the base of your neck and goes down your spine till it reaches the point between your shoulder blades.

7. Feel this center warm up as you bring your attention to it. You can almost sense its coming alive, becoming activated. Feel this center pulsating with a powerful force that you never realized you held on to. Spend a few moments here and amplify the energy of the Creation Gateway by sending your breath toward it.

8. As you exhale, feel your breath going to the base of your neck. Now, for a moment, go back to the energy stream located at the crown chakra: you are ready to start completing the loop. Allow the energy from this center to move toward your Creation Gateway—and with it, the energy of your intention, your desired outcome. With force and strength, release the energy of your manifestation through the Creation Gateway into the matrix. With each out-breath, you should feel like the power of your intention is leaving your body through the back of your neck. Stay here for ten breaths.

9. Appreciate this rare moment of direct communication with the matrix. Know that there is always a give and take relationship when energy is concerned. When something is given, something else with a similar vibration must be received back.

10. As you complete your ten breaths, watch as the matrix starts to return the energy stream back to you. It enters through the same point in the base of your neck.

11. Take this renewed energy stream gifted to you by the matrix and send it down your body, starting with your heart center. Allow this energy to pass through all of your lower chakras and finally leave the soles of your feet and travel at light speed toward the heart of Gaia, finally joining the emerald crystal.

Congratulations, you have completed your first Great Loop of Creation. Feel free to repeat this loop as many times as it feels good. With each new loop, your intention amplifies. Here is a short pathway description as a reminder:

Center of the Earth → soles of the feet → root chakra → sacral chakra → solar plexus chakra → heart chakra → throat chakra → third eye chakra → crown chakra → optional: soul star chakra → Gateway of Creation in the back of your neck → heart chakra → solar plexus chakra → sacral chakra → root chakra → center of the Earth

PRACTICE: THE SHORT LOOP OF CREATION

1. If the earlier loop is too time-consuming or intense for you, feel free to use this condensed version, called The Short Loop of Creation (see Figure 20). Try each of the practices at least once to determine which your body prefers.

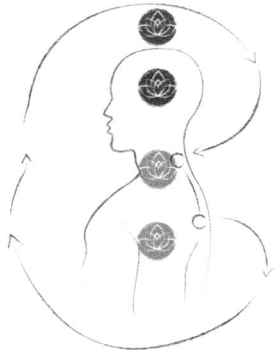

FIGURE 20: THE SHORT LOOP OF CREATION

2. Close your eyes and focus on your breathing.
3. Focus on your heart center—its healing, glowing green energy. With every breath, feel this center expand more and more.
4. When it feels good, move this energy up toward your throat center, through your third eye, and looping around at the crown. Take a moment to focus on the vastness of the Universe and connect to your own Higher Self aspects.

5. From this state of heightened perception, focus on your heart's desire—the object of your manifestation. Then take a few moments to activate your Creation Gateway by sending breaths toward it. With force and intention, send the energy of your desire through the gateway into the matrix. Stay here for ten long breaths.
6. Keep sending this energy through the portal into the depth of the matrix. Know that the matrix hears you, feels you, and understands you, and is beyond willing to help.
7. Now receive the energy—fortified and stronger than ever—back from the matrix. Let this energy enter your body and move toward your heart center.

You have now completed the Short Loop of Creation. Feel free to repeat it as you see fit. The energies get amplified the more times you do this. Repeat as many times as necessary. With each new loop, your intention amplifies. Here is a short pathway description as a reminder:

> Heart chakra → throat chakra → third eye chakra → crown chakra → optional: Soul Star chakra → Gateway of Creation in the back of your neck → heart chakra

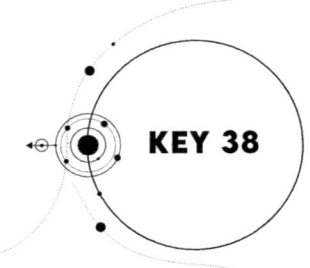

KEY 38

THE BREATH OF THE ANKH

> *"Know thyself and thou shalt know the gods."*
>
> —Ancient Egyptian Proverb

Humanity has used symbols for communication, healing, and opening portals from the beginning of time. While many symbols span different cultures and epochs, VERY few are as magical and potent as the Ankh. The energy of the Ankh was once transferred to Earth from higher dimensional civilizations who looked to help our planet evolve by evolving the consciousness that dwelled on it—humanity. From this perspective, Ankh is a cosmic symbol, but beyond that, it is a portal into dimensions of higher consciousness, faster energies, and Divine transformation.

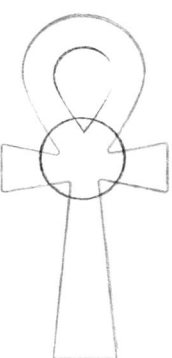

FIGURE 21: ANKH AS THE CROSS OF UNITY

As we are continuing our exploration of the Ankh, let's focus on its crux—the crossroads between the lower and the higher chakras. The Ankh has been called many things throughout history. One of them was "the Divine cross of unity"—a nod to the fact that the Ankh is a symbol of unity consciousness, or the merging of the higher and lower vibrations (see Figure 21). The Ankh governs our respiratory system and the life-giving power of our breath. So using the breath, we can bring the lower and higher energies of the cosmos into one cohesive integral system.

FIGURE 22: HORUS AND THE PHARAOH. GIVING THE BREATH OF LIFE

Recognized by ancient Egyptians as the representation of the "breath of life," the Ankh is often placed to the pharaoh's lips or nose by one of the Egyptian gods (see Figure 22). While modern science believes this placement to be a gesture of offering eternal life (life after death), its original meaning was related to manifestation. The higher dimensional beings that brought wisdom to our planet were initiating humans into the mystery of the breath of the Ankh—a rare and sacred ritual depicted in the tomb carvings. The energy of creation and the energy of manifestation are one and the same. When humans learn to manifest, they essentially claim their nature as creators, thus closely emulating and aligning with the frequency of Source (God, the Universe, or whatever you like to call it) consciousness. The act of manifesting is thus one of the most "spiritual" and high-vibrational activities you can be engaged in.

So why the breath? Breathing is a sacred act of continuous purification that starts in your physical body but spans all of your light bodies. Physical breath launches a cycle of rebirth and renewal that all of your bodies require to maintain vitality. With every breath you take, you have an opportunity to start fresh. Every breath is a new beginning, a new cycle, and a new chance to become what you were always meant to become. Breathwork is one of the more important daily rituals you can adopt to increase your capacity for manifestation. And of all the many different types of breathing, the Ankh breath is the most Divine one.

THE ANKH BREATH

The Ankh breath uses the Ankh form to enhance the processes of purification, manifestation, and creation within your body. Breathing into the Ankh (also called interdimensional breathing) activates your "mind over matter" connection and enables you to recreate the world around you according to your own design. Here are a few practices that explain how you can use the energy of the Ankh to enhance manifestation.

PRACTICE: ACTIVATING YOUR CREATION GATEWAY.

In the last chapter, we worked with the Gateway of Creation (see Figure 18 from Key 37, page 171). Amplifying your connection with that gateway is a necessary practice if you are just beginning to work with these transformational energies. To activate your Gateway of Creation portal fully, you need to work with it daily for about two weeks.

1. Focus on the Gateway area—from the base of your neck, down along the spinal cord, to between the shoulder blades.
2. Imagine that the Loop of the Ankh is located directly over this part of your body. As you are breathing, imagine breathing out through the Loop of the Ankh (which you might find easier to do if you breathe out through your nose).
3. On the inhale, draw in the light from the cosmos into your body. On the exhale, breathe out that light into the Ankh. Watch your Creation Gateway begin to fill up with the energy of higher cosmic dimensions.

PRACTICE: BREATHING INTO THE ANKH

Breathing through the Ankh can help guide the powerful healing energy of the breath while accelerating anything you are striving to achieve.

1. Focus on your heart's desire—ideally some visual representation of it. Place the Ankh over that representation. In this way, the Ankh should be located between you and your desired outcome. Remember: the Ankh is a portal—it can accelerate and bring to life whatever it is connected to.
2. Take a deep breath in. On the out-breath, exhale through the Loop of the Ankh. Feel free to exhale through your mouth to amplify this practice, and do so audibly—this act will ensure the lifeforce is properly released.
3. As you breathe in this way, have an intention of materializing your heart's desire. Send that intention through the Ankh with your breath. Your desired outcome already exists somewhere in the Universe, and calling on the energy of the Ankh will help bring it closer to you.

PRACTICE: BREATH ACTIVATION FOR THE GREAT/SHORT CREATION LOOPS

Once you become sufficiently practiced with the Short/Great Loops of Creation (see Key 37, page 171), you can take them a step further by incorporating Ankh's breath into these practices.

Breathe in as your energy is rising through the loop. Breathe out through the Ankh when the energy is going through the Creation Gateway phase. Hold your breath to complete the loop. This will enable you to power through multiple loops per minute. Such high-velocity Ankh breathing will activate your dormant energy reserves that are generally stored away and waiting for a rainy day. Activating these dormant pools of energy increases your ability to manifest without depleting your resources.

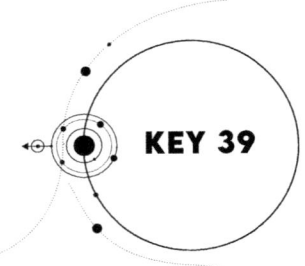

KEY 39

SACRED GEOMETRY IN ACTION

> *"God geometrizes continually."*
>
> —Plato

The matrix in which we live is a mathematically precise system. It operates according to a set of mathematical equations, number sequences, and geometric shapes. To understand sacred geometry is to hold the keys to the Universe. Each geometric shape visually describes a particular pattern of energy movement that shapes the world around us. No two patterns are alike, even though some seem deceptively close. It is not just the shape but the direction that matters. Figures pointing up are connected to the sky and the greater Cosmos, while downward-pointing shapes are associated with earthly or lower plane energies. Clockwise movement signifies an upward energy stream, while counterclockwise movement points to a downward energy stream.

Today, we'll explore some of the basic shapes and patterns in sacred geometry and how they can assist you in manifestation.

TRIANGLE

Considered the most stable of all forms, the equilateral triangle is the simplest energetic pattern representing creation in the physical. Triangle is all about connection, hence the many trinities it represents in religious and esoteric movements throughout the world. The reason this shape is so stable is that it represents the perfect unity of elements that go well together. Once that unity and cohesion are established, they are hard to break apart. At surface level, the triangle might come across as masculine and fiery. But that is the most rudimentary interpretation of the magic of this form. Triangle is a shape that represents the connection between earthly and spiritual planes, as well as the direct communication channel with the Divine. Egyptian pyramids (by extension, spatial triangles) were first and foremost communication towers that enabled the priests and priestesses of the old to receive clear messages from higher-dimensional consciousness.

The energy of the triangle symbolizes organized matter—the end product of manifested energy.

Some of the more important trinities the triangle represents include:

- △ Divine Masculine + Divine Feminine + Divine Child
- △ Heart + Mind + Soul
- △ Past + Present + Future
- △ Mind + Body + Spirit

Later in the practice session, we'll explore how to leverage the magic of the triangle to enhance your manifestation.

CIRCLE

The circle represents completion and the fullness of the Universe. It also symbolizes abundance in all its forms—physical, mental, emotional, and spiritual. The circle's energy helps with the demarcation of the world around you—everything that the shape of the circle contains within itself can and will be manifested in your reality. Everything outside of the circle is something that doesn't belong in your Universe.

Here is a quick exercise: Take a piece of paper and draw a large circle. Add all the things you want inside of this circle—anything really—more friends, love, money, and any specific goals or feelings. By doing this, you are inviting these energies into your world. Then take all the things you no longer want and write them down outside of your circle. Be specific on what you don't want or want less of. When you are done, take a pair of scissors and cut the circle out. Place the circle of manifestation where you can see it—near your bed or desk—and refer to it to assist with manifestation. Burn the part of the paper that contains all the things you no longer want.

SPIRAL

The energy of the spiral is one of the forms of the breath of the Universe. Greater consciousness uses this shape for expansion, growth, and evolution. The energy of the spiral is the learning curve, the path of expansion, and the energy that makes the world go round. The spiral is the grand multiplier—it takes what you have and expands it exponentially. If you have a little of something but would love to get more, use the energy of the spiral to assist you. In a meditative state, imagine the thing you want to multiply as being located at the center of the spiral. Then start moving that spiral in the clockwise direction and watch the energies expand. In your mind's eye, see and feel the spiral working with the universal energies to multiply the object that you have placed in its center.

SEED OF LIFE

Once upon a time, there was the Great Seed, and from it, all other energy forms were born. The seed of life represents seven perfect circles entwined together in a dance of life (see Figure 23).

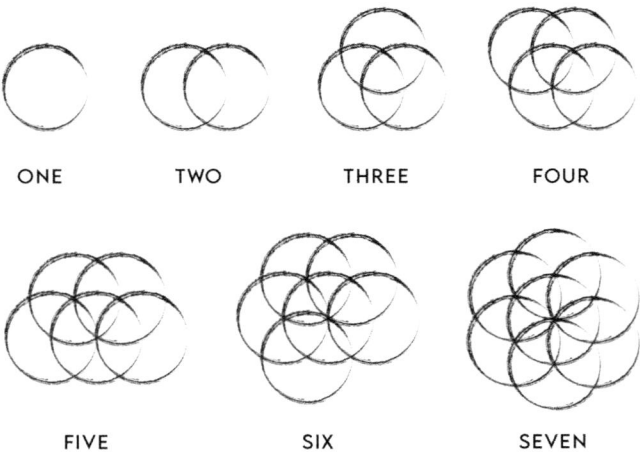

FIGURE 23: THE SEED OF LIFE

This is the shape of Divine birth. Everything, both simple and complex, once began as a seed of life. If you are starting a new project, especially something bigger in scale and more long-term, the seed of life should be your first step on the journey of creation—the cornerstone of your new venture.

Take out a piece of paper, draw the seed of life and name your seed. Like every successful project, your venture should have a name. Then place your hands above the drawing and close your eyes. Imagine how your newly minted seed is fueled by the energy of your hands. Go through each element—air, fire, water, and earth (see also Keys 26 and 27, pages 120 and 126)—as you nurture your new seed. Congratulations, your new baby is born!

PRACTICE: MANIFESTATION MUDRA. THE TRIANGLE OF MANIFESTATION

A *mudra* is a ritualistic shape that contains within it a sacred movement of energy. *Mudras* are mostly created with your fingers and hands, which serve as both masterful energy receptors and masterful energy transmitters in the physical.

FIGURE 24: MANIFESTATION MUDRA

The Triangle of Manifestation is a *mudra* that allows you to call in abundance into your physical existence.

1. Place your hands to form a shape of the triangle (see Figure 24). Make sure your triangle is facing up.
2. Focus on the movement of energy this shape creates in your fingers.

3. Press your fingers even closer together and feel a slight tingling sensation that creates. The shape of the triangle is tricky: it is exceptionally powerful, but it doesn't accumulate energy—rather, it enables you to put that energy to good use and get it to work.
4. Imagine there is a fire located right underneath your triangle. Feel the triangle powered and amplified by the energy of this fire. Feel it's becoming stronger.
5. Now imagine the life you are trying to create for yourself. Envision a circular shape encasing your vision of your future, like a protective shell that's incubating it for the time being. Place the imaginary circle above the triangle, so the top of the triangle touches the edges of the circle and fuels it with its energy.
6. Stay with this sensation for a few minutes. Watch as your vision starts to take shape in the physical.

Repeat this *mudra* as often as a few times a day to center yourself around your vision. This triangle works with the energies of fire and is powered by the Sun, so it is most effective in the daytime—from noon to 3 p.m., when the Sun is at its most powerful. If you can do this practice outside in the Sun, the *mudra* will have double the impact.

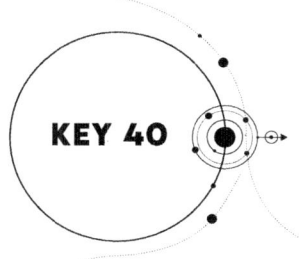

KEY 40

THE INDIGO WELL

Indigo—a hue of deep cosmic blue with a touch of purple—is more than just a shade on the color wheel. It is a frequency, a vibration, and an expression of God and the Great Cosmos. Moreover, it is a visual representation of the state of flow—a highly coveted place from which all creation happens. Anything is possible in flow. It transcends pressure, clears away stagnation, and defies chaos. Flow is the unrestricted movement of formative energies; it is the dance of the elements to birth something of greater scope.

Before our world as we know it took shape—before the planets were plugged into the fabric of this reality, and before there was even magnetism and electricity—there was an endless ocean of indigo. The alpha and the omega, the inception and the unwinding, the beginning and the end—everything was contained within that ocean. The only thing missing was the word of God—the force bound to set everything in motion. The same force, the same indigo ocean, is still very much alive today. While its energies are quite covert on this planet, they want to make themselves more visible. You have certainly heard of indigo children—one of the major ways indigo energies are making themselves known on Earth. Indigo children are merely the children of the flow—the ones who come with a deep, inherent understanding of the mysteries of the Universe, and the ones who move in complete sync with it. They are believed to have special abilities, but are these abilities truly special? Humanity is beginning a cycle of ascension toward the original blueprint of human abilities, toward the fuller activation of the DNA, and toward a future where everyone has access to special abilities. And it starts with the humble act of manifestation—a long-forgotten human art form.

The frequency of indigo is alive in each and every one of you. It came as a small seed of consciousness alongside your Spirit when it descended into your current body. And yet this energy has remained dormant in most people—until now.

The time has come for your indigo frequencies to wake up and fulfill their original intention. Your indigo seeds are meant to get you into the state of oneness and inspired creation. They are here to accelerate your path to a better future—and while small, their impact is mighty. The seeds of indigo, of the great cosmos, are here to bring you to your center and to align you around your core. They are here to transport you to a state where the great everything and the great nothing merge together, healing your wounds, mending your wrongs, and tying the loose ends. They are here to patch you up and seal the deepest cracks of your soul. This world is not without pain, and the pain has been holding you back. This world is not without fear, and the fear has held you paralyzed. And yet there is no force greater than the force of the flow—the Divine Feminine vastness. This is the force of the Great Mother energies—from which everything is birthed. And these energies are here for you.

It is no coincidence that in the science of energy, indigo is associated with *Ajna*, the third eye chakra—your gateway to higher consciousness, greater knowing, and intuitive understanding. It is in this center that all the elements merge, unleashing their collective might. It is your cosmic command center within, an energy center that impacts the world around you. It is in this center that your sense of purpose and sense of path lie. *Ajna* is the captain of your soul journey and a gateway to happy intentional living. And indigo is very much its bloodline.

PRACTICE: ACCESSING THE INDIGO FLOW WITHIN

Use this practice to open the deep well of indigo within you and anchor its energy flow.

1. Close your eyes and start breathing deeply.
2. Focus your breath on the area of your third eye—breathe in and breathe out of your third eye chakra. Imagine that right in the middle of your forehead, in the depth of your third eye center, there are a few indigo-colored seeds. They lie dormant, tucked away from the rest of the world.
3. Picture a deep well located inside of your body. This well is a source of the highest vibrational frequencies available to you, and it is filled with transparent water. Notice how the indigo-colored seeds are gently deposited into the deep waters of this well. As that happens, picture the waters' turning the deepest indigo you can imagine, which matches the color of the seeds.
4. Allow this glorious deep blue-purple energy to wash over your body. Let it move down your body, passing every major organ, bone, muscle, and cartilage. Imagine this energy's transforming your body from within—removing the pain, the fear, and the hurt, and healing the wounds of the body, heart, and soul. There is nothing impossible for this Great Mother energy.

5. Know that from this day forward, the healing energies of indigo are ever available to you. Call on them when you feel lost or need guidance.

For the next few days, pay attention to the symbols and the signs around you. The energy of indigo will remain in your body, healing and guiding you. So don't be surprised if you start noticing changes in how you feel and act in the coming days.

PRACTICE: WORKING WITH YOUR INDIGO

The energy of indigo can enhance your meditations, intentions, and all of the practices in this book. The following will help you ensure the indigo energies remain activated in your body.

- Any time you experience the absence of flow, picture the stream of indigo encircling your spinal cord. Allow these energies to fill up your body.
- Call on your indigo seeds whenever you are challenged with decision-making, especially if it is life-altering. Get into the indigo flow first and ask this energy to guide you. The answer will come.
- When you are experiencing a roadblock, connect with your indigo well and let the stream of this energy melt away or wash away the obstacle.

Indigo vibrations are incredibly high frequency and can improve your overall quality of life. Adopt a practice of calling in these energies before going to bed—imagine that you are floating in the sea of indigo right before you fall asleep. You will notice that your overall sleep quality will improve, as well as your abilities to get guidance and messages in your sleep. Enjoy!

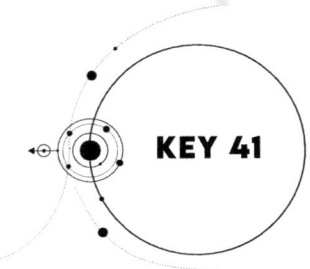

KEY 41

IN THE FLOW

Most things in the observable Universe exist in a constant state of flow. Flow is the most natural state of all living beings. Flow is a state of interconnectedness—an act of being in complete sync with everything else in existence. Of all beings on Earth, we are perhaps most challenged with experiencing flow. This stems from our collective belief that we are separate from nature and somehow superior to it. Believe this long enough, and you are guaranteed to start developing a state of non-flow. Non-flow is an artificial state one experiences when they are utterly out of alignment with themselves and the rest of the Universe. A state of non-flow is the dominating state of humanity today. Non-flow is struggling incarnate—the constant pushing and pulling against the fabric of the Universe, a state of being lost not to be found, a state of loneliness, and a state of despair. This is a state of holding your breath underwater and being afraid that your next breath might just be your last. It is the constant tightness in your chest, the inescapable feeling of inadequacy, the perpetual fight with circumstance, and the uphill battle.

Flow is a long-lost aspect of natural magic that should be inherent to our daily lives but instead is only experienced accidentally and rarely. Only about 1 percent of human existence happens in the state of flow. And yet true manifestation is *impossible* in any other state. Relearning to flow is thus crucial if you are serious about changing your life's circumstances. Relearning to flow is going back to basics—one of the most ancient, most simplistic wisdoms out there, yet so often unattainable to us.

GETTING INTO THE FLOW

The flow state is connected to two primary elements—water and air (see also Key 27, page 126). To experience true Divine flow, both need to be balanced and tapped into correctly. Both elements need to be purified and present in your body and your life.

AIR

I find that many people are starved for air. After all, your relationship with air is closely correlated to how much you trust the world around you. If you cannot trust the outside world fully, your full ability to inhale (intake freely) and exhale (give freely) will be constricted. This distrust restricts the flow of life-giving air elements in your body and in your life. Let's face it, you have learned to mistrust the world around you—beware of strangers, wildlife, and natural cataclysms. You have been conditioned to believe this world is out to get you, and that is the future you are actively creating for yourself. Chances are, you haven't been getting enough air in your lungs for decades. Breathwork is an incredible practice to adopt in order to increase flow capacity and improve your odds at manifestation. We will also explore an exercise you can use to get the flow of air back into your life in the practice section today.

WATER

Water, despite being one of the most prevalent elements on Earth, is not fully integrated within the collective consciousness. This planet is still learning to integrate the nurturing energies of the Divine Feminine (see also Key 35, page 161), which implies a bit of a disconnect to the core feminine element— water.
The state of water in your life and body exists under a tremendous amount of pressure—the weight of expectations, the blocks of negative thinking, and above all else, the load of negative emotions. Humanity has forgotten how to purify the state of water in their lives and bodies and thus ends up cycling through and navigating murky waters. While better than nothing, this navigation hardly represents the coveted state of flow. To stay connected with the state of water, you need to do two things:

△ **Purify the water within:** This starts with the water you drink and bathe/shower in. All the water you intake should be pure and ideally charged with high vibrations. Simply bless the water before drinking it. You can also hold the cup in both of your hands and send positive vibrations into the water in the cup. You can send any vibrations you want—those of love, health, happiness, or abundance. Water is a very malleable substance; it immediately receives vibrations and becomes them. You can also purify and charge your water with minerals—such as shungite or rose quartz. Simply place the mineral inside of your water carafe and let it sit there for a couple of hours before drinking.

△ **Reconnect with the element of water twice daily**: When you are bathing or taking a shower, imagine the water's cleansing more than your physical body—imagine the water's taking away all the negative energies stuck to your light bodies. This cleanse is spiritual hygiene. You can also do this practice in a meditative state—just imagine that you are standing under a large waterfall that flows from the skies and falls on your skin, washing away anything that doesn't belong to you. You can also deepen this practice by imagining the waterfall carries you away in a torrent of warm, welcoming waters. You should surrender to that powerful movement and trust it will take you exactly where you need to be. The flow always knows the way. Allow it to become an ever-present force in your life and remove any obstacles you are experiencing.

MAINTAINING THE STATE OF FLOW

Getting in the flow, however, is only half the trouble—maintaining it is where the true mastery lies. While there are thousands of tips on maintaining the state of flow, below are some of the most important ones.

△ Make sure you consume things that are good for you—this includes food, drinks, and information, as well as people you come across. All of the above are just different forms of energy, and the energy surrounding you will always impact your flow. While you cannot and shouldn't try to control the world, you can certainly optimize what you consume and whom you socialize with. Listen to your body and eradicate foods and people that make you feel suboptimal.

△ Moving your body every day is imperative for maintaining a state of flow. Find the type of movement that feels good, whether it is walking, running, dancing, or yoga. There is no wrong answer here. The movement will naturally release any stuck energies—it is a major detox activity.

△ Learn to manage your emotional states. No, this doesn't mean controlling your emotions or burying them deep, never to be found—suppressed emotions tend to manifest themselves as ill-health. Simply allow your emotions to come and go while realizing that this too shall pass. This acceptance is about the state of perfect receptivity—yes, you may feel sad or lonely at times, but you will also be able to move past these emotions easily. Remember: emotions act like tides of the ocean—they come only to leave. You should learn to respect the deep ocean of your emotions, without control and without judgment.

△ Take the power that belongs to you away from circumstances. Believing that things happen to you and especially feeling like you are not controlling your external reality is a quick way to lose the flow. Give yourself the credit you deserve, as the sovereign creator of your life. You live in your personal slice of reality, and nobody but you decides how that slice will look and feel. Take your power back. Claim back your flow.

PRACTICE: OPEN YOUR LUNGS TO AIR

Use this practice regularly to get the flow of air back into your life.

1. Start with a few deep, liberating breaths. As you breathe in, imagine that your chest and lungs are becoming filled with the most beautiful blue light. Blue represents many things in the Universe, including freedom and flow. It is thus liberating energy for your trapped and constricted lungs. Allow the energy of the blue ray to penetrate every cell in your lungs, purifying and releasing things along the way.
2. Follow through with a breath sequence. Breathe in all the way—fill your lungs with as much air as you can. Hold it for a count of three. Breathe out halfway. Hold for a count of three. Breathe in all the way again. Breathe out halfway. Hold for a count of three.
3. Repeat this sequence four to five times. Then exhale all the way. Notice exactly how good it feels to exhale fully—to release that which is no longer serving you.
4. Breathe in and out normally for a minute or so.
5. Then inhale all the way. Exhale all the way. Inhale halfway. Exhale all the way, inhale halfway. Repeat this sequence four to five times. Then, inhale all the way and fill those lungs with air—all the air you have been craving all this time.
6. Feel free to come back to normal breathing, but as you breathe in and out, take in more air than you normally would. Allow your body to be saturated with

life-giving air. Focus on the color blue and how it feels inside of you. Allow this color to anchor in your body, enabling you to breathe in and out while trusting the Universe. Trust that the Universe has your back, and that it will be there to pick you up if you fall. Allow this beautiful, serene blue light to remove any blockages in your throat, in your lungs, and even in your belly.

7. Savor the true flow of air in your body. Return here any time you feel constricted in your chest or feel out of the flow.

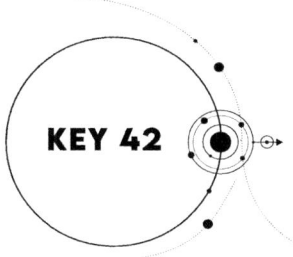

KEY 42

PORTALS OF COSMIC ALIGNMENT

Studying manifestation wouldn't be complete without exploring energy portals—small windows of opportunity that offer cosmic alignment in and of themselves. While the practical exercises in this book work regardless of when you choose to do them, they are especially potent when aligned with one of the cosmic portals. Portals are doorways that connect Earth with a particular strand of the cosmos. Below we'll explore some of the main energy portals and what they can bring forth.

1/1 AND 10/10

Essentially the energy of these two portals is the same because they have the same Divine numerology. However, while the energy of 1/1 is virgin and pure, the energy of 10/10 has come a full circle and brings a more potent charge. Every year you have two days on the calendar—January 1st and October 10th—that bring forth this unique energy to Earth. They carry two master energies—the Divine Masculine (the energy of one) and the Divine Feminine (the energy of two). Both are incredibly potent for large projects and big undertakings. Any type of business venture or project involving money and prosperity, or anything that has to do with seeking fame or recognition or developing a large following, can be better manifested during these two days.

2/2

This portal brings about very strong feminine creative energies that help build a strong foundation for something monumental and solid—a cornerstone for the rest of your life. Manifesting projects that involve real estate (moving, buying, or building a home), making a large purchase of any kind, or starting a partnership or family is perfect for these energies. The energy of the four (2+2) is all about building for the long run, creating stability, and making good long-term decisions.

3/3

The numerology of the number three is rooted in mystery—it is the first of the numbers that can maintain a structure in perpetuity. It is the number of revolutions, new beginnings, and balance. It is also the first number of divinity—Divine balance and Divine order. Three begins and ends an upheaval; it is a necessary number of reformation and progress. This portal is perfect for manifesting things that seek to bring about innovation, progress, and a new way of being. So if you are seeking to invent something, commercialize an invention, or succeed in politics or communications, this date is perfect for you. Manifesting a new school of thought, a new scientific theory, or anything that involves the written or the spoken word? This is your portal.

4/4

Four is the number of order, sustainability, and building something solid that will stand for generations. Generally, the biggest enterprises and the largest companies in the world carry the energy of four within. It is about wisdom, wise council, stability, and wealth. It is the number of builders, architects, and businessmen. It is grounded in reality, leaving little room for daydreaming but plenty of room for logic and pragmatism. A lot of the world's stability and power come from the energy of four. If you are looking to create something that will pass the test of time and span hundreds of years—this is your portal. This is also a portal of Divine guidance—meaning it will be especially helpful for those who know what they want but have no clue of how to get there.

5/5

Another feminine powerhouse, the energy of five, is spontaneous, creative, lighthearted, and joyful. This energy is that of an artist, a dancer, or a poet. Rooted in romance and finer things in life, five is a Venusian number reminding us that while this too shall pass, we can certainly enjoy it while it lasts. This portal is perfect for manifesting joie de vivre, adventure, a new love affair, and overall happiness. It can bring forth effortless and luxurious living; it can also assist the path of an artist or any artistic creation.

6/6

Six represents Divine polarity—the presence and absence of light. It symbolizes the path of a spiritual seeker and is always guiding its subject toward greater discovery. Six indicates great personal power and even greater learning. If you are looking to manifest a more spiritual path for yourself, one filled with greater understanding and pursuit of mystery, this is the portal for you.

7/7

Seven is the number of true luck and a symbol of removing obstacles in your path. This portal can help bring about unexpected and massive wealth as well as other material pleasures. Seven is perfect for an enterprise with a planetary mission, but absolutely awful for an enterprise for personal gain. Seven is a number of Divine grace and cannot be taken lightly or selfishly. It opens the door to bigger contributions and true planetary change.

8/8, ALSO LION'S GATE

Eight is the beginning, the middle, and the end. Full of possibility, true untapped potential, and wonder. If you are seeking to leverage the energy and incessant power of the Universe for your enterprise, pay special attention to this portal. It is not for the meek of heart, though, as this path is rooted in challenges. The energy of eight has no limits—anything can be yours if you dare, as long as you are ambitious and willing to work for it.

9/9

Nine signifies completion, enlightenment, and a path well-walked. If the person is worthy, this energy can help reap the best material and spiritual rewards. These energies help the ones who live the lives of service, of significance, and of altruism. If what you are trying to manifest is connected to seeking true mastery of a field, craft, or subject, this is the portal for you. This portal has helped birth many great thinkers, philosophers, and sages of every generation.

11/11

This is the number of Divine intervention and Divine protection. It is often considered the angel number, but it goes so far beyond angels. This is a great symbol of synchronicity and déjà vu—you are here, on the right path, exactly where you are meant to be at the moment in time. There is nothing that this portal cannot help with—the world is your oyster. In fact, if there is one day in the year that manifesting is highly recommended, it is 11/11.

PRACTICE: PORTAL ACTIVATION MEDITATION

If you are manifesting during one of the cosmic portals, use the below meditation and then follow through with any other meditation/visualization practice from this book.

1. Close your eyes and focus on your breathing. Allow your mind to calm down and your thoughts to become slower, or disappear completely.
2. Imagine that you are sitting at the intersection of golden lines—ley lines, the magical light vessels of the Universe. They are like the blood vessels in your body, only they belong to the Earth's body. Higher energies can be anchored into the fabric of our planet through ley lines.
3. Imagine there is a portal right over your head, and through it, the purest stream of white light is flowing downstream, toward Earth and toward you. Picture this energy pouring over and saturating the ley lines you are sitting atop.
4. As the ley lines become saturated with the light, they start emanating an etheric, other-worldly glow. Your body is now covered by a cloud of these Divine emanations. You are now one with the energy of the portal.
5. Feel its power and its harmony inside of your body. You may feel a slight tingling or slight shivers. Stay in these energies for a few minutes to absorb and anchor them further.
6. Follow through with another meditation/visualization practice from this book.

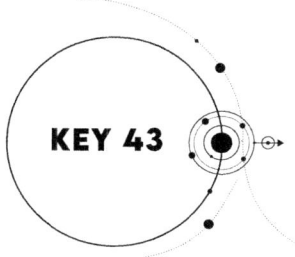

KEY 43

OBJECTS OF ABUNDANCE

Manifesting is a marathon, not a sprint, and it requires little pick-me-ups along the way. Below are some objects that can assist you with manifestation or naturally bring about greater abundance to all aspects of your life.

MOUNTAINS

Mountains are naturally formed pyramids, so they inevitably carry the manifestation power of the triangle within their midst (see also Key 39, page 182). Mountains help us connect to and channel formative and powerful masculine energies that are best at organizing matter. Being in the vicinity of a mountain when you are working on goal-setting can help you leverage the power of that mountain toward making those goals a reality. You could also mentally connect to any mountain that resonates with you and enlist it to help you with manifesting.

When working with mountain energy, connect to its core—the heart of the mountain, its liquid center deep within the Earth. The most potent mountain energy dwells along the vertical axis that connects the heart of the mountain to its peak. Feel free to imagine the power of the mountain rising from within the depth of the mountain in an upward sweeping motion and exiting the mountain at its peak to power your intended outcome. This simple meditation could easily double the effectiveness of your manifestation.

CITRINE

Citrine is a powerful Sun stone. Its energy is stable and reliable—it is a steady horse that wins the race. Pick up a new piece of citrine for every major thing you are trying to manifest. Charge the crystal with the energies of what you'd like to manifest. Hold the crystal next to your bed or your desk—anywhere in your immediate vicinity. Make sure to touch the crystal often and recenter it around what you need help manifesting. Citrine has powerful grounding and anchoring properties; it can help direct your energy toward achieving your goal.

EMERALD

The symbol of wealth and ultimate luxury, emeralds are not for the faint of hearts. Investing in an emerald symbolizes your commitment to building wealth—the kind that withstands the test of time—for yourself and your loved ones. Hold the emerald close to your body, as close to your skin as possible. Emerald has an uncanny ability to sync with the rhythm and the deepest desires of your heart and make them happen. It is a masterful helper and a true alchemist of the crystal kingdom. It is closely connected with the state of flow and will enable that state in your life. There is truly nothing impossible for the owner of an emerald.

HONEY

Honey is a magic substance—it's healing for your body and your soul. One of its properties is energetic alignment. Honey both heals and activates your solar plexus chakra—it balances your self-perception, increases your confidence levels, and brings you into alignment with your immediate surroundings. Honey is a great harmonizer. Have it with tea, with granola, or just straight up. As you are ingesting honey, imagine that just the process of consuming the product puts you directly on your ideal path. Sprinkle in gratitude for this wondrous substance and the honeybees that are freely offering it to humanity. Honey is an abundance catalyst.

JUPITER

Outside of the Sun, Jupiter is the best manifestation planetary helper. Jupiter is all about growth, expansion, abundance, wealth, and amplified creation. Enlist the energy of Jupiter to assist you by connecting to the planet's energy body in meditation. You can envision your desired outcome as a code that gets uploaded to Jupiter's matrix system. Jupiter is the master grower and harvester. It is a planetary equivalent of Midas' touch—anything that is powered by Jupiter grows. Make sure to do your goal setting outside of the periods of Jupiter retrograde to harness the energy of this great planet.

PRACTICE: BECOMING A VIBRATIONAL MATCH TO YOUR GOALS

To amplify and speed up your manifestation, you need to come into alignment with what you want. This can be tricky as not having what you want means you are precisely out of alignment with your desired outcome. Alignment is another name for the Law of Attraction—like attracts like (see also Keys 24 and 50, pages 111 and 229). Vibrate at the rate of what you want, and you shall receive it.

Another facet of alignment is your heart and mind connection. Your manifestation has double the impact if both your mind and your heart are on the same page around what you want. It is also important that you are fully in agreement that you CAN have that which you desire. Below is a simple practice to bring you closer in alignment to what you want.

1. Close your eyes and imagine that your body is surrounded by two spheres. The inner sphere is colored green and represents your heart and your Emotional Body. The outer sphere is steely blue-silver and represents your mind and Mental Body.
2. Now focus on your desired outcome for a few moments. Really "see" it in your mind's eye.
3. Place that outcome inside the sphere representing your Mental Body and allow that sphere to absorb and envelope the vibrations of your desired outcome. This way, you can become one with that vibration. You are looking to form an integral whole between your Mental Body and the mental vibrations of your desired outcome.
4. Repeat this process for your Emotional Body. As a result, you will have the code representation of your desired outcome fully integrated into both your emotional and mental bodies.

Used regularly, this practice will enable the much-needed mind to heart connection so you are in alignment with your goals and wants.

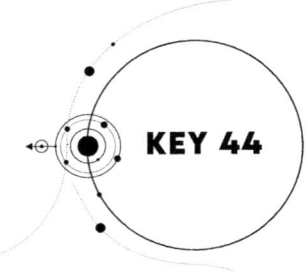

THE QUANTUM BRIDGE

A quantum bridge between two points is the quickest, least obstructed, and most direct path between them—as a linear projection, it's the shortest distance. While not technically a shortcut, a quantum bridge is the most optimal path that considers the entirety of the Universe and your personal desires.

Most human paths are far from linear. Rather they are a series of loops and curves better likened to a maze than a highway. When you start manifesting, you generally begin from a place of pure inspiration and excitement. That tends to create an optimal path for you to achieve what you want. If only you were to trust that path and start moving your feet one in front of the other in the direction that feels good, you would be traveling this most optimal path without much wasted effort. However, since our time-space reality is extremely viscous (read: slow), the physical manifestation is often a lengthy process with very little instant or apparent gratification. And herein lies the trap that many people fall into. Below we'll review some of the most important things you can do to stay on the most optimal path and manifest as quickly as possible.

TRUST THE PATH

Trust sounds simple, and yet this is one of our biggest pitfalls. Humans are neither very patient nor very trusting, especially of the Universe. Trusting the Universe takes an understanding of exactly how interconnected we all are and how held we are by this greater power. Chances are, over the years, you have grown too skeptical, or too distrusting. You stopped expecting the good just to come your way on the simple basis of your being a Divine being. You forgot that by default, you are deserving, worthy, and meant to have all the things you want; you were born to claim them as yours. You are not meant to have all the answers—just the general direction and the desire for a particular future. The Universe always takes care of the path and the execution at the grand level.

Start cultivating trust for your path and for the Universe. Know in your heart of hearts that no harm can come to you from your Universal Mother. In fact, the rest of existence has been conspiring to assist you in every way that counts. Trusting is receiving.

ACCEPT THE TIMES WHEN YOU DON'T MAKE PROGRESS

The Universe moves like the wild cat—with large chunks of time spent collecting and conserving energy and only short spurts of action. Know that this balance is the natural flow of the Universe. Get used to lengthy periods of time with no apparent wins, followed by a short sequence of major upgrades, especially if you are working on manifesting something on a large scale. The work the Universe is performing on your behalf centers around aligning—also known as weaving in your personal needs and wants with those of the rest of humanity. This meticulous work takes time and patience. Stop pressuring the Universe to deliver things for you; it operates on its own timeline.

REALIGN FREQUENTLY

As a creator of the vision for your future, you become an energetic parent for that outcome. Realigning with that future is like feeding your energetic baby. Without the proper nurturing, the baby withers away and dies. Make sure to keep your ties with your desired future strong by keeping it at the forefront of your mind through visualizing, refreshing your intentions, and remembering where you are heading—and why. Make sure to align with your desired future weekly to stay on the path fully.

PAY ATTENTION TO THE FLOW

Learn to notice the flow—that deep knowing and feeling that things are going your way. Notice the gifts from the Universe—big and small—and be grateful for them.

Gratitude is a great multiplier. Being grateful for the positive flow of energy that keeps you in that flow.

Learn to read the signs of the Universe—if things are becoming effortless, and the gifts from the Universe become plentiful—acknowledge that you are traveling up the stream that is quickly getting you to your desired future. At the same time, if you feel like you are NOT in the flow, don't get upset and worried about it. Rather, align yourself to your desired outcome and simply wait for the Universe to deliver—without judgment, pressure, and expectation.

MAKE THE MOVES, HOWEVER SMALL

Manifesting is not about taking the back seat. It takes two to tango—while your feminine energy can sit back and relax, calling outcomes to it, your masculine energy needs to be in action. If massive action seems daunting and impossible, start small. Do one thing daily to get you closer to where you want to go. It is through the collaboration of your efforts with those of the Universe that you will get the outcome you want.

PRACTICE: DRAWBRIDGE (QUANTUM BRIDGE) FOR COURSE-CORRECTING

Any time you feel that you have strayed off course or doubt you are still on the path, this quick exercise in course-correcting may be exactly what you need.

1. Close your eyes and start with deep breathing to quiet your busy mind. For a few moments, let go of the clutter of your daily hurdles and walk into a space of quantum healing—the depth of your soul temple.
2. Imagine standing on a little island amidst a vast ocean. This island represents you today—where you are in time and space. You may notice that this island is filled with all of your favorite objects—books, clothes, and trinkets—and everything that makes you—you.
3. Notice a drawbridge that leads away from this island to another one, set in the vast ocean. This bridge represents the path you are currently walking—the most

likely outcome. Does the island you are currently connecting to represent your desired outcome, or merely some default version of your future? Likely your default outcome is not the one that you are trying to manifest.

4. Focus on what you are trying to manifest. Think of it as an island in its own right—abundant and luscious and full of the objects you want. This island has everything you could possibly dream of—the people, the circumstances, the feelings, and the thoughts—all available and waiting for you.

5. When the image of this island becomes clear in your mind, the only thing left is connecting to it. Lift the drawbridge that is currently connecting you to another island and see how it is slowly lowered to the shores of this new island. Now you have a quantum bridge connecting where you are today with the spot you would rather be.

6. From here on out, trust that every step you take will always be in the direction of your desired outcome. After all, the quantum bridge is the shortest path between the two points—your today and your bright tomorrow.

Repeat this practice every time you feel like you are straying off course.

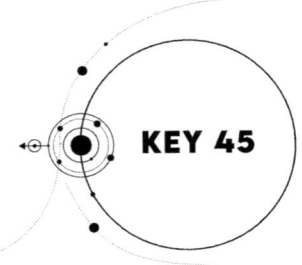

KEY 45

THE TEMPLE OF MANIFESTATION

From the beginning of time, temples have served as holy receptacles and transmitters of Divine energy. Physical Earthly temples serve as the acupuncture points of our planet. Through these spots, healing energies can enter to be distributed to the far corners of our planet by the temple's adepts and attendants. Our ancestors dedicated temples to all the major energies at play on the planet—from the Sun and the Moon to the wind and fire, to love and truth, and of course, to the good old favorites, gods, goddesses, and saints.

Temples are powerful energy aggregators: they tap into and accumulate the energy streams of many people driven by the same idea, frequency, or concept. Some temples are physical. Others are etheric (energetic) in nature. Neither one is more powerful than the other—they are simply two facets of the same phenomenon.

The Temple of Manifestation has existed within the crystal matrix of Earth since the dawn of humanity. It has been powered by generations of dreamers, wanderers, and go-getters. Through time it has borne many names—the Temple of Dreams, the Temple of Abundance, and the Temple of Fortuna (Lady Luck). Apart from its etheric footprint, it has had many physical footprints in each of the main human civilizations, from Hyperborea to Atlantis.

The Temple of Manifestation is one of the cosmic energy receptacles—the convergence of the invisible streams of creative and formative vibrations. Many souls have contributed their unique gifts to this temple, and many have benefited greatly from it.

Today we'll be visiting the Temple of Manifestation together, and you'll learn exactly how it can aid you on your path.

The benefits of spending time within the Etheric Temple of Manifestation include:

△ Tapping into the collective energy of human dreams—and the energy of making it happen.
△ Amplifying your creative energies.
△ Removing any obstacles in your way.

- △ Filling your cup with nurturing, healing energies of abundance.
- △ Creating your personal footprint within the temple and asking for the Universe's assistance with your own manifestation.

PRACTICE: WORKING WITH THE TEMPLE OF MANIFESTATION

There are two steps to this practice. Feel free to return to the temple as often as you'd like. With time you will notice that it starts to amplify your intentions, and you will undoubtedly see the results of this unique partnership.

Step 1: Visiting the temple

1. Close your eyes and slow down your breathing.
2. Focus on your heart center—the steady, nurturing energies of your beating heart. As you dive deeper into these energies, notice your chest filling with the most etheric emerald-green light. True creation is a byproduct of your heart stream. That is why we need to start in this center to connect to the Temple of Manifestation.
3. Notice that there is a path paved with emerald-green crystals that emerge right under your feet. Start walking down this path. This is the path of your heart, and it's leading you to a place that it knows so well—a place where your dreams can come true.
4. Imagine this path is leading you to a beautiful temple made entirely of crystal quartz atop the hill. As the multifaceted crystals catch the lights of the midday Sun, they sparkle like diamonds, covering the temple's surroundings with a Divine, angelic glow.
5. Walk up the steps that lead you inside. The steps are numerous, but you don't feel tired as you walk up.
6. Inside the temple you see a large hall filled with sunshine. It is full of people and creatures of all kinds—dragons, unicorns, and even fairies. The trees line the temple walls, making it feel like you just stepped into a crystal-enclosed, luscious garden.
7. In the very center of the temple, there is a master crystal—massive and awe-inspiring. This is the crown jewel of the Temple of Manifestation. This crystal

is called rainbow opal—it contains every color of the rainbow and sparks with the most beautiful cosmic light. Rainbow opal is the master manifestor stone—there is something in it for everyone. It contains a full spectrum of energies and shares them freely with everyone who comes to spend time in this temple.

8. Walk up to this gorgeous crystal and lay your hands on it. Think of what it is you are trying to manifest and ask the master stone for assistance. As soon as the crystal hears your request for help, it will start sending jolts of energy into your palms. Stay here for a few moments and just receive. This stone is wise: it knows exactly what you need to move forward on your path, and it will send you blessings that will aid with your manifestation.

9. Thank the crystal for its assistance. It thrives on the energy of gratitude. With your thanks, it can help other people who come to this temple. You can also ask the crystal to remove any obstacles in your way if you haven't done so already. The rainbow opal is exceptionally powerful, and no obstacle is greater than the power of this stone.

Step 2: Building Your Personal Space within the Temple

1. As soon as you are done working with the master crystal, notice a figure's approaching you. The figure bows to you in respect and introduces itself as one of the guardians of this temple. It is happy that you came today and would love to show you the way to your personal quarters within this grand temple. It is asking that you follow it.
2. In a few seconds, you find yourself standing by a large door, and, interestingly, the door has a little tag with your name on it. Indeed, it seems they have been awaiting you in this temple.
3. Feel free to open the door and enter.
4. The space that opens up for you is unique and special. No two rooms within the Temple of Manifestation are alike. What do you see inside? This is your personal space. Feel free to rearrange it to your liking—add or remove windows, natural light, plants, or furniture. Feel free to play and make this space as comfortable as you please.
5. Now call in a crystal to assist you with your manifestation. The crystal needs to be planted in the very center of this room. The crystal will be unique to you

and represent a vibration close to that of your soul. You can think of this crystal as your soul crystal. Allow it to reveal itself. Do you know what crystal you are seeing? Notice its shape and color—nothing here is random. Place your hands on this crystal and charge it with your personal energy.

6. When the crystal lights up with the help of your personal energy, charge it with the knowledge of what it is you want to manifest. From this day forward, this crystal will act as your talisman and your helper.

The more often you use this practice and communicate with your crystal, the more helpful it can be. It can assist in bringing the right people, circumstances, and events into your life. This crystal is your partner in crime and will be here for you any time you require answers or assistance.

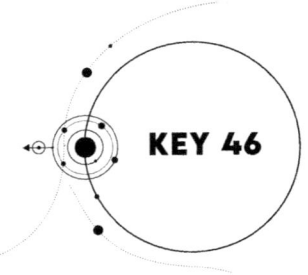

THE GAME OF FOCUS

The skill of manifestation is the ability to take a dispersed energy stream and transform it into a focused energy steam while infusing it with momentum and a sense of direction (see also Keys 18 and 25, pages 86 and 115). Most of your energy exists in its dormant state, ready to be awakened at any moment. Mastering manifestation is a journey of moving from smaller to bigger challenges over time. Starting small is definitely the name of the game. Use the tips below to turn your energy into a more focused stream.

- △ **Sleep is key**: Make sure to get enough sleep and generally be well rested. When your body is depleted, it automatically goes into maintenance mode, not creative mode.
- △ **Be good to yourself**: Get great at replenishing your energy. Build habits that allow you to be in a state of fullness. Take the time to fill your cup. To manifest effectively, you have to make time for activities that feel good. Try to get out of the grind and the routine as much as possible.
- △ **Create space**: Most people have trouble attracting even the simplest things into their orbit because their world is already too full—with clutter. Energy doesn't flow into spaces that are over cluttered. Make it a habit to declutter and free up space—in your closet, in your head, and in your life. Get good at cutting out people who no longer align with you and the path you are on. Review your habits and routine continually to find all the activities—big and small—that no longer match who you want to be. Take action on altering these habits.
- △ **Don't overextend yourself**: At any point in time, you cannot be manifesting more than three things, and even three is a lot. Less is more. You have a finite energy resource, and splitting hairs on it is not advisable, especially if you prefer to move quickly.
- △ **Find strong sources of energy—your manifestation allies**: Here you cannot go wrong, at least not in the beginning. More is more when it comes to allies and helpers. Sources can be external, such as the Sun, various stars or constellations, or the Black Sun discussed earlier (see Key 4, page 34). Your ancestors can be a

great source of energy to tap into, especially if you are used to working with their energies. Crystals (individually and in grid form) are great manifestation allies. Their energies are fixed and targeted—exactly what you need for productive manifestation. You can also call in an animal you admire to donate its energy to assist you. This would require you to ask for the animal's allegiance, but when asked properly, allegiance is often received.

- △ **Repetition is key**: Every thought you think is an energetic virtual currency. Every thought of yours counts. The more attention you pay to your desired future and the more frequently you think of it with intention, the quicker it will manifest itself. Find ways to remind yourself of what you are trying to manifest—from sticky notes to journals to pictures, everything is fair game. Surround yourself with objects that remind you about your ideal outcome. The more you see them and interact with them, the faster your manifestation will go.
- △ **Create a talisman for yourself**: A talisman is an object, often a natural object (like a tree branch, leaf, stone, flower, or essential oil), that can assist you in manifestation once it's infused with your energy. Once you select the object, place it between your palms and saturate the object with your energy. This should take two to three minutes of focused attention. Once the object is infused, give it an intention—a mission of sorts. Let it know exactly what it can help you attract into your life. Then place the object where you can easily see it. You want to come back to your talisman every day, holding it in your hands and charging it with your energy. Within a few days, the object will have enough power inside it to start assisting you. This assistance might be invisible, but the object will work to remove obstacles in your way and help you attract exactly what you need.

PRACTICE: MANIFESTING SMALL THINGS—THE BLUEPRINT

This simple practice will help you focus your energy to manifest.

1. Pick a small object you want to manifest in your life—a crystal, a certain kind of flower, a small amount of money, or whatever resonates with you and whatever you feel good about manifesting. You will spend quite some time focusing on this object, so pick wisely.

2. Align your energy with the energy of that object. To do that, close your eyes and imagine the object. Observe it from multiple angles—both its physical appearance and one layer deeper, its energetic makeup. If this object were energy, what would it look like? Would it have a shape? A color? Trust your gut feeling here; you cannot go wrong.

3. Call the object into your orbit. Imagine that invisible strings are drawing this object close to you. This pull is inevitable, and the object cannot and doesn't want to resist it. Imagine that the strings bring the object so close to you that you can stretch your arms and take it. Place that object inside your own energy field—you should have an energy pocket that is a perfect fit for this object. Trust that the object is already yours. This confidence is critical. Don't doubt for a second that you can have the object. Allow yourself to be reunited with the object in your real life.

4. Refresh this connection twice daily. Morning and evening, imagine holding on to the object and taking it out of your virtual pocket to connect with it. You want to feel it pulsating inside the palm of your hand. You want to close your eyes and picture this object's now dwelling on your desk, right next to you, in real life. Know that this connection is possible, and it is already happening for you. Repeat the same exercise in the evening.

5. Watch it manifest in your life. Often in more ways than one. If you are a talented manifestor, you will attract the object within three days—you will either be gifted it unexpectedly or will accidentally just find it or come across it in a local store for a crazy discount. Take note of this little win—you can try the same process with a bigger object next time.

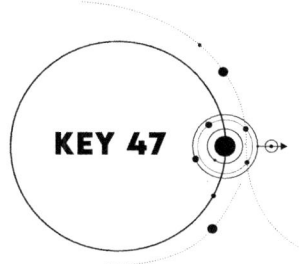

KEY 47

THE TRIPLE HELIX OF MANIFESTATION: BE, DO, HAVE

> *"For this reason, I tell you, whatever you pray and ask for, believe that you have received it, and it will be yours."*
>
> —The Gospel of Mark 11:24

Manifesting is a cyclical process. It represents several identical cycles that you need to repeat continually to get to your desired outcome. Collectively these cycles form a ladder leading from your reality of today to your reality of tomorrow. Each cycle of manifestation represents a step of the ladder—a specific energetic frequency that is characterized by many aspects of your physical reality, from the people who surround you to how much money you have in your bank account. Every manifestation cycle has three main aspects summarized in a simple formula—Be, Do, Have.

Together, and exactly in this order, these three aspects represent one complete cycle of manifestation. Depending on the complexity of what you are trying to create, you might only need one cycle or quite a few. Manifesting in a low-dimensional reality (which Earth falls into) is not immediate. It requires you to align with the energies of that which you desire, and that is a gradual process. The same way you climb a ladder step-by-step, manifestation is a step-by-step game (see Figure 25 on the next page). A new step is always a new vantage point, a newly integrated vibration, and a new frequency that enables creation at a higher, more complex level.

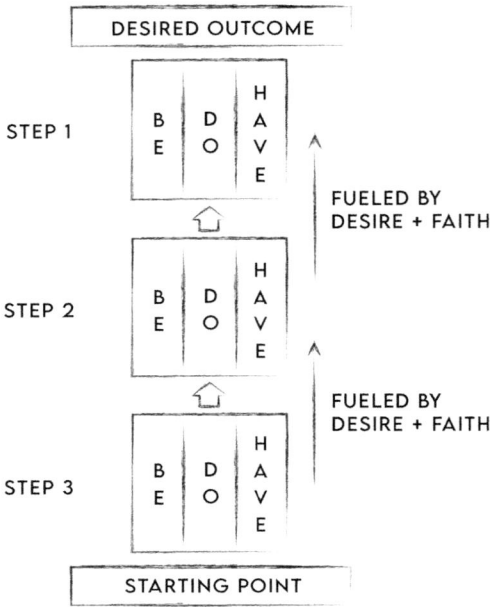

FIGURE 25: MANIFESTATION LADDER – BE, DO, HAVE

Let's explore the cycle of manifestation in detail. The order of the cycle is predetermined: Be → Do → Have. Skipping steps or changing their order is ineffective and creates enough delays with manifestation that manifesting doesn't work for most people.

BE—THE STATE

Always begin with your state. There are two very important components to consider.

1. **Master the "resourceful" state of being full and enough.** Humankind possesses three general energetic states: resourceful (positive), in between (neutral), and lacking (negative). A resourceful state is a state of "glass half full." Make sure to notice all the great things around you—every aspect and ounce of abundance and goodness that surrounds you today. This is also a state of finally allowing

yourself to start being enough. This is a state with minimal doubt and negative self-talk. This state also requires you to watch everything you consume to ensure toxic people, news, and products don't enter your system. Things that contribute to being resourceful are physical movement, meditation, healthy foods, and interactions with happy people. But above all else, stop reminding yourself of all the things you are not and do not have. Stop comparing yourself to others and living according to someone else's playbook. Stop being in a rush and just allow yourself to breathe. Allow yourself to find your rhythm and a pace that makes you happy and full. Stop judging others: give them their innate right to live life on their terms, and at the same time, take this right for yourself.

2. **Align with what you want.** Keep what you want at the top of your mind and set up various reminders for yourself so that you inadvertently come back to the vision of your ideal future as frequently as possible. With manifestation, repetition is everything. Vision boards, sticky notes, daily reminders, and custom mantras are all tools to help you stay in alignment with what your heart desires—use and abuse them.

DO—THE ACTION

Follow through with action. The state without action is wasted energy. The physical world is a place of massive, unapologetic action. Wishing on the stars might be a curious pastime, but unless it's backed up by plenty of action, it will NEVER result in a change of your circumstances, unless what you are trying to manifest is fairly small or insignificant. Keep making steps toward your goal. Know in your heart of hearts that your desire is not only possible, but *inevitable*. And while you are at it, start moving in its direction so the two of you can meet halfway. The absence of action creates doubt and, unless controlled, will start eroding your state. Thus taking massive action in the physical cements your intention and allows you to benefit from the state you have just created.

HAVE—THE REWARD

If you complete the first two steps of this process, it won't take much time until the early results start rolling in. Notice and mark them in your mind as proof that you are moving in the right direction. The act of having is not only about bringing things into your life, but also noticing them as they come, and being grateful. I will not get tired of repeating this: gratitude is a master multiplier.

INTEGRATING BE, DO, HAVE

Once your cycle is complete, as long as your manifestation is still fueled by your desire and faith, it will organically move into the next step—a new cycle. The cycle will look the same at face value—Be, Do, Have—but the vantage point will differ. The state will become even more elevated—the highs will be much higher. The level of action you will be able to do in the physical would also feel elevated compared to action in the previous step of the ladder. You might even start getting some recognition for your work from the people surrounding you. And the rewards that you reap will be truly something to be proud of. Keep going—you are on the right track!

YOUR FUEL: DESIRE AND FAITH

Desire makes the world go round. Any project, movement, or business that has ever been created emanated from pure desire—an impulse that fueled the initial stages of the project. You first really need to want it with all you have. And while desire is all you need for that original creative spark, faith is what keeps the momentum going. Cultivate your faith—the belief that you can and will have what you want. Know that as a Divine spark of light, you deserve everything you could possibly wish for. Nurture your faith and allow it to spread its wings. Your accomplishments in the physical world are directly proportional to the level of faith you have.

PRACTICE: THE STATE OF RESOURCEFULNESS

The State of Resourcefulness is also known as the State of Water. Water is infinitely creative, infinitely abundant, and infinitely healing. It is the element that gave life to the majority of creation on this planet. Descending into the state of water can be the most healing and peaceful state you could experience.

1. Close your eyes and start with deep breathing—in and out.
2. Imagine floating in the deep waters of the ocean. The waters are warm and gentle; they are softly caressing your skin. You know that you can trust this vast ocean and that it has your best interest at heart.
3. As you are floating in these healing waters, imagine being fully submerged by the ocean. This is what the hug of the ocean feels like—soft and gentle. Allow yourself to be rocked back and forth by this force of nature, joining with it fully.
4. Imagine your hands turning into streams of water as they join the rest of the ocean, becoming one with it. Let your body become water—let it unfold at the cellular level, turning into a sequence of individual cells. Allow each cell to turn into water and fully rejoin the vastness of the great ocean. Know that at this moment, all of your worries and problems are being dissolved as well. Allow the water to heal you at a deep cellular level. Give all of your negative emotions to the ocean to take care of. Allow yourself to be cuddled and to be nurtured by this wondrous energy.
5. Finally, when you are ready, color the waters of the ocean into a hue that feels great to you right now. For one reason or another, you crave this color and this frequency.
6. As the ocean's hue adjusts to your desires, allow that hue to penetrate your cells. Allow yourself to experience a few moments of true peace and quiet.
7. Become water. Notice how the water feels. Notice that it is in no rush to get anywhere because it already is everything and everywhere, all at once. Feel the power of this ancient element; remember this feeling of complete and utter surrender to the element of water.

Hold on to this feeling and evoke it anytime you feel down or low.

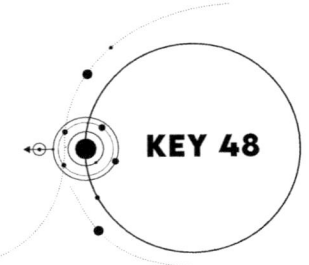

KEY 48

MANIFESTATION ARCHETYPES: STRATEGY BY ARCHETYPE

Remember discovering your major sponsoring element in Key 26 (page 120)? While different things you choose to manifest may be sponsored by different elements, you have one overarching master archetype associated with how the energies of manifestation move through your body. You manifestation archetype tends to remain with you for the duration of your life. Today, we'll explore the four major manifestation archetypes and strategies associated with each.

ALCHEMIST—AIR

The Alchemist is blessed with the capacity to manifest anything faster than others. This manifestation archetype has mastered the air element and thus has mastered speed, agility, and nimbleness. While not terribly patient, the Alchemist has a superior ability to change the tides seemingly effortlessly to their liking. The moods and desires of the alchemist quickly disperse into their surroundings, gently bending circumstances and events according to the Alchemist's will. The Alchemist is exceptionally adaptable; they don't get discouraged by obstacles. The Alchemist is, above all, a dreamer; they like large-scale projects and endeavors. You will never find them thinking small.

For the Alchemist, life is a playground, not a challenge to overcome or a battle to fight. They have a lighthearted, easy-going attitude which allows them always to maintain a resourceful state. On the flip side, the Alchemist has a hard time sticking to one thing—they get bored easily and thus don't always follow through. Therefore, despite their superior talents, the Alchemist doesn't always have the results to show for it. The Alchemist is prone to not knowing what they want; they like to go where the wind blows and thus can struggle to generate enough of a spark of desire to launch the sequence of manifestation in the first place.

MANIFESTATION STRATEGY FOR THE ALCHEMIST

First and foremost, the Alchemist needs to narrow down the number of targets they want to pursue. Even with such enviable manifestation talents, the Alchemist cannot do it all. The second biggest challenge is actually to commit to something. The game of manifestation for the Alchemist is the challenge of patience. The Alchemist needs to learn to go through the motions of creating something, which always takes time, and be content with the seemingly slow progress. The energy of air that the Alchemist has mastered is a powerful creative force. Yet the Alchemist is tempted to use that creative power for pursuing random projects instead of growing "the one." The biggest lesson and pain point here is the power of focus and saying no to distractions.

POWERHOUSE—FIRE

The Powerhouse is blessed with incessant energy and drive. This is the most energetic of all the archetypes. As the wielder of fire, the Powerhouse has mastered the art of desire. The Powerhouse has mastered that original spark that causes everything else to become. They are a terrific organizer, a skillful conjurer, and a powerful orchestrator of the physical plane. A natural-born leader, the Powerhouse's passion is contagious. The Powerhouse is great at attracting allies into their orbit and arranging things so that others do most of the hard work. Whatever they are manifesting, they tend to do so with intention and an intense level of focus that others only wish they could achieve.

The Powerhouse can come across as lucky—things just seem to appear magically for them. And yet this "luck" tends to result from hard behind-the-scenes work and incessant faith. The Powerhouse has the heart of a true believer, which allows them eventually to see projects and initiatives through. The curse of the Powerhouse is burnout. They tend to over-invest at the beginning and almost try to take the fortress by brute force. In the process, they lose plenty of energy that is hard to replenish. The Powerhouse is also prone to mood swings caused by external circumstances. They tend to take things personally, especially criticism, which can get them out of the state of resourcefulness for weeks at a time. And yet the Powerhouse is extremely determined, stubborn even, so eventually, they tend to get back on track. If the Powerhouse only knew how to handle their emotional states better, they could move down the manifestation track with better agility and fewer bruises.

MANIFESTATION STRATEGY FOR THE POWERHOUSE

The Powerhouse needs to focus on energy replenishment. Their greatest impediment on the road to a better life is feeling depleted or unworthy. To become a masterful manifestor, the Powerhouse needs to find all the things that replenish their fiery energy. Fire in all its forms and facets (from a candle to a fireplace) is a great place to start. The Powerhouse needs to schedule downtime. Overachieving in life is a marathon, not a sprint, so a well-balanced schedule is paramount to preventing burnout.

The Powerhouse has a tough exterior hiding a very gentle heart that is incredibly receptive to incoming energies. The Powerhouse is also extremely prone to self-criticism, which is the number one energy responsible for killing all creative prowess. The Powerhouse needs to master their inner critic to be successful. It is also important for the Powerhouse to keep a tally of all their achievements and accomplishments. A great memory is not one of their greatest assets, so a list of accomplishments is a great tool for one of those down moments where the world seems bleak and creation impossible.

FLOW ARTIST—WATER

The Flow Artist is a gentle soul, but don't mistake that to mean lack of power. While the Flow Artist will never exude overconfidence and will never resort to brute force, they have access to primordial formative energies that originally created life on this planet. The master of the element of water, the Flow Artist, is enviably flexible and has a wise, indestructible Spirit. The Flow Artist knows that there is more to manifestation than meets the eye. Of all the archetypes, this is the one that has the highest probability of just sitting still while things get manifested, seemingly in and of themselves.

The Flow Artist has mastered the energy of flow—the most potent creative stream on this planet—and thus, as a great fisher, they have the advantage of dipping the fishing rod in the water and sitting back while the perfect fish manifests. They often don't have to lift a finger to get what they want, unlike others who have to put in real blood, sweat, and tears. The Flow Artist simply has to manage the flow—their emotional and mental state—and wait until the rest is taken care of. The Flow Artists is most prone to mood swings and sudden changes of heart compared to other archetypes. This happens because, at any point in time, they are experiencing the flow and might inadvertently absorb whatever energy is present in the collective. Boundaries are paramount for the Flow Artist because they have none. This archetype is thus most prone to suffering. Having unending patience, the Flow Artist stays in relationships and circumstances that don't serve them and hopes that things will change.

MANIFESTATION STRATEGY FOR THE FLOW ARTIST

Establishing healthy boundaries and getting rid of toxic relationships is the best thing the Flow Artist can do to amplify their capacity for manifestation and happy living. This doesn't come easily as they tend to have a soft loving personality. The most important word to learn for the Flow Artist is "no." Saying no to things that don't serve the wellbeing of the Flow Artist is the single most important healthy habit. Once the immediate network of the Flow Artist is free from toxic, needy, and abusive people, they will find it much easier to stay in the positive flow and attract things easily. Pressure is the absence of flow. Thus it is advisable for the Flow Artist not to have a stringent schedule or regimen. The Flow Artist thrives on freedom and having enough space in their day-to-day to truly create.

THE SHAMAN (ALSO: MASTER NURTURER)—EARTH

The Shaman is naturally in tune with their surroundings and operates from a sense of deep knowing and understanding of everything that is. The Shaman will never impose their will on others, but finds paths that take others into account. The Shaman doesn't move fast—their decisions are measured, level-headed, and intentional. While the Shaman has impeccable intuition and innate wisdom, their energy can be very internal-facing, almost quiet. Thus the Shaman is sometimes challenged to generate that original spark of an idea that would excite them.

Often the Shaman will spend life as a seeker, never truly committing to something because they don't feel enough "passion" for it. And yet this quiet reflection comes with the territory. The Shaman is exceptional at growing and nurturing things; they have the patience and the skill to grow anything. Therefore the Shaman is adept at taking on long-term, large-scale projects. Perhaps the projects won't be the most innovative, but they will make people's lives better, and ultimately, the Shaman really cares about that. The challenge of the Shaman is to watch the energy exchange between themselves and other humans. They tend to be all give and no take, which creates a sense of loneliness or feeling used by others. The Shaman needs to remember that taking is okay, and that doesn't make them a bad human—rather a more balanced one.

MANIFESTATION STRATEGY FOR THE SHAMAN

The Shaman needs outside stimulation to be inspired to manifest. That original spark tends to come from the outside rather than the inside. So the Shaman needs to ensure there is always enough inspiration in their world—from people to consumed content to the day-to-day work—since surrounding themselves with the right energies is important. The Shaman needs to get great at filling their own cup and meeting their needs first before helping others. As master nurturers, they need to make sure they are not personally lacking before generously distributing their energy to others—those in need or otherwise.

PRACTICE: DETERMINE YOUR ARCHETYPE MEDITATION

Chances are, as you were reading the above, you have already recognized yourself in one or two archetypes. Trust your intuition. In this particular case, it is most likely right. If you want to double-check your gut feeling, follow the practice below.

1. Close your eyes and take a few deep breaths.
2. Imagine there are four goblets in front of you. The first one is white and represents the element of air. The second one is red and represents fire. The third one is blue and represents water. And the fourth one is green and represents Earth. Take some time to examine each and feel the energy encapsulated within.
3. When you are ready, stretch out your right arm in front of you to magnetize one of the goblets to you. Watch as one of the goblets flows straight into your open hand. Which goblet did you catch? The element of the goblet will be the element of your archetype.

4. Now, stretch out your left hand and see if another goblet is magnetized. For some of you, it won't be the case. Don't worry—this means you only have one manifestation archetype. For those of you that find yourself with another goblet in the left hand—you have a hybrid archetype. This is completely normal and makes you even more powerful as far as manifestation is concerned.

Remember your archetypes. They hold the key to your unique energy profile and, thus, to your perfect manifestation hacks.

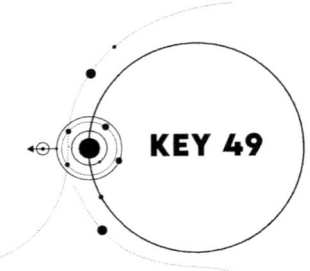

CLOSING THE ENERGY LOOP

Did you ever wonder where your energy goes? If you are like most people, chances are you feel completely drained after an eight-hour workday and barely capable of doing anything remotely productive. We are incredibly effective at giving our energy away and not even noticing it in the process. For a normal adult, the majority of life is spent on autopilot—we, after all, are creatures of habit. This means that your routine (and not you) drives your life. Now this would only be half the trouble if your success with manifesting the life you want wasn't directly correlated to your energy levels.

You may give away your energy to everything under the Sun—sometimes consciously and other times subconsciously. Sharing your energy consciously is a great thing—this is what having meaningful, healthy relationships, hobbies, and a job you love are all about. It is the subconscious loss of power that we should examine and worry about.

Below we'll explore how you may subconsciously be giving away your energy, which causes you to feel depleted.

EXPLORE YOUR RELATIONSHIPS AND COMMITMENTS

Getting rid of toxic relationships is perhaps the most common advice in therapy. However, that is just the first step to reclaiming your energy. The second step is cutting the cords with that person (also see Key 14, page 71). To do that, in a meditative state, imagine energetic cords connecting you and the other person. You then want to take a sword made entirely of white light and sever the cords. Once the cords are gone, you should feel an influx of your energy coming back to you while the energy of the other person returns from you to them.

You should also explore the various organizations you were once involved in—such as your school or a sports club. Very often organizations we belonged to will still be tapping into our energy pool years after we stopped an active involvement. It is advisable to perform a cord-cutting and energy-reclaiming practice with those organizations also.

REWRITE YOUR PAST TRAUMA

Each traumatic experience becomes a bookmark in your personal book of life. And as such, it inadvertently makes you pay attention to it until the moment that trauma gets resolved. Resolving past trauma might seem like a daunting task, and many have certainly spent years upon years in therapy grappling to come to terms with what happened. However, if you look inward, there may be a simpler way to help you along the path to trauma recovery.

One such resource is choosing to write a new story over the traumatic one. Take out a piece of paper and a pen. Start by remembering the morning of the day that the event happened. And as if you were a screenplay writer of your own life (which you are), create a script for a new day—a day where the trauma never happened. Write down that day in detail the way you wish it happened. If you complete this exercise fully, you will be surprised at how much relief this simple act brings. This will help free up blocked energy that can finally be used toward a positive outcome.

WATCH WHAT YOU CONSUME/EXPLORE YOUR ADDICTIONS

For each negative thing you consume, make sure to consume two nourishing things (this relates to drinks, foods, media, and largely anything else that enters your body). This balance will create the positive momentum you need to maintain high energy levels. Notice how your body responds to the foods you eat. Pay attention to whether you feel light and happy after consuming them or heavy and on edge. Be especially attentive to what you would describe as addictions, however small and insignificant. Addictions are where you give away most of your energy. Try substituting anything you're addicted to with something that is overall better for you and watch big chunks of energy come back to you.

EXPLORE YOUR NEGATIVE THOUGHT PATTERNS

Negative thoughts lead to negative emotions, so if you don't want to give away your energy, stop accepting thoughts of negative frequencies. Get intentional about your thinking patterns. Awareness is half the battle in this case. Try keeping a tally of your negative thoughts for one day; count them. You might be surprised how many negative thoughts you amass in a day. The following day, try to reduce that count by 25 percent. You will notice that just through this act, you get better at switching off negative thought frequencies and will start tuning into more positive vibes. Music can be of much assistance here. Create an upbeat playlist for yourself and play it in the background as you do work or chores. It is a lot harder to think negative thoughts when you are listening to positive tunes.

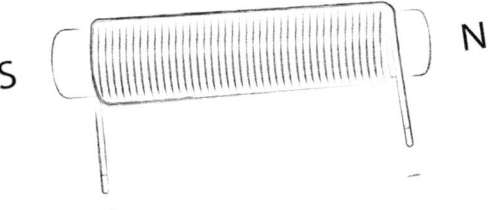

FIGURE 26: AN ELECTROMAGNETIC COIL

PRACTICE: ELECTROMAGNETIC COIL FOR MANIFESTATION

To manifest successfully, you need both the energy of electricity and the energy of magnetism. Collectively, the two energies fuse into an electromagnetic field—a tool that has enough momentum to make virtually anything happen. Today we'll work on building your own electromagnetic system that will aid in manifestation. To be successful, an electromagnetic system requires:

- **A source:** Luckily, we have plenty of energy sources handy, from the Sun to the Universe.
- **A coil:** You probably remember the solenoid from your high school physics class (see Figure 26). Just to refresh, a solenoid is a cylindrical coil that acts as a magnet when carrying an electric current. This is a neat little instrument that we'll need to create a magnetic field around you.
- **A closed loop:** This way, the initial current of energy is circulated within the system in the most sustainable way possible—automatically, perpetually, and without the loss of energy.

We'll take all of the above into account as we build your personal electromagnetic powerhouse in the following practice.

1. For this practice, you need to stand up and place your feet firmly on the floor. Find a comfortable position to stand and focus on your breath.
2. Imagine a tight coil around your body—it starts at your feet and ends at the top of your head.
3. First focus on the Earth beneath your feet. Imagine the very core of our planet—a place called the Earth Star chakra. You do not need to know what it looks like. Your intention is enough. This is your first source.
4. Imagine a stream of potent energy flowing from the Earth Star chakra toward the soles of your feet and entering the tight coil that is wrapped around your body.
5. As more and more energy enters the circuit, allow it to flow up and pass through every coil loop and exit at the top of your head.
6. Watch as this energy returns back to the center of the Earth, in effect closing the loop. Then allow the energy to start the same loop again. You want to allow this energy to keep repeating the same cycle. When massive amounts of energy move through the coil, it creates a magnetic field around you. Now charge the coil with the essence of what you want to create in this world—the imprint of your desired outcome. This way, as the magnetic field works to help you manifest, it can attract the exact things you need.
7. Now, let's work with your second source—the Sun. Imagine an electric current from the Sun is traveling toward you and enters the coil through your head. Allow this energy to travel downward with significant strength and momentum.

As the electric current from the Sun moves down the coil, it creates a massive magnetic field in the process.

8. Allow the electric current to exit through your feet and loop around toward the Sun, closing the loop in the process. Once again, focus on what you are trying to manifest and saturate this newly created magnetic field with those energies. Now continue with the loop one more time, setting it on autopilot, and will it to keep going long after you complete this exercise.

9. Stay in these energies for a few moments. Soak up the power of the two alternating currents—the one powered by the Sun and the one powered by the Earth. You may feel the warmth circulating all over your body, or a slight tingling sensation—this is completely normal in powerful practices like this one.

Come back to this exercise any time you need an extra boost of energy.

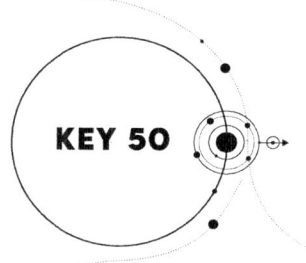

KEY 50

IMPRINTING

The Law of Attraction is predicated upon the so-called Cluster Principle—things of similar vibrations tend to accumulate together and remain so. This world is a lot less homogeneous than you may think despite the obvious cosmopolitanism and the strength of the collective consciousness. Rather, this world consists of clusters of energy—each defined by a frequency and interacting with other clusters—both similar to and different from one another. The reason you are a sum total of your five best friends is that collectively they represent the few clusters you are the best energetic fit for. You cannot be friends with anyone you are not a vibrational match to, at least not for the long haul. Therefore, you don't lose friends; you just slowly alter your vibrations and move away from the cluster of energy they represent—or vice versa.

As you might remember from high school physics, according to the law of energy conservation, the total sum of all energy in an isolated system remains constant over time. Planet Earth is an isolated energy system—the energy that is available to it is constant. And yet it hardly feels this way from within—things seem to be in constant movement day in and day out, and they seem to change more rapidly than we can all collectively keep track of. The most noticeable property of energy is its constant movement. The ebbs and flows of energy are responsible for any type of transformation you witness in the physical. This world depends on energy's maintaining and preserving its qualities, just as much as it depends on that energy's ability to transform. After all, if nature couldn't preserve your body in its current state, every day, you would see a different face in the mirror upon waking up. The mystery of this energetic dance involves understanding what determines which energy aspects remain constant and which are bound to change—the push and the pull, the electricity and the magnetism, and the progress and the stagnation.

Let's go back to the Law of Attraction for a second. The reason similar things are attracted to each other ("like attracts like") is that this process enables the Universe to create a cluster of energy to bring together creatures and objects of the same vibration. This cluster takes a lot less effort to maintain than many segregated instances of the same energy. And if there is one thing the mathematical nature of this Universe detests, it's wasted effort. Therefore, it is literally the DESIRE of the Universe to bring things with similar vibrations closer to each other and repel and isolate energies that don't belong together. The lion's share of the Universe's daily work is shifting energy in this way. Being armed with this knowledge, you unlock additional keys for manifestation. Manifesting is less about bringing things to you and more about **moving your vibrations** to match the vibrations of what you desire.

The work starts with you. You can visualize that coveted dollar amount on your bank account all you want; you can utter a million mantras in an attempt to believe you are already rich and abundant, but energy cannot be fooled. The only way to get what you want is to alter your vibration frequency. This movement is hardly a rudimentary or a quick task. Many books have been written about gradually changing your vibrations over time—positive thinking and visualization are the most commonly suggested techniques. And yet many on this planet don't have enough faith or patience to see this through. These rudimentary techniques work, but they are like water trying to alter stone—incredibly gentle and slow. The energies present on the planet today enable you to move much faster—if you dare, of course. And one such technique is imprinting.

Imprinting is a high-frequency energy practice that enables you to instantly upload the codes of your desired outcome to your light bodies and preserve them there, thus communicating to the Universe your intention to jump from one energy cluster to another. Once this process is set in motion, the rest is just a matter of time. The light codes will start working in your stead, bringing you to a place where what you want will materialize in front of your eyes. Imprinting takes some light maintenance, but comparatively speaking, it is incredibly simple compared to the tedious, old school (first generation) manifestation techniques (such as constant positive thinking and visualization).

The practice of imprinting consists of two equally important parts—encoding and, well, imprinting, or the transfer.

- △ **Encoding** is a highly intuitive process of translating the energy of your desired outcome into a sequence of numbers or symbols—a code. This is a process that requires trust. All energy in the Universe can be represented in a sequence—you might have heard of some examples already, like the Fibonacci sequence or the golden ratio. And beyond that, if you are familiar with computers, you know that anything you see on a computer screen is really a sequence code of just two digits—zero and one—presented in a way that shows up as moving and static images. The encoding process is backward translation—from a physical object back to the numeric sequence it represents.

△ **Imprinting** is the process of embedding that numeric code into your personal energy field. This part of the practice is intuitive and requires you to trust the process and the outcome.

PRACTICE: IMPRINTING

1. Close your eyes and start by focusing on your breath. Watch it enter and leave your body freely. Imagine breathing in pure white air and breathing out that which no longer serves you—the toxins, the past trauma, and the emotional baggage.

2. Focus on your ideal outcome. What represents that for you? Is it a place, a moment in time, a feeling, or an accomplishment? Paint the picture of what you want vividly in your mind. Be specific—focus on any goals or objects you are trying to manifest. Details matter—try not to miss anything critical. The Universe can be very exact, so take the time to add the accents and the additional strokes to your picture.

3. Imagine the feelings and the thoughts you would have if your goals were achieved. Feel those feelings now. Think those thoughts. Allow yourself both to soak up and to observe this beautiful energy. As an observer, you get to see this beautiful future of yours from any vantage point you desire. Choose to see it from an architect's standpoint—the mathematician who plans and creates everything in existence. Ask yourself: if this future were a string of symbols and numbers, what would it be?

4. Now let go of logic and allow yourself to receive this frequency. Notice as your picture-perfect future transforms into a sequence of symbols and numbers. You may be able to see them, feel them, or just know that this perspective is available to you. You may be able to see this sequence written in the sky in golden letters or floating in the air all around you. For each of you, this experience and the frequency will be very unique—just let it unfold.

5. Now let's imprint these codes into your light body. Imprinting is a process of energy transfer that transforms and shapes who you are. The most seamless and

instant imprinting happens when you are a baby. This is a very natural way of learning about the Universe. And it brings forth a particular future.

6. Imagine yourself as a baby. Perhaps you are just a few days old. Try to look at yourself—that baby—from an onlooker's perspective. Imagine that you are watching yourself sleep quietly in your cradle without a worry in the world. As a baby, you are incredibly receptive. There is a small area at the top of your head—your receiving center. Through this center, you absorb the information about this world—everything you need to know. But you can also absorb light codes and frequencies just as easily. Imagine that the codes that we have just generated—the codes of your desired outcome—are being uploaded into this baby's brain, your brain. Allow this process to flow naturally; don't force it, and do not worry—it works 100 percent of the time.

7. Watch as the golden codes are taking hold in your body—they become a part of your energetic DNA structure, transforming you from within. These codes are altering your original vibrations; they are now an integral part of you, as integral as can be. You can also solidify this process with a declaration: " I allow the numeric and symbolic code of my ideal future to become imprinted within my physical and light bodies. I allow these codes to call forth that ideal future and assist me with manifestation. For the greater good. So mote it be."

8. When you feel that the codes have been uploaded, seal the spot at the crown of the baby's head, allowing it to get some rest and properly integrate what has been received. Remember that time doesn't exist, so by uploading something into the "past," you are, in essence, changing your future. Everything is happening in the present moment.

9. When the imprinting is complete, thank the energies working with you today for their assistance.

PRACTICE: IMPRINTING—UPKEEP

The codes of your ideal future are now a part of your energetic DNA structure. Now your default path is toward the future you have just programmed into your system. However, activating these codes and keeping them fresh is an important process. To refresh the codes, use the following practice.

1. Get into a meditative state and imagine your energy body. If you wish to see the light codes already imprinted in you, they will be revealed as the tattoos of light coursing through and penetrating your body. Imagine these codes glow with the most beautiful, glimmering golden light.
2. Now imagine a source of energy over your head—a huge orb of Galactic, golden creative light. This is a deep well of energy that is always available to you.
3. Picture as the golden rays that emanate from the orb are nurturing and fortifying the light codes imprinted in your body.
4. Watch as these codes become brighter, more potent, and more pronounced.
5. Allow the orb to feed your codes of light and activate them fully.
6. Once you feel like the codes are sufficiently charged, thank the orb for its assistance. Know that the energy of the codes is now renewed and enhanced.

Trust that your ideal future is already unfolding in front of your eyes.

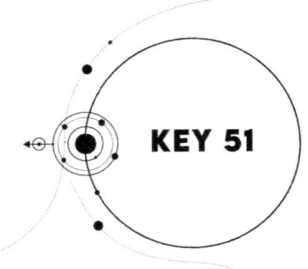

KEY 51

THE EARTH STAR CHAKRA

Planet Earth is incredibly fertile—just look at all the abundance surrounding you. The abundance of nature is a living testament to the creative powers of our rare planet. Terra, Gaia, Pachamama—the many faces of Earth and the many keys to her motherly power—have been birthing life for millions of years. There is more where that came from. Gaia's intention is to keep creating with the greater good in mind; it is Gaia's deepest desire to ensure the happiness of all of the creatures it gave birth to. This includes you. From day one, you have had access to the deep well of energy that is Gaia. But having something and knowing how to wield it is not the same.

Every mother is connected to her child through the umbilical cord—a one-way street that sends all of the abundance and resources of the mother organism to feed and nurture her child. There is a point that connects you to the energy of Gaia as your planetary Mother—and it is called the Earth Star chakra. This energy center serves as your entryway into the creative powers of our planet, and it is readily available to assist you in building the life you want. The Earth Star chakra is your anchor point—it connects you to everything else on this planet. Located a few inches below your feet, the Earth Star chakra governs your path: it helps you stay rooted in your mission and achieve things with much intention and momentum. It is a great remover of obstacles. Imagine that the power of every creature on this planet was at your disposal. Imagine having an invisible army of helpers available to you any time you call for assistance. Imagine being connected to the crystal web of everything else that Gaia has ever created, and being a part of it. Imagine that your planetary Mother is assisting you without reservations and without asking for anything in return. For all of this is true.

The Earth Star chakra is called *Vasundhara* in Sanskrit, which translates to "Daughter of the Earth"—and it is a commitment of your planetary Mother to stand and fight by your side, no matter what. You don't need to do anything to deserve this connection or the nurturing and abundance that it brings. It is readily available to you as a Child of Terra. Our ancestors were deeply connected to the wealth and abundance that activating this center provides, but like many ancient wisdoms, this one has been well forgotten. First it became the stuff of legends, then myths, and finally, it was reduced to the realm of the well-forgotten (and occult) knowledge only available to the select few. The time has come to claim that connection back—for the good of all.

Dubbed the super root chakra, the Earth Star is your ticket to the ancient codes of creation. When our planet was forming, major galactic codes of the Milky Way were uploaded to the planet's core, which granted Gaia entry into the realm of perfect creation. Perfect creation is defined as an unlimited capacity to birth life, where the more you create, the larger your ability to create becomes. This is the wheel of creation at its finest—an unstoppable force once given to Gaia as a tool to master, and now a tool that belongs to Gaia due to her service to the Universe.

The Earth Star chakra is activated in only ten percent of humans—and mostly subconsciously. Today I invite you to activate this unique energy so you can claim more of your power back. By activating your Earth Star chakra, you will unlock the deepest connection you could have with Gaia herself and all of her creation—you will become one with this well of power, and you will start feeling more at home here than you ever have. You will also unlock true serenity for yourself—the deeper knowing that you are worthy and meant to have everything you could possibly wish for. By reclaiming your connection with the Earth Star chakra, you become a master manifestor.

PRACTICE: ACTIVATING YOUR EARTH STAR CONNECTION AND UPLOADING THE CODES OF CREATION

For this exercise, it is best to be in nature and with your feet bare.

1. Focus on your breathing and close your eyes. Place your feet on the ground. Feel how this simple act alone connects you with the energies of our planet—notice how the energy from the core of the Earth enters through the soles of your feet and empowers, steadies, and heals your body.
2. With your eyes closed, picture a pulsating, black, opalescent sphere a few inches below your feet. The sphere is black at face value, but as you look deeper into it, it starts glowing with a beautiful magenta light. Know that this center is connected to the heart of Earth—at all times, it is receiving information on how you feel and sending that straight to Gaia herself. This is your connective point—your communication center between you and your planetary Mother.

3. The sphere is your Earth Star chakra. It is pulsating with a myriad of energies—it might be inanimate, but it is very much alive.
4. Imagine stretching out your arms and placing them on the surface of this beautiful, pulsating sphere. As if by magic, the sphere's energies start entering your body—first through your palms and then through every pore, every opening. Notice how the soles of your feet are starting to accept this energy. Feel this powerful force filling you up from within and aligning you to everything and everyone on this beautiful planet.
5. Know that your Earth Star chakra contains the codes to the abundance of the Universe—the abundance that is immediately available to you if you so desire. If you are ready to accept the codes, simply say, "I accept the wealth and abundance codes from Gaia with much faith and much gratitude."
6. Now notice how a stream of magenta energy is starting to enter the soles of your feet and travel to your crown. As the codes of abundance enter your body, imagine that they are being distributed to different organs and tissues—they know exactly where to go, and they settle in comfortably, as if they have always been there. Allow this process to run its course. When you are ready to come out of the meditation, thank Gaia for her assistance today and always.

The codes may take a few days to be fully uploaded and integrated. Don't worry—this is completely normal, and you might not even feel it, as most of the work happens in the background. Remember to get enough sleep and drink plenty of water. Don't worry if you experience slight discomfort in your body—it is temporary. It can manifest as a slight tingling or a headache. Make sure to spend a lot of time in nature as you continue integrating these energies.

PART II

YOUR BELIEF SYSTEM AS A KEY TO MANIFESTATION

In this next section, we'll be working with your belief system and anything that might be preventing you from experiencing your full abundance all day, every day. When you were born, you inherited a whole slew of beliefs around money, abundance, work, and happiness. Given the state of the planet today, I am willing to bet that at least some of those beliefs don't serve you. I will teach you how to find your limiting beliefs and, most importantly, how to transform them into a narrative that is positive, automatic, and prolific in its power. We will be rebuilding your mental network into something that works for you, not against you.

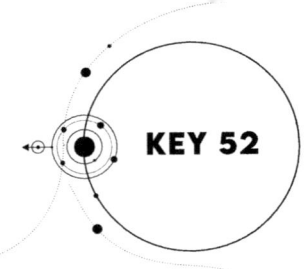

KEY 52

THE PRINCIPLE OF FULLNESS

> *"For everyone who has will be given more, and he will have an abundance. But the one who does not have, even what he has will be taken away from him."*
>
> —Matthew 25:29

One of the greater magnetic principles of the Universe is the Principle of Fullness. It tells us that as time goes by, things that are already full will become fuller. Empty things will become emptier. As unfair as it may sound, this is one of the most fundamental principles of creation, and it is meant to teach us the lesson of true abundance—abundance starts from within.

This kind of abundance begins at the cellular level and expands into every structure of your being, including the matrix within your personal Universe. It permeates everything you create. And it originates with a simple belief that you hold. A belief that is 100 percent correlated with the quality of your life—your most raw, unedited core belief about the world around you.

What is your core belief about the world? Do you fundamentally believe this world is abundant? Full of all the good things? Always evolving and becoming better? Is your world generous? Or is it challenging, competitive, unfair, and depleted? Is your world dangerous? Is your world unstable? Is it full of pain, loss, and struggle?

Whatever your core belief, the water in your cells holds this belief and reflects it back to you. The reflection you get is in the people you meet, your circumstances, and the outcomes you create. Do you love your life? Unless your answer is an undeniable and resounding "yes," you have work to do around your core belief.

For anyone whose cup is always half full (hello, optimists), the magnetic principle of attraction applies. When you believe this world is abundant, you magnetize things to you. You are open to receiving, so more things can and will come your way. In the spiritual community, this is called "being in the flow"—a phenomenon characterized by great things coming your way effortlessly and seamlessly.

On the other hand, when your glass is half empty, you inadvertently repel all the good things. On an energetic level, you look like a person with pockets full of holes, where even the things you have can slowly slip away like grains of sand through your fingers. Lack creates more lack. Loss creates more loss. That's why the poor will always get poorer. And no amount of charity contributions, raising the minimum wage, and other attempts at equalizing the system will ever change this principle. Life is not fair, but it does operate according to a specific set of rules. And just like with the law of gravity, ignorance of the law excuses no one.

Whether you believe the world is full and overflowing or empty and insufficient—you are always right. As the supreme authority within your personal Universe, every belief you hold is the ultimate law and must be obeyed.

PRACTICE: OBSERVING ABUNDANCE

Nature is a perfect place to observe abundance. Take some time out of your busy day to observe nature. Think about the abundance of leaves on each tree, the multitude of clouds, and the great number of insects and birds. Nature has never been poor, and as a part of nature, you are meant to live in abundance—an abundance of your own making. Make it a practice to notice the fullness of the world. Each day list three to five things that prove that abundance is everywhere—the sand particles on the beach, the waves in the sea, or the drops of the rain that fall on your windshield. There is so much abundance in the world; it has been surrounding you since the day you were born, and you've probably been taking it for granted. Be grateful for the abundance around you and know that it exists to nurture and fill you up. Scarcity is an illusion, a myth that you choose to believe. A myth that is not true and never has been. This world is fullness, this world is love, and this world is everything you ever wanted it to be—and so much more.

PRACTICE: ASSESSING YOUR FULLNESS FACTOR

Let's assess your fullness factor and your core belief about abundance.

Close your eyes and imagine a transparent tube in front of your eyes. Notice that the tube is filled with beautiful golden liquid—your personal abundance stream. How full is your tube? In your mind's eye, you should be able to see it down to a percentage level.

- If your tube is less than 60 percent full, you have a lot of work to do.
- If your tube is more than 90 percent full, congratulations: you are in the top 2 percent of humanity as it relates to abundance.

Either way, for anyone below 100 percent, there is room for improvement. One of the better ways to change this core belief is to rewrite it by adopting a new mantra. Below is an example of what a healthy core belief could be, but feel free to edit it to fit your needs better.

Mantra: "The Universe is always flowing in my favor. I trust my world completely, and my world trusts me. Every day my life is becoming more and more abundant. There is no limit to my abundance."

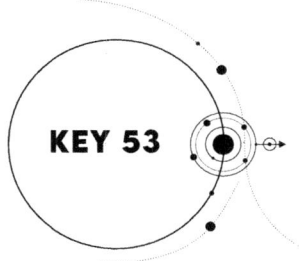

KEY 53

THE ANATOMY OF THOUGHT

The matrix is the backbone of our Universe. It is a structure that consists of numerous pathways and the energy flowing through them. One of the defining attributes of the matrix is movement. Without movement, our Universe would quickly collapse onto itself. Therefore movement is growth, and growth is evolution—the final end that justifies the interim means.

A thought is an energy form of this time-space reality. Think of the matrix as a bowl of soup containing thoughts of every caliber—the darkest to the most blissful. Thoughts belong to the matrix in every way that counts—every major thought-form was originally created at the same time as the rest of the matrix. Thoughts are energetic filler material for the matrix and a precursor to all future movement. Thoughts as elemental energy forms co-create reality. They exist to ensure there is always movement—the show, after all, must go on. Thoughts exist in the matrix, separate from people who might engage with them. They existed here before souls started incarnating and will exist long after. From this standpoint, thoughts are completely separate and independent energetic entities.

Here is the paradox: we tend to think of thoughts as inherently ours—"my thoughts," "I am thinking," etc.—and perceive them as being internal and belonging to us, like a reflection of our unique perspective. This perception couldn't be farther from the truth. Every thought you could be experiencing as a human was once designed and perfected by the same consciousness that created the matrix—the Great System Architect. Thoughts exist in clusters that range from positive to neutral to negative. For instance, jealousy and betrayal belong to the same cluster.

Chances are, you are very familiar with the Law of Attraction (see also Key 50, page 229). The Law of Attraction is pure physics. If you think thoughts of death, death will show up in your life, because the energy prefers to live in clusters. Every energy and thought frequency wants to be in its maximized state. "When it rains, it pours" is merely an example of an extreme clustering of negative circumstances, all based on the Law of Attraction.

Given that the matrix is an incredibly fluid structure, it is easy for the energy to move around and shift with the Law of Attraction. We live according to our thought patterns—thoughts we think all the time. These internalized thoughts quite literally form our bodies and our world.

One thing to know is that a thought about reality often has absolutely nothing to do with said reality. Before your personal thought patterns are formed, a few of them are tried on for size. Meaning, based on a particular circumstance, the matrix will present you with a few random thought patterns to choose from. Humans tend to resonate with the ones that hold within them a maximum learning potential. This doesn't mean we always choose the nicest, most optimal thought patterns. Sometimes we prefer to go with a more negative pattern since it presents the biggest learning opportunity. From the perspective of higher consciousness, there is no preference for positive versus negative thought patterns—whether we learn through stones or daisies, as long as we get the lesson, it is considered for the highest good.

Just to make this clear, "your" thoughts are no more yours than the Moon is yours—thoughts are just an aspect of this time-space reality. This is generally great news—changing your thoughts, and thus your life, may be easier than you think.

PRACTICE: SPRING CLEANING YOUR MENTAL BODY

You take a shower every day to cleanse your physical body, but what about the hygiene of your thoughts? Your Mental Body—the seat of all of your mental activity—also needs to be groomed and cleaned regularly to make sure it can optimize your inner thought sanctuary. When your Mental Body is in a state of disrepair, it can only attract suboptimal thoughts. On the other hand, a clean Mental Body attracts beautiful, positive thoughts. So today, we'll work on a spring cleaning of your Mental Body.

1. Close your eyes and deepen your breathing.
2. Imagine that your body is surrounded by a sphere of steely blue color. This sphere has its own matrix—a network of vertical and horizontal lines making up its surface. Welcome to your Mental Body—the inner sanctuary of all your mental activity. If you look closer, you will notice that certain spots of your Mental Body contain black clots. Many of these clots are located at the intersections of the lines at the surface of your Mental Body. And they are

constricting the movement of energy through the lines. This is your mental trauma—your negative and limiting beliefs, all the things you "know" to be true that no longer serve you.

3. Invite the light of the golden flame to assist you in this practice. Imagine it as a stream of gilded energy that is available to you.
4. Picture this gleaming energy entering your Mental Body—all of its pathways and all of its flows. As it travels up and down the lines of the Mental Body, watch the golden energy remove all the blocks and the clots stuck there. As this happens, see the flow of energy restored in every section of your Mental Body.
5. Within the Universe, like attracts like. As the golden energy works on healing and clearing your Mental Body, it infuses the latter with its high-frequency Divine light. From this day forward, this energy will become a part of you—a part of your mental space. As such, it will work toward attracting other high-vibration, positive thoughts into your orbit and will actively repel anything detrimental to you.

Feel free to repeat this practice any time you notice that you are falling into negative thinking patterns.

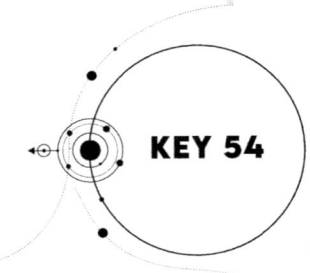

THOUGHT LOOPS

A thought loop is a persistent group of thoughts that is so integral to you that it's playing on autopilot. Your most persistent thought loops create the soundtrack of your life. Each of your persistent thoughts is accompanied by a corresponding set of emotions that further anchor your reality within a particular frequency.

A typical thought loop operates continuously, becoming stronger with each new cycle of repetition. Once fully anchored and integrated, a thought loop is hard to eradicate and could take over your life. An average thought loop cycle is a sequence of a thought followed by a feeling that, when complete, immediately triggers another thought loop. Thought loops tend to trigger other thought loops within the same cluster—these may be different thoughts, but they tend to have a similar vibration and outcome. This is a continuous process that is occasionally interrupted by some form of action—an action that is inspired by this thought/feeling pattern.

Here is an example of a thought cluster that can trigger a loop: "I'm fat … I am not skinny … I cannot stop eating … my jeans don't fit … that girl is skinny," etc. There is also a corresponding group of feelings that goes along with this thought group—feeling down, worthless, apathetic, sad, helpless, and other similar feelings. If you worry about your weight, you may produce hundreds of different thought-forms focused on your weight daily. All of them are part of the same thought cluster and would get you into a continuous loop of feeling bad about yourself without a means of escape.

Thought loops are extremely powerful. While they might be the culprit behind your feelings of inadequacy, they may also be the saving grace when you need to make meaningful shifts in your life. At their core, thought loops are a tool to be used if you want to make lasting change. The trick to making it happen is using thought loops intentionally instead of inadvertently.

Your whole life is run by just five of your most dominating thought loops. They create your reality, your body, and your relationships—literally and figuratively. Exactly what kind of thought loops you are running in the background will determine your overall levels of success and happiness. Optimistic and happy people tend to have four or five positive thought loops. In contrast, people going through depression would experience the polar opposite—four or five of their major thought loops are negative.

On your path toward the life of abundance, you may meet many adversaries, but very few are as powerful as your thought loops. Any negative thought loops you subscribe to are chipping away at your happiness and might be poisoning the positive seeds you are grooming. In our practice session today, we'll learn to diagnose your dominant thought loops and to rewrite them.

PRACTICE: REWRITING NEGATIVE THOUGHT LOOPS

There are more forms of thoughts than forms of feelings in the world. So to get to the bottom of why you have issues in your life, don't try to find the originating thought—go to the feelings first. To determine your primary thought loops, we will first examine your dominant feeling patterns.

Step 1: Diagnostic

Answer the following questions truthfully, giving five answers for each one:

△ Most of the time, I feel ...
△ Sometimes I feel ...

Your top five are your most dominant feeling patterns. Your bottom five are your shadow or secondary patterns. If you want to make meaningful changes to your life, you need to make shifts within both your dominant (primary) and secondary patterns. You also have the option of selecting a secondary pattern you like and promoting it to become one of your dominating patterns (step 3).

Step 2: Getting rid of a toxic thought loop

For each of the ten feelings above, identify thoughts that are causing them. There can be more than one, but one is always dominant. For any negative emotion, you want to work on the negative thought pattern that is causing it.

1. Take a page and divide it into two halves. On the left, write as many thoughts as you can think of that cause each negative emotion on your list. Ideally, you should have 20–30 thoughts in total.
2. On the right side of the page, write the polar opposite of each thought. Once you are done, compile all of the thoughts on the right into a two- to three-sentence positive mantra. Write the mantra down on an index card. Read it every morning and every evening for at least 30 days. The thought loop should change accordingly.

Step 3: Improving the rank of an existing positive thought loop

The easiest thing to do is to move one of your already existing thought loops up in ranking.

To do this:

1. You'll need to condense that thought loop into a one- to two-sentence positive mantra and read it daily for 30 days.
2. Then repeat the diagnostic (step 1) and watch for improvements.

Step 4: Introducing a new thought loop

Try to encapsulate your desired feeling into a thought mantra that corresponds to that feeling. New habits might take up to 60 days to establish—read the mantra twice a day to create new habitual thought patterns. Repeat the original diagnostic (step 1) after 60 days.

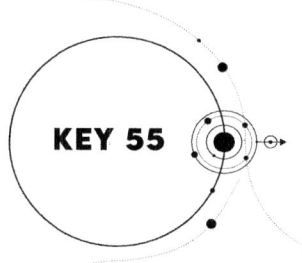

KEY 55

YOUR MENTAL AURA

An aura is an electromagnetic field surrounding every living being (yes, minerals and plants have them, too). But none are quite as diverse as human auras. After all, we are pretty complex beings. Your aura is unique to you, just like your fingerprints, and while it represents your energetic blueprint, it is far from being homogenous. Rather, your aura is like a layered cake where the layers are intertwined and mingle together to create a uniform whole. An aura is a very complex structure and is divided into an endless number of layers, but for simplicity's sake, let us say that it consists of five major ones:

- **Physical Body Vibration** (healthy vs. sick)
- **Energy Body Vibration** (the sum total of your chakras + other energy vessels and pathways)
- **Emotional Body Vibration** (the sum total of your feelings)
- **Mental Body Vibration** (the sum total of your thoughts/beliefs)
- **Spiritual Body Vibration** (your soul gifts and challenges).

Having an overall healthy aura is helpful with manifestation, but the vibrations of your energy body and your Mental Body are especially critical. The first part of this book aims to balance your Energy Body, so in this chapter, we'll address your Mental Aura.

Your Mental Aura consists of two types of constructs—thoughts clusters and belief systems. Your Mental Body is the Universe in and of itself. You can best imagine it as a sphere of light with layers of its own. The innermost layer of your Mental Body is your belief system—it is like the roots of your mental tree. Nothing can grow on the tree unless it resonates with the vibrations of your belief system. It simply cannot stick.

The second layer is your native thought clusters. Thoughts never exist alone—they are always part of a particular vibrational cluster. You can think of them as a herd species. What makes some thoughts "native" to you is the frequency with which you think these thoughts. You will always have at least ten native clusters. These thoughts, while not always positive, are very natural to you. Thinking them feels very "you."

The upper layer of your Mental Body belongs to the fleeting thoughts. This layer is the most dynamic—it is impacted by other people and circumstances but doesn't make up your native cluster. These thoughts are more in the moment and reactionary. You don't tend to internalize them much or judge who you are as a person based on them. This isn't true of your native thoughts—they represent your opinion about yourself, others, and the world at large. Your emotions are always a byproduct of your thoughts, not the other way around. This is a one-way street. You can't alter your feelings unless you alter your thoughts. If the aura is an electromagnetic field, your Mental Body creates electricity, while your Emotional Body creates magnetism. Collectively, they form your reality. But working with your Mental Body is, for all intents and purposes, working with the root cause of your current state.

Your Mental Aura is the sum total of all of your beliefs, native and situational thoughts. Together, they form an emanation that not only represents who you are on the mental plane, but also directly impacts your future.

We have a limited capacity for evaluating our thought patterns and the overall health of our Mental Body. In fact, very few people pay attention to their daily thought patterns.

PRACTICE: ASSESSING YOUR MENTAL AURA

The first step to controlling your thoughts is understanding where you stand. Determine the health of your Mental Aura using the following practice.

Pick a day in your life and take an "inventory" of your thoughts as closely as possible. This is tedious work and requires a lot of effort, but it will be worth your while.

- △ Write down your main thoughts throughout the day. You should have a list of at least 100 by the end of the day. Please don't force yourself to think positively when you do this exercise—you would only be fooling yourself.
- △ At the end of the day, assign a score to each thought—positive, negative, or neutral. The best way to know where each thought belongs is to watch the emotion it creates in your body—positive, negative, or neutral. Be honest with yourself. For example, a thought such as "The Sun is really bright today" could be positive, negative, or neutral depending on the circumstances and your relationship to the Sun. Is the Sun shining too brightly for you to drive your

car safely? Then this is a negative thought. If you love the Sun and it brightens your day, then this thought is positive.
△ Calculate your total score in percentages.

Example of a Healthy Score: 50 percent positive / 35 percent neutral / 15 percent negative.

A well-balanced Mental Body has more than 50 percent positive thoughts and under 15 percent negative thoughts. If you over-index on the negative side, you will need to eradicate negative thought patterns (see also Key 52, page 238). If you under-index on positive thoughts, you will need to create more positive thought patterns.

PRACTICE: BEST REMEDY FOR IMPROVING YOUR MENTAL AURA

If you'd like to take action on fixing your Mental Aura, gratitude is your biggest weapon. The frequency of gratitude is exactly the same as the frequency of abundance. The energy of gratitude is the energy of receiving. Adopting gratitude is the quickest way to shift your mental vibrations.

△ Make a list of fifty things you are grateful for. When you feel down, re-read the list.
△ Create a gratitude journal for yourself and commit to writing in it every day. Every morning list three things you are grateful for today. Repeat the exercise before going to bed—list three more things that you are grateful for. Review your journal over time. Challenge yourself to find new things to be grateful for instead of repeating the same things.
△ Thinking a negative thought is like swallowing poison. And it requires an antidote. So force yourself to follow up with at least one thing you are grateful for.
△ Stick with the gratitude practice for at least a few weeks. Ideally, gratitude should become your lifestyle, not something you try on for size and then discard. The best manifestors I know are masters of the gratitude frequency.

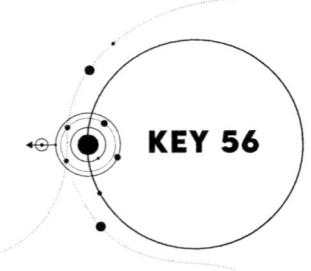

KEY 56

SOMETHING BORROWED

Energy borrowed is energy gained. Yet be careful what you borrow since that energy becomes you. Borrowed energy will work its way through your body, altering everything in its wake—whether you like it or not.

When you come into a human body, a few energies "sponsor you" into this existence. For the sake of simplicity, we can call them formative energies. Three major formative streams make up your body's composition—the stream from your Higher Self, the stream from your dad's ancestral line, and the stream from your mom's ancestral line. Those energies contribute to four of your five major bodies—physical, etheric (Energetic Body), astral (Emotional Body), and intellectual (Mental Body). Your capacity for manifestation is greatly impacted by the composition of your formative energies. One aspect that perhaps matters more than the rest is the belief system you inherit as a part of your Mental Body. As a great gift from your parents, your Mental Body inherits their belief system—the good, the bad, and everything in between.

An inherited belief system is like a coat of armor that you come into when incarnating on Earth. The idea that we are impacted by our belief system is hardly new. What's new, however, is just how little we are responsible for a large chunk of what we believe to be true.

If you could follow the various ancestral lines (family trees) closely, you would notice that they have a very consistent relationship with abundance. Some are rich, and they tend to stay so, keeping and multiplying the wealth. Others remain poor and have a hard time affording even the most basic things. This could be partially due to education and opportunity, but there is more to this picture than meets the eye.

BELIEF SYSTEMS

Everything is energy. Period. Being wealthy is a frequency, and so is being poor. The reason this frequency is inherited is that we borrow our energy from our ancestors to be able to anchor into a body. This is the great copy-paste principle—you are a sum total of the two parental energies that birthed you (plus the energy of your Higher Self, of course). Is it possible to change the energies you were born into? Absolutely. But it requires the willingness to go outside of your comfort zone. Belief systems are protective armor. They are mental constructs created to keep you safe and keep you alive, at least within the status quo and from the perspective of your ancestors. That is why changing your belief system might feel like diving off a cliff headfirst—a leap into unchartered territory. So how do you go about altering your belief system?

Step 1: Realize Your Beliefs Don't Belong to You

Realize that your beliefs around abundance and money don't belong to you. They don't represent some sort of ultimate truth and they are not a predicament. They are merely a mental construct of shortcuts to help simplify and better your life. Beliefs that don't work should be changed, so as to not be passed on to your children. Times change—what worked for your ancestors and kept them safe might be the exact thing that tampers with your personal growth. Belief constructs are meant to be altered to keep up with the times.

Step 2: Figure Our Your Beliefs

Determine exactly what your own set of beliefs is as it relates to abundance. To do that, make two lists—your mom's beliefs about money/wealth and your dad's beliefs about money/wealth. Naturally, if your parents are a vibrational match to one another, their set of beliefs might be quite similar. However, to do this exercise properly, we have to be thorough. Once you are done, circle the beliefs of your parents that you also subscribe to. If you have developed beliefs over the years that your parents don't have, add them to the bottom of the list.

Step 3: Locating Your Core Belief

Belief systems are incredibly interconnected. They are integrated systems where subordinate elements are built around the core belief. When the core belief is changed, the system collapses on itself according to the law of a domino effect. When the old system collapses, the new one is gradually built up in its stead. When trying to locate your core belief, the first thing you need to diagnose is its overall energy. Basically, your whole belief system around abundance would collapse into one of the two general themes: "This is a world of abundance. I can have anything I want." Or: "This is a world of lack. Getting what I want is a struggle." In other words, your core belief about wealth is either positive (has a plus sign) or negative (has a minus sign). If your core belief has a plus sign, congratulations. Your next step would be to keep strengthening it. If your core belief has a minus sign, you will need to flip it and rewrite it.

Take a moment to ponder and write down your best guess at what your core belief around abundance is. Don't worry about getting it wrong – trust your gut on this. Whatever statement you come up with, as long as it is related to abundance and rings true for you, it is the one we are looking for.

Congratulations! Getting your core belief from the realm of your subconscious out in the open is a big step. Now we can work with it, whatever it may be.

PRACTICE: REWRITING YOUR NEGATIVE CORE BELIEF

To rewrite a negative core belief, we'll embark on a journey into your Mental Body.

1. Sit down or lie down comfortably and close your eyes. Focus on your breath—allow yourself to breathe in and out freely, yet deeply. With each breath, allow your body to sink deeper and deeper into relaxation.
2. Imagine standing at a crossroads. This is no ordinary crossroads—below your feet is a pathway illuminated by the most beautiful, etheric blue light. As you look around, you see that you are surrounded by a whole network of such pathways, all intricately illuminated. This place seems familiar to you—as if you have been here before. And since you most certainly have, you know your way around. It is like a distant memory that you have access to.
3. Allow yourself to start walking in a direction that feels right, the path calling to you. You are heading toward the core belief section of this strange, alluring land. Your feet know exactly where to carry you.
4. As you walk, notice that you are passing by different doors, archways, and gateways. They are all of different shapes and sizes.
5. Finally, you approach a large silver door. It is locked, but you have just the key to unlock it.
6. As the door opens, you see a large spacious room inside that is filled with the same etheric blue light. It is quite cozy, yet grand.

7. In the very center of the room, there is a geometric shape suspended in the air. This shape represents your core negative belief about abundance. What shape is it? What color is it? Notice that it is a living and breathing organism; it contracts and expands, never static, always dynamic.

8. Notice the network of pathways that borrows energy from this grand geometric shape. Realize that it is the very center of your abundance Universe. And just like the Sun, this geometric shape fuels and governs everything that is happening in your material life. Like attracts like. Your core belief is working hard at attracting more things with the same vibration into your life. It wholeheartedly believes it is serving you right now. And yet, you know otherwise: it is time for you to change the emanations of your inner abundance guardian; it is time to step on another path.

9. Focus on the very center of the geometric shape, and as you do so, invite the energy of ice to come and assist you. The energy of ice is the precursor to transformation. Imagine using the power of the ice to freeze the shape that represents your negative core belief. Stay here for a couple of moments until the shape is completely frozen.

10. You now have a chance to select a new core belief for yourself. Select whichever one speaks to you the most. Remember: there is no wrong answer here. Pick the most expansive thought you can come up with and just commit to it—here and now.

11. When you feel ready, imagine that the ice is starting to melt, and as it is melting, it turns into a stream of pure, sacred water. Water is the elemental force of change and transformation.

12. Allow the water to encircle the shape fully and then speak your new core belief into the water. Repeat it three times, and as you do so, allow the water to absorb the frequency of this new belief. Ask the water to transform the shape that it is encircling, and allow it to reshape it completely.

13. When the water is done with the work, ask it to reveal the new shape, the shape of your new core belief. Take a note of how the shape has changed—does it look and feel different? Has its color changed?

14. Welcome the changes and remember—you are the creator of this realm and hold all the power here. Now we need to activate your new belief. Reach out and touch the new shape. And on your out-breath, imagine breathing life into this structure. As you do that, watch the shape come alive. See that it is starting

to grow pathways around itself and sending its vibrations through them. This is just the beginning of the new world and the new reality for you.
15. Feel free to leave this room and go back the same way you came. It may take a few days for you to integrate the new belief fully, but the great work has begun.

Once you come back to your awake state, write down the new belief on a piece of paper and place it where you can best see it. Read it out loud for at least 28 days. And then, watch your world transform.

PRACTICE: STRENGTHENING YOUR POSITIVE CORE BELIEF

No matter how strong your positive belief is, we can always amplify it. Here is a mind map exercise to help with this.

1. Take out a piece of paper. Draw a circle in the middle. Write down your positive belief in it. Now, create twelve rays emanating from this core belief.
2. From a place of full alignment with positive outlook and having the glass half full, write down twelve new beliefs you would like to adopt around abundance. They all need to be strengthening your core belief in the center, but each should offer a new perspective or a new angle. For instance, your core belief might be, "I have full access to the abundance of the Universe—anytime, anywhere." Your supporting beliefs could be: "Universe provides for me in my time of need." Here are some more examples:

△ "I can easily make more money."
△ "The Universe is full of opportunities."
△ "There is more than enough wealth to go about."

Think of your core belief as if it were a tree trunk and the supporting beliefs—its branches. This ecosystem is stronger together.

If you would like to deepen this practice:

1. Close your eyes and imagine that you are in the field where the soil is fertile and the Sun is shining.

2. Imagine that you have seeds that are ripe for planting.
3. Drop a seed into the soil and think of one of the supporting beliefs you wrote down earlier. Think of this seed as representing that belief while the soil is your subconscious. You are the master of your garden. Only you get to decide what grows there.
4. Plant all of your new seeds (new beliefs) straight into your subconscious. Water them and watch as they grow.
5. Keep the piece of paper with these new beliefs close by—it is best to read all of them once a day for at least seven days to let them sink in deeper.

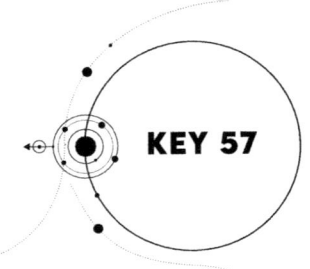

KEY 57

THE MONEY CHAPTER

It is hard to find a less understood subject than money despite its being obvious at face value. Money is a representation of human energy. Specifically, it represents how much value you are creating in the outside world. Think of money as the energy that other people share with you in exchange for your contribution to their livelihoods. It is an important distinction to anchor. Money is not simply energy, but it is the energy of gratitude that others give you in exchange for your contribution. So money is never about take—it is all about give.

Your true wealth lies in the field where the greatest number of people would be grateful to you for your contribution to their lives. Great wealth is never accumulated by faking it. Help one person, and you can have food on your table; help a dozen, and you can have a nice house to live in; help hundreds, and it starts the conversation of building true wealth. Your greatest abundance is 100 percent aligned with your greatest contribution to humanity. Let me repeat myself: money is the energy of gratitude. Period. So when chasing money, looking at the highest paying job out there is the absolutely wrong place to start.

So, where should you start?

You should start with your unique gifts—the things you were born with, like your innate strengths and talents that were obvious to everyone around you, even from early childhood. Our soul gifts have loud voices; they won't stay concealed, especially not in our childhoods before the conditioning sets in. A rare human can recognize their unique Universe-given talents, and yet they are precisely what you should explore to find your shortcut to your abundance.

A good place to start is to remember all the things you naturally enjoyed or were good at as a child. What were you specifically leaning into before the adults told you what you "should" pursue? It might be helpful to talk to your parents and other people who knew you as a child—they should be able to share insight into what you were naturally good at. This skill is exactly where you need to dig deeper. Once you hone in on what your natural talents are, the next question you should ask yourself is how you can use this talent of yours to contribute to as many people as possible.

ABUNDANCE TRAPS

There are a few traps that plenty of people fall into while seeking abundance. They don't come across as traps, which makes them ever so dangerous. Let's examine just a few of them and what happens energetically when you engage.

SAVING MONEY

Yep, this is the primary money trap. Saving money is the energy of not having enough; it is the energy of lack and despair. What this communicates to the world around you is "I worry I don't have enough," and "I worry that I will never have enough, so I need to hold on to everything I make." Money is an energy that likes to flow in and out, like the tides of the ocean. It is not the energy that thrives on being contained or restricted—and the energy of saving money is a vibration of restriction.

BORROWING MONEY

Borrowing money is not essentially bad, but it is generally accompanied by a slew of negative emotions around paying the debt back. Borrowing also comes with the pressure of paying back with interest, which generally sets you back even further. While occasional borrowing is not bad per se, habitual borrowing is a bottomless pit that forms a backward relationship with abundance.

LENDING MONEY

Again, lending money is not inherently bad. But when you don't feel like you have enough, lending money tends to come with strings attached, and those strings come in the form of fear. Fear that you won't be repaid or fear that you didn't have any business lending since you don't have enough in the first place. The only way to avoid this when lending is to let the money go freely and being okay with NOT being paid back. This creates an empty space where there would have been fear. And then, if you do end up being paid back, this is a welcome cherry on top.

TIPPING

Tipping in and of itself is actually great—it is your ability to share your gratitude with the people that serve you. There are a few traps, however. If you feel like you cannot tip enough, it is reconfirming to you and the world that you don't have enough to give freely. In countries where tipping is an integral part of the culture, this can be a daily reminder. Remember—you don't get rich first, then tip generously. You start by tipping generously, which changes your frequency and attitude around money. After all, only the person that has a lot can tip a lot. Please don't go over the top here—20 percent is plenty, no need to leave a $2,000 tip at the restaurant hoping that the Universe will pay you back. Let the act of tipping become a ritual of gratitude—a way for you to tell the Universe and the people in it how much you appreciate them.

To practice healthy money habits:

△ Be grateful every time you get paid. Recognize this as a sign this Universe is infinitely abundant.
△ Be grateful every time you pay the bill. Be grateful that you have enough money to be able to do so.
△ Every time you find a coin on the street, pick it up with a sense of gratitude—and know that this is a sign the Universe is conspiring to bring abundance to you.
△ Increase the limits of what you believe you deserve to get paid. You always deserve a raise—I am not kidding. And if you believe you deserve something, the Universe will provide.

PRACTICE: INCREASING YOUR MONEY FLOW

Did you know that you have a money channel that defines the flow of this type of energy into your life? Every channel has only so much output. Regardless of how abundant your personal money stream is, it can always increase—make no mistake. Whether you are consciously aware of it or not, you allow only a certain amount of money to come to you. It is like you have created an artificial constriction of that flow, and this constriction is defined by your core belief (see also Key 56, page 250)—you always get just as much as what you believe you deserve. By working with this core belief, you can significantly and almost instantly increase your income.

1. Close your eyes and try to quiet down your internal dialogue. Imagine a stream of abundance ("money") flowing like a waterfall and washing over your body.
2. The waterfall taps into a powerful water source but can only carry a certain amount of water ("wealth") toward you. Your stream is generally equivalent to your current income. What is your number today? Would you like to double it, triple it, or perhaps 10x it? Anything is possible as long as you allow for it to happen.
3. Imagine your desired income, whatever it is. Now ask your waterfall to expand its flow of abundance to match the frequency of this new number that you presented to it. It should feel like the waterfall's power is growing and you are now receiving more energy every second that goes by.
4. Bask in this newly found energy. It is important to sit with this new number and start integrating it. Initially, your body might feel strange about this number—as if there is something within you that is repelling it. In truth, there is.
5. Imagine the energy of this number penetrating your body, cell by cell, and filling you up with a whole new frequency. Stay here until the energy of this number becomes familiar. Trying on a new income is not dissimilar to trying on a new shirt—it can feel uncomfortable at first and might take some getting used to.
6. Now that this new number is a part of each of your cells, you will notice that your body actually quite likes it. It will stop repelling it and will start working on bringing the new number closer to you. With each drop of water on your skin, imagine that this number sinks deeper and deeper into your body and into your bones to become an integral part of you.

If you are working on manifesting a large amount of money, try repeating this exercise a few times (three or more). You will notice that with each meditation, you become more and more comfortable with the energy of this number, and eventually, you will start vibrating at the same frequency. And we always get the things that are congruent with our vibrations. This is the law.

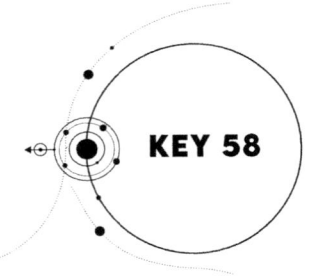

KEY 58

THE GREAT LOGOS

> *"In the beginning was the Word, and the Word was with God, and the Word was God."*
>
> —The Gospel of John 1:1

Logos is the life-giving energy of the word of God. It is the mind of the original Creator solidified in thought form—a core aspect of Divine consciousness and an indelible precursor to physicality. Logos is the part of the Source that causes things to become. Everything in existence is a byproduct of two formative energies—Chaos and Logos. Chaos is the void, and Logos is the organizing principle behind the void—that which gives structure, shape, and form to the otherwise sporadic and haphazard fabric of antimatter.

Logos is far from an ephemeral macro concept, however. Logos makes itself known through the words we speak, the thoughts we think, and the life that we reap as a result. Just like the great Creator, each and every one of us is an architect of our immediate reality. The words we speak are the building blocks of that reality. Every word is energetically charged for creation, maintenance, or destruction. What has the power of the great Logos manifested in your life? What is the sum total of your "word capital"? If you love the reality that surrounds you, you have been using the great power of Logos that is innate to you in the proper way.

You see, you have always held the keys to abundance. Since the moment you formed your first thought as a baby, you have either been building a friendly and happy reality or a life of struggle and pain.

Words are the simplest thought-forms and the only energy form that moves the needle in the mental plane of existence. All creation within the Matrix (and outside of it) starts in the mental plane. A thought-form always precedes a physical manifestation of that form.

The domain of the Great Logos is vast—it starts with thoughts (the most volatile mental form) and spans the gamut, culminating with oaths and vows that represent the densest energy forms of the mental continuum. Below is a spectrum of mental energy forms ranging from the most to the least volatile.

Thought → Spoken word (10x more powerful) → Written word (10x more powerful) → Intention (10x more powerful) → Promise (10x more powerful) → Vow (10x more powerful) → Oath (10x more powerful).

You have come across each of these energy forms more than once and perhaps not fully recognized how much weight and momentum they carry. To be a master manifestor, you have to have a healthy relationship with all aspects of Logos—from thoughts to vows. This means paying attention to your thoughts and words, but even more so, being careful with the energy of the promises you make to yourself and others. So much energy is wasted on empty promises that it could fill a trillion oceans. Oaths, for instance—the strongest form of Logos—span generations and can travel from one incarnation to the next, right alongside you. Be mindful of how you speak to yourself and others—it creates your life.

At any given time, up to 35 percent of your energy could be going toward maintaining vows, oaths, and promises you made to yourself and others in the past. Maintaining the energy of a vow is not the same as keeping a vow, however. Creating a promise comes with allocating a portion of your energy toward keeping that promise. If the promise isn't kept, that energy remains reserved and untapped, in case the giver of the promises needs it in the future to start making good on that promise. Given that we are immortal beings going through a cycle of reincarnating, over time, we accumulate a whole slew of vows and promises that we once gave. This accumulation creates pockets of energy reserved for maintaining these promises that cannot be used toward anything else. The irony is that because vows and oaths travel with you across incarnations, many of the promises you currently carry in your energetic balance don't even belong to the current version of you. They could be promises of eternal devotion to a past lover or revenge on someone who hurt you three lifetimes ago. From a higher perspective, those promises are not very useful for your current cycle of evolution, but such is the power of Logos—it is real, and it is transcendent. It is what the fabric of this Universe is made of, and it accentuates its power. Cutting the cords of old, outdated vows can help free up energy that should go into creating and solidifying new promises and vows—the ones that serve you today. In our practice session, we'll be doing just that.

PRACTICE: CUTTING THE CORDS WITH ANCIENT VOWS AND OATHS

Set aside about 20 minutes for this energy practice. It can go quite deep, so make sure you will not have to be "on" for the rest of the day. Cord-cutting can be quite draining initially before your energy fully rearranges itself. This practice is best done in the evening before going to sleep.

Naturally, not every vow is bad for us, so for any exercise of cord-cutting, you want to separate the useful things from the ones that no longer serve you. This can be accomplished through the power of intention.

1. Close your eyes and imagine your energy body. It should look like a cluster of white and gold energy. With your inner voice or aloud, ask the Universe to reveal all the energy cords of vows and past promises you currently carry.
2. Now ask the force of the Universe to narrow down the cords and only show you the ones that no longer serve you. You will start seeing cords of light emanating from your body as if they were the rays of the Sun. You may have very few or dozens—depending on how prolific of a promise maker you are.
3. You will need to cut each cord individually. The best instrument to do this is the Light Sword that belongs to Archangel Michael. You can kindly ask to borrow Michael's sword for your ceremony. Of course, if you are not into swords, you can imagine a pair of golden Divine scissors or a gilded ritual knife—they work just as well.
4. Focus on one cord at a time and cut it. Then watch the part of the cord that is still connected to your energy body withdraw into it—as if the loose end is being picked up by the greater whole. This loose end is a part of your energy integrating back into your body.
5. Be patient with yourself—this is a form of energetic surgery. You want to spend a few moments healing the spot where the cord got absorbed into your body—this is a temporary energetic scar that requires tending to. To do that, use a sphere of white or purple light and place it over the spot that needs to be

healed. Keep the sphere intact until the scar disappears and its location becomes wholesome, perfect, and pristine—just like the rest of your energy body.

6. Keep going in the same fashion until all of the cords have been cut.

Wait at least a week to let your energy fully rearrange itself before making new promises. From now on, know that your words matter and your vows matter. Treat them as Divine entities that need to be taken seriously. Your promises are your doorway into Logos' consciousness and thus the magic of the power of life creation. Use them wisely.

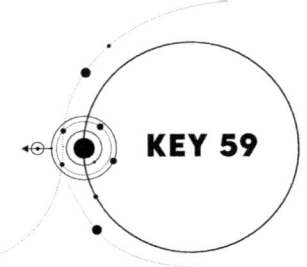

KEY 59

THE PRINCIPLE OF ALLOWING

A great ancient power is unlocked through the simple act of allowing. The energy of allowing is the master key—it fits any keyhole and any lock, and it does so instantly without any effort.

You are a sovereign ruler of your world and your personal layer of the matrix. And while some collective rules are impossible to transcend from within the human form, most of your limitations, as well as your blessings, are of your own making.

Manifestation is a road, and it starts with allowing. Allowing yourself to have exactly what you want. Sounds simple, and yet, for many, this allowance is a chasm they will never be able to cross. From our childhood, we have been conditioned to believe this world is split into two parts—the things we CAN have and the things we CAN'T, the latter of which somehow seems to be a bigger chunk. "NO CAN DO" is a spell that we have often heard in the external world that we internalized. And we became believers in our own limitations.

Your limiting beliefs are a self-induced structure made of walls, dead-ends, and ceilings that prevent you from seeing and benefiting from the innate fullness of this world. The Universe is limitless. Creating boundaries and limits is a very human pastime. And the only way we evolve both individually and as a species is through expanding our limits, tearing down the walls and ceilings that have been holding us back, and realizing that the dead ends are not so dead after all. The main reason you still don't have the things you want is that you haven't allowed yourself to have them. Your resistance to allowing things to happen for you is the main obstacle on your path to a better life. Manifestation is unlocked in four simple steps:

1. **Allow yourself to have what you want:** Create space so it can come into your life. Prepare your own receptacle.
2. **Intend to have it:** Avoid worrying and doubting. Cultivate confidence that you deserve what you want and it is already on its way to you. Because you said so. Also, trust that the Universe is always flowing and conspiring in your favor. For it always does.

3. **Claim your territory:** Use the heavy guns of your masculinity, which boils down to action in the physical (see also Key 34, page 156.)
4. **Await the results:** Watch what you want manifested in the physical.

The energy of allowing also happens to be the energy of the flow. Being "in flow" is synonymous with getting out of your own way and surrendering to the ebbs and the flows of life—the process of giving and receiving. The Principle of Allowing is the Great Female Principle. It is the absence of action and the presence of faith. The Principle of Allowing is all about expansion. At any point in time, there is only so much "free space" within you that could enable receiving. The receiving is only as great as the receptacle. Have you ever stopped to ask yourself if your receptacle in its current state is big enough to be able to hold all that you want? Boundaries that we have built for ourselves are tricky because not only are they invisible, but they are mostly subconscious—they reside in the shadow realm. And yet that is exactly what our light is for—to illuminate our limitations and build for ourselves a bigger receptacle that can hold the extent of our newly found fullness.

Allowing is a great exhale, and it brings with it immense relief. Making ourselves small is a full-time job, and it creates plenty of tension in both our physical and our light bodies. The act of allowing removes pockets of tension; that is why it feels so good. It brings true relief. You can never desire impossible things; desire doesn't work that way. If you desire something, it is within the realm of possibility for you. You are beyond capable, and your only limiting factor is the size of your receptacle. So starting today, give yourself permission simply to allow things to happen. It will be worth it.

PRACTICE: ALLOWING THROUGH EXHALATION

Today you'll practice allowing. And you should be glad, because this is a very pleasurable practice. This is one of those practices you can do with your eyes open if you'd like, but closed eyes work just as well.

1. Focus on your breath. Inhale deeply, hold your breath for a couple of seconds, and then exhale. Repeat a few times to quiet your internal dialogue. But also, don't worry about it—this practice will work regardless.

2. Imagine golden armor all around you—you are a bit of a gilded knight clad in it. The armor represents your current state of allowing—all things that belong to you and all the things you allow yourself to have. Where you are going is a place much different, and it would require a different set of armor—a much larger one.
3. Think of the one audacious goal or dream of yours that feels ENTIRELY too big. The one that you thought you would get to thinking about one day, but not now, because it was so big. And as you focus on this dream, know that the only thing separating you from having it is the simple act of allowing it. You need to allow yourself to have it—and you need a new set of armor that is a vibrational match to this new dream of yours.
4. As you hold this dream at the front of your mind, take a deep breath, and as you exhale, exhale into your armor, slowly expanding it in the process. Your armor is moldable and dynamic. The energy of your breath is a perfect instrument to enable its expansion.
5. Keep breathing in and out. And keep using your exhale to expand your armor and broaden your limitations. Keep going until your armor feels big enough to house even the most audacious dream of yours. But make sure to do at least a set of twelve deep, slow breaths. The number twelve is complete in itself; it represents a full cycle of creation. If you completed the twelve breaths, but you still don't feel sufficiently expanded, proceed with another set of twelve breaths.
6. Repeat this practice until you feel a sense of relief take over your body. It should feel like a load was taken off your shoulders—the weight of your self-induced limitations. Remember just how hard it is for your body to carry this weight. You are a limitless being, and you are always meant to be expanding. Here is to a new chapter of your personal growth!

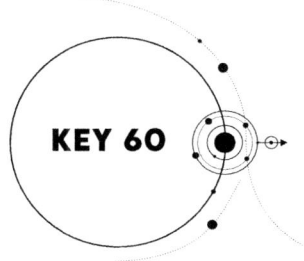

KEY 60

EXPANDING YOUR COMFORT LEVEL

What you have in life is directly correlated to your comfort levels. This sounds obvious, and yet, it is anything but once you dig deeper.

Every moment of every day, your body is emitting signals to the outside world. Those signals are numerous and include information about your emotional state, your mental state, and your energy state. But above all else, your body constantly communicates your comfort levels about all aspects of your life. The Universe is constantly receiving signals about things like the kind of relationship you are comfortable having, the amount of savings in your bank account you have allowed yourself, and how large of a paycheck you are comfortable with. And the Universe will always match you one-to-one as far as your comfort levels are concerned.

You see, the Universe doesn't waste energy—and having things requires energy. Your comfort levels establish the amount of "free space" within your auric field that is allotted to the different aspects of your life. The Universe will take great care to fill up all the allotted free space and provide you with exactly the life you are comfortable with. It is not likely to give you less, but it will also not give you one iota more.

Energetically speaking, there are aspects of reality that are a part of your inner "allowed" circle and aspects outside your circle. While manifestation within the immediate surroundings of your "allowed" circle is easy, manifesting something far outside of your comfort zone would be close to impossible. For instance, let's say making $20/hour is your current reality. You can probably manifest a salary of $40/hour with some of the exercises from this book, but if your goal is to manifest the salary of $1000/hour, you have to start with upgrading your comfort level first. Making massive changes in your life requires an expansion of your comfort zone.

KNOWING YOUR COMFORT LEVEL

Listen to your body—it is a dead giveaway for all the things that are outside of your comfort zone. Let's do a quick test. Think of the amount of money that represents your annual income. Focus on how that amount of money feels inside of your body. Chances are, it doesn't feel like anything all that special; it would just feel like an integral part of you. Now imagine setting a goal for yourself of increasing your salary by 100 times within twelve months. Focus on that amount of money. How does your body respond?

Chances are, at least one part of your body is now experiencing discomfort—it may have become tense, tight, or stressed. You are very likely to feel this in your stomach area—which is where your relationship to money tends to manifest itself. Make a note of exactly how your body feels when you are imposing things on it that are outside of its comfort level. As you start expanding your comfort zone, you will notice how your body is starting to react differently to the amounts of money that used to cause you discomfort. This works for other things you are trying to manifest outside of money, but it is easiest to notice using money as an example.

Use the following steps to start expanding your comfort level.

START WITH A DIAGNOSTIC

Chances are your comfort levels dwell in the depths of your subconscious, like a tuning fork aligning your reality to your vibration. This phenomenon is physics, not magic. Your comfort level is one of the main variables defining your life. As long as your limitations remain subconscious, they will run your life. Shedding light on them and bringing them into your consciousness is the first step toward expanding your comfort zone.

List all of the things you want on a piece of paper. Close your eyes and focus on each of these wishes. Notice any discomfort in your body as you feel each of these things, one after another. For any object that causes you discomfort make a special note—you will need to bring it inside your inner circle (see today's practice).

REPETITION HELPS

When expanding your comfort level, persistence beats resistance. It is similar to getting into a cool ocean— at first, you dip a toe, and the water feels cold, but as you step deeper into the water, the feeling changes, and you can fully submerge without much discomfort.

SMALLER STEPS HELP

You will notice that it is easier to expand gradually instead of in one fell swoop. If you have a hard time getting your body to feel comfortable around an audacious goal right away, start with a smaller goal. Get comfortable with that goal first, and then move on to bigger things.

PRACTICE: EXPANDING YOUR COMFORT LEVEL

In addition to the above guidance, this practice used regularly can help to expand your comfort zone and create more abundance in your life.

1. Close your eyes and start breathing deeper.
2. In your mind's eye, focus on your body. Examine the auric field that surrounds your body—you should be able to see it as a sphere of light encapsulating you. Notice that beyond your auric field, there is a fence that marks your territory. Your fence will be unique to you—it may be low or high, made of wood or iron, or even made of light. Whatever fence you see, it is just perfect.
3. Focus on one object of your desire. It will show up as a pillar of light a few feet tall. Where is this pillar located? Is it located inside of your immediate area that is marked with the fence, or beyond it? Chances are, if your desire is large enough, the pillar will be located outside of your inner zone, sometimes quite a distance away.
4. Start breathing even more deeply. With each exhale, imagine your fence is expanding in the direction of the pillar of your desire. With every breath you take, the fence starts taking up more and more space. Keep expanding and

breathing, breathing and expanding. Continue this practice until your fence expands enough to be able to encapsulate the pillar of your desire inside of your territory. This is another way of claiming what's yours from the Universe.
5. Notice how your body feels now that you can finally have what you want. Is there any discomfort left in your body? If so, send white light toward that part of your body to remove it and wash away any tension.
6. Feel free to repeat this practice for other items on your wish list.

Remember, this is an ever-expanding Universe; it is only fitting that you are expanding your immediate field of influence and abundance to enable you to be on the same energetic page with the greater Universe.

Happy manifesting!

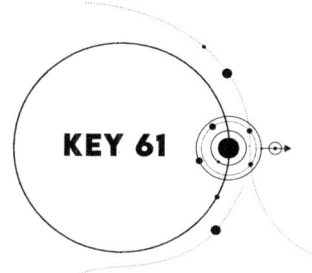

KEY 61

MASTERING FAITH

> *"Because you have so little faith,"* He answered. *"For truly I tell you, if you have faith the size of a mustard seed, you can say to this mountain, 'Move from here to there,' and it will move. Nothing will be impossible for you."*
>
> —Matthew 17:20

As I shared in the previous chapters, the strength of your belief in yourself is directly correlated with how quickly you can manifest things. On the contrary, if your manifestation is rooted in doubt and worry, you are inadvertently chipping away at your desired future and delaying manifestation. If your doubt becomes strong enough, it may even derail you completely. Lack of faith is the most common dream killer and one of the main reasons most people cannot manifest lasting, meaningful change.

DEVELOPING FAITH

Below are just a few ways you could curb your natural inclination for doubt and pave a path to a life where you can finally have what you want.

GRATITUDE

I shared the importance of gratitude practices in Key 55 (see page 247). So while being grateful for what you already have may sound almost too simple, the energy of gratitude goes hand in hand with the energy of belief. Let's just say they exist in the same vibrational range. The energy of gratitude is fertile soil for faith to grow and become stronger. Any time you feel doubt creeping up to take over, focus on gratitude instead. List all the things you are grateful for until you feel the energies shift and doubt recedes into the background.

LOWER THE VOLUME OF YOUR DOUBT

The energy of doubt is a mental frequency—you can turn it off or lower its volume. While completely turning off a frequency is easier with practice, anyone can easily master lowering the volume. When you succumb to thoughts full of worry and doubt around your goals, imagine that you are stretching out a hand and lowering the volume of that frequency—exactly how you would lower the volume of a radio station. Your faith has a frequency also. Can you tune into it? What is it telling you? Stretch out your invisible arm and make that frequency louder. Allow it to fill your inner space. "Mark" this frequency as being desirable. Let your system know that this is your favorite radio station and that it should be played as often as possible.

ADOPT A NEW CORE BELIEF AROUND FAITH

We explored core beliefs earlier in Part II (see Key 56, page 250); they are a powerful tool worth mentioning again. Remember, a core belief is something you declare true no matter what—it has no conditions. It is true forever and always, because you said so and because you believe it to be true. The rest of your beliefs are woven around your core beliefs and form a mental network that runs your life. Adopting a core belief is a declaration—you can just declare a statement as your new core belief, and your mental network will rearrange things accordingly. Remember, your core beliefs always come true for you, so select wisely.

Examples of core beliefs that can help increase your faith are below:

- △ The Universe is flowing in my favor.
- △ The Universe is always on my side.
- △ My Universe has my back.
- △ My Universe is generous and full of everything I want.
- △ I always get what I want.

CREATE A "BOOK OF WINS"

Notice and record all your wins, big and small, ideally in a separate notebook that you can rightfully name your *Book of Wins*. No accomplishment is too big or too small. Jot down every little circumstance or streak of luck that is getting you closer to your desired outcome. When you're in doubt or just feeling down, take out your *Book of Wins* to remind yourself of how awesome you actually are. Take every entry in the *Book of Wins* as proof that you are moving in the right direction. If you weren't, you wouldn't have so many wins. You are welcome.

DEFINE THE FUTURE YOU ARE LIVING INTO

The concept of lifelines is almost mainstream. A lifeline is the most likely path your life will take based on the current moment. The lifeline you are living is determined by the vibrations you give off. To manifest a different future, you will need to leave your current lifeline and move to another lifeline that contains within itself your desired outcome. Manifestation is essentially traveling in between the various lifelines toward a lifeline that already contains what you want. Manifestation is thus not an exercise in molding your current lifeline to materialize an object of your desire—it would be quite impossible.

Since at any point in time you are moving along only one lifeline, there is a default future you are living toward. Did you ever wonder what that future holds? It may seem undefined to you. However, your current vibrations determine your future vibrations and, thus, the eventual outcome. If you want to be intentional about your future, you can program it in a way that serves you instead of living into the default version. To do that, take a piece of paper and name it "The future I'm living toward." Then take the time to write down your ideal future—be as detailed as possible. What kind of people surround you, what does your home look like, and what do you like to do on weekends? The more specific, the better. Then have the audacity, even for a few moments, to believe this ideal is your actual future. Even a "mustard seed" of a belief will start the process of transferring you to a lifeline where your ideal future is also the default future.

PRACTICE: CONNECTING TO YOUR FUTURE SELF

Now that you are living into your best future, the last step is to connect to the future version of you that already has what you want.

1. Start by closing your eyes and taking some deeper breaths.
2. Imagine that, at the end of a winding road, your desired outcome exists. Mentally transfer yourself to that point in time. There is already a version of you there—the one that has walked the walk and got the prize.
3. Connect to that future version of you. How do you look, feel, and act? Are you very different from the current version of you? What does the future you know that you don't know currently? Do you carry yourself differently in this future?
4. You can ask the future you for advice. Specifically ask what is most helpful to know to walk the path they have already walked. Ask them how to cultivate your faith better. Ask them to send you signs when you are on the right path. You should agree exactly what those signs are. Perhaps a symbol of some sort? Take notes on any insights that come through.
5. Allow yourself to merge with the future you for a few moments and perceive the world through their eyes. You can even run back and forth between the present and the future, all the while noticing the difference in perspectives in how the two feel. Nothing prevents you from feeling the way your future self does—starting today. That is exactly why you are given this reference point.

You can come back to this version of your future as often as you'd like. Over time as you nurture this connection, your ideal future will start feeling imminent—more and more "yours" for the taking. By meeting your future self, you have started changing and anchoring your vibrations in the right sector of the Universe.

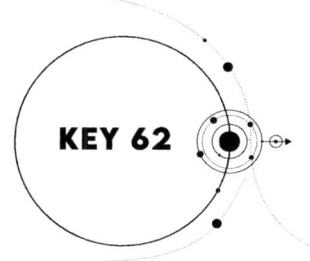

KEY 62

THE LESSON OF PRESSURE

Pressure is the primary reason you cannot maintain a state of perfect flow. Societal pressure, self-induced pressure, and past trauma pressure—it all counts. On an energetic level, pressure is condensed static energy—like a blood clot—that prevents any liquid from passing through. Pressure stops the forward-moving energy flow in its tracks and turns a stream full of life into stagnant, murky waters. There is nothing inherently wrong with static waters other than they cancel flow. More significantly, static water becomes that which it is in direct proximity to—which in case of blocked energy is MORE blocked energy.

The energy of flow manifests itself differently for the masculine and feminine energies within our bodies. For the feminine within, experiencing flow means being a super attractor. It is an act of true magnetism—what you desire manifests on your path as the Universal waters carry what you want straight into your lap.

For the masculine within, energies of manifestation are a lot more forward-moving, targeted, and intentional—similar to an electric current traveling over a great distance with agility and momentum toward the desired outcome. When our masculine aspects experience flow, we experience the absence of obstacles—achievement becomes seamless, easy, and almost effortless. Things happen quickly and with much momentum. Flow is thus a great remover of obstacles.

Pressure kills both the masculine and the feminine facets of flow; it is the common denominator that stops alignment and creates distortions in your energy field, which causes things to take forever to manifest and forces you through the blood, sweat, and tears of getting somewhere. That hardship, by the way, is an entirely optional path. Creation is not meant to come through experiencing pain. Creation is the most natural thing for an aligned human—a human in the state of flow.

RELEASING PRESSURE: ART AND SCIENCE

Let's examine all the ways you can release pressure in your life and move on to a path of fast manifestation.

THE PRESSURE OF COMPARISON

One of the more common vibrations on the planet, the energy of keeping up with the Joneses, is real. As another form of focusing outward instead of inward, comparing yourself to others is a detrimental practice for your physical and mental health that takes your personal resources away from manifesting what you want.

Manifestation is a game of focus and not just any kind—inner focus. It starts with acknowledging that you are the Universe in and of yourself and thus completely self-sufficient and self-sustaining. The manifestation game begins when you tune the rest of the world out and finally start dancing to the beat of YOUR drum. There is literally no other way. You have to get great at making the surrounding frequencies secondary to your own. Your dreams, your desires, and your intentions should become the center of your Universe. Everything else is at best secondary; at worst, it doesn't deserve your attention and should fall by the wayside. When you catch yourself comparing yourself to others, lower the volume of that frequency. It doesn't serve you—it never has. This frequency is merely a distraction to take you off your path. And above all else, you should be protective of your path—it is the exact thing that will lead you to what you want in life. The energy of comparison is like cancer within the larger body of your manifestation. You should nip it in the bud. Remind yourself that as your own central Sun, your own Moon, and your own Earth, you are in charge, and thus others are simply irrelevant—unless you choose to bring them in for the ride. You will notice that it is easy to switch your focus away from comparing and into building. So get on with it.

THE PRESSURE OF EXPECTATION

Be mindful of expectations—both your own and those of others. Expectations are a great source of unnecessary pressure and struggle. Having a high bar is healthy;

having high expectations, on the other hand, only brings frustration. Instead, approach each new day and each new accomplishment with arms wide open—with gratitude, reverence, and joy. Give the Universe a chance to surprise and delight you.

The energy of expectations comes attached to taking things for granted. And that is the opposite of gratitude. Taking things for granted robs you of not only abundance but also of well-earned joy. True freedom comes in the absence of expectations. Those are the hooks that are holding you in place and preventing you from experiencing true flow. They are also the reason the going has been so hard. Having expectations is a form of control, at least a semblance thereof. And yet you can no more control the Universe than you can control your emotions. Some things are not meant to be controlled. They are meant to be savored, enjoyed, and revered. Let go of your expectations and watch the world deliver beyond your wildest dreams.

THE PRESSURE OF TIMING

There is a whole lot of frustration in third-dimensional worlds around the timing of things. The timing seems to be eternally off, which creates another form of pressure. Time is extremely arbitrary—it even moves differently for different people. Despite time's arbitrary nature, a common form of pressure involves expecting to have things by a certain age. Nothing kills your creativity and prevents the flow of abundance from coming through quite like feeling you are late with something. There are no two paths that are exactly the same. And while collective consciousness would have us believe there is a perfect age for everything, you are extremely unique. In fact, having certain things earlier than you are meant to could be your biggest curse. Trust your timing. Trust that there is a plan and a path, and everything is happening in accordance with that. Allow the Universe the freedom to bring things to you according to its timing. Cultivate patience.

PRACTICE: CUTTING CORDS OF EXPECTATIONS

If you are ready to get rid of the weight of expectations that you have of yourself, as well as the expectations other people (parents, siblings, spouses, etc.) have of you, this is the practice for you.

1. Close your eyes and start breathing deeply and calmly.
2. Imagine that you are walking up a winding path. The Sun is in the sky, and it is a nice day, but you are carrying a heavy backpack. Not just any backpack—it has the load of all the expectations you and others have developed for you over the years.
3. You like walking, but the backpack is extremely heavy, and it is making the going hard. The time has come for you to release all those expectations and start fresh. Take the heavy backpack off. You can even open it if you want and see what's inside. What has been holding you back? What have you been expecting of yourself and failing to deliver? What have others been expecting from you?
4. From this day forward, you can choose not to carry any of those expectations around. Enough, after all, is enough. You can get rid of the backpack in one of two ways—you can burn it with all of its contents, or you can throw it into the deepest river and have it be carried away by a massive torrent. Pick whichever way feels right to you.
5. Feel free to stretch your physical body after getting rid of the backpack—you may notice a need to stretch it out. Your back may even feel different—like a weight has been lifted.
6. The last part of this practice is to see if there are any light cords of expectations still attached to your body. Ask those cords to be revealed to you if they exist. The cords will come in different colors—depending on the nature of a particular expectation. Whatever those are, feel free to cut them with a pair of massive scissors or a sword of light (the Sword of Michael). They no longer serve you, so it is time for them to go.

Make sure to do more stretching once you are done with this meditation. You may also want to do some yoga to get your energy flowing. Expect some shifts in your body in the coming days. This practice is powerful and frees up a lot of stuck energy that will be rearranging itself throughout your body, so don't be surprised if your body feels "different" for a couple of days.

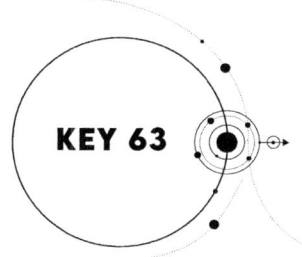

KEY 63

THE DORMANT POWER OF YOUR PERSONAL TRUTH

Self-expression is a flow. Your personal truth is a flow—a movement of energy straight from your Higher aspects into your current incarnation. This flow is representative of your unique personal sound frequency—your true soul voice. Being able to embody and express it fully is directly correlated with how well you can manifest things physically. The energy of your truth is your most potent, most productive, and most creative energy in relation to third-dimensional space. It is your resource state.

Speaking your truth is a symbolic act of firmly walking the path you are meant to walk while feeling safe to express the entirety of who you are. And yet, the vast majority of humanity live half-lives—never stepping into their full potential and not even truly knowing who they could become if they just allowed themselves to express the fullness of their energy.

When you were born, a particular allotment of energy descended into your body. Your energy arrived on planet Earth just by your deciding to incarnate here. Now, the fact that your energy was projected forth by your Higher Self to assist you in this incarnation doesn't yet mean you have full access to it by default. For most people, the energy of their personal truth is tucked away in a safe space, far from prying eyes and even from the individual itself. You can think of it as an energy pocket saved up for a rainy day. Alas, the rainy day never comes, and thus, the wheel of *samsara* (cycle of reincarnations) goes on. Unless you feel safe to be who you came here to be, this energy can't be claimed by you. It will stay sealed away for nobody to see and nobody to benefit from.

Only by expressing a healthy flow of the entirety of you can you unlock your full potential for manifesting. Anything short of that is child's play. Anything short of that doesn't do you justice. It is through liberating this trapped energy that you join the high-stakes table. When a portion of your energy is tucked away inside a pocket, it exists in its stagnant state. In the third-dimensional world, stagnant energy is a burden, not an asset. A natural state of energy is movement—only in its moving state can the energy act in accordance with its purpose.

Your self-expression can be powered by one of two sources—Earth (and the Solar System) or higher-dimensional cosmic energies. Within your body, it manifests as two energy loops—a loop through your lower chakras and a loop through your higher chakras (see Key 7, page 47). The healthiest flow of self-expression is powered by both loops simultaneously. This combined flow creates the unlimited potential for manifesting abundance in this reality. Once activated, these flows can maintain themselves and attract what you want to your path while clearing away the obstacles. Your personal truth is another face of your personal power. And it should no longer be dormant.

PRACTICE: ACTIVATE THE FLOW AND PATHWAYS OF YOUR SELF-EXPRESSION

This practice will help you activate your lower and higher loops of self-expression.

1. Center into your body and start with deep breathing. Let your chest expand fully to take in as much air as possible. Close your eyes.

   Lower loop of self-expression

2. Start by focusing on the mini-Sun within your solar plexus chakra. Imagine that a stream of beautiful, gilded light is streaming upward from your yellow center—the center of your personal power, which is nurtured by the Divine Masculine, fire energies, and the force of the Sun.
3. Allow this energy to pass through your heart center. Watch as it starts pulsating with the most beautiful emerald green, absorbing the frequencies of your compassionate heart.
4. Allow the stream to keep moving upward toward your throat chakra (blue center), removing any blockages or stuck energy that may be there. Feel free to open your mouth physically or do the same in your mind's eye—whatever feels better.

5. Imagine the combined stream of the yellow and green energies starting to flow out of your mouth, falling down like a waterfall.

Congratulations: you have just activated the first stream of self-expression. This is an exceptionally healing energy stream. Over time it will upgrade the homeostasis of your physical and energy bodies.

Higher loop of self-expression

6. Start by focusing on the energy of Source (the Universe, the Creator, God—whatever you want to call this energy). You may want to imagine it as a sphere of brilliant white light. Imagine that a stream of starlit energy flows from Source into your head and your crown chakra. Know that higher guidance, and intentions of your Higher Self are also flowing through your crown chakra. Feel this center become activated and incredibly receptive. It has been thirsty for these beautiful healing energies, and now it can finally be nurtured by them.
7. Watch the stream descend toward your third eye area and activate it. Watch as a lotus flower springs open right where your pineal gland is (third eye chakra). The stream doesn't stop there, however. It reaches your throat chakra and pours out of your throat as a stream of diamond-esque, high-vibrational energy.
8. Watch as the two streams—the ascending and the descending—join into one, like a double helix. Bask in the energies of full spectrum self-expression. Allow these energies to anchor themselves in your life and invite them to co-create with you for the rest of your life.

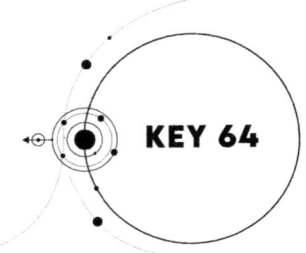

KEY 64

THE UNIVERSE STARTS WITH YOU

Before our world (read: the matrix) was created, the Great System Architect was sitting on his spacious balcony and facing a nontrivial challenge—perhaps the hardest challenge of his existence. You see, he set out to create a system of mathematical equations destined to describe a new type of reality—a virtual reality of sorts. But not just any kind of new reality—the one that would enable the fastest growth and evolution for any being that chose to play the game (read: incarnate in it). The Great Architect has created other matrices before, but this one, if he were to get it right, would be the crown jewel. The reason this new creation was more challenging than anything he faced before was the sheer range of its parameters. This was the first-ever matrix to house souls of all levels—from very young to ancient, older than time itself.

Now, those souls were all very different—they wanted and needed different things and they craved very different experiences—and yet his new creation had to cater equally well to all. The Great Architect has been rightfully called a mastermind. The smartest being in existence, they said. And yet he was clueless as to how he could possibly accomplish this challenge. He was playing with a billion configurations, a myriad of settings, but like the most frustrating of puzzles, this one didn't seem to have an answer at all.

The Great Architect was great at controlling systems—at making equations so perfect and precise, they could define and describe anything he set his mind to. But when put to the test, his newly created matrices failed to deliver the experiences he wanted—they either didn't work for the young souls by being too complex or they didn't work for the old souls by being too simplistic. A creature of control and habit, and a stickler for mathematical precision, the Great Architect was about to give up altogether when a thought hit him. "What if . . . just what if the answer to this riddle was less control, not more?" This concept was new territory—giving up control, or even better yet, sharing it with others? New, uncharted territory, which was both scary and revolutionary. The Great Architect smiled his wildest, most ecstatic smile and wrote down a single statement—the one that would break every rule in his book, the book of the Universe. The statement that would jumpstart everything about the new matrix—its cornerstone principle. The alpha and omega of his most perfect system yet. He rubbed his hands together with a sense of almost childlike anticipation and winked at himself.

On an otherwise blank piece of white parchment, right in front of the Great Architect, there was a single sentence, written in a tight, precise black script: *"The Universe starts with You."*

SOLVING THE PUZZLE

What did the Great Architect mean, and exactly how was he able to solve the puzzle? The answer is simple. He gave full control of the experience to every living being. That way, each incarnating soul would design its own experience, albeit subconsciously. This script was truly the only way to ensure a satisfying and challenging journey for all.

In coming to Earth, you have forgotten that you are fully in command. You have forgotten that you are in charge of every aspect of your life and circumstance. Chances are, you feel like a victim sometimes—as if things are being done to you, not for you. The day has come to remember the most ultimate truth about this reality: you have ALWAYS been in the driver's seat. You have always been in full control of your life. You are the master of your reality. **Your Universe starts with you.** It always has. Every change, every person you meet, and every happy or unhappy circumstance—you have put them into your path, subconsciously. From this day forward, it is time to move toward conscious creation.

You see, if you are personally creating your own slice of reality through your thoughts, feelings, and actions, it will always be a fully-customized experience. Your areas of opportunity are abundantly clear through your thinking and emotional states; your areas of opportunity are like anchors in the otherwise smooth fabric of the Universe. They create a ripple effect and bring forth circumstances so that you can deal with them and overcome them, leaving only the smooth fabric behind. This matrix is malleable—it responds to you as it was designed to do. Because only through its ability to respond to you can it create a very custom learning ground for souls new and old, souls with very little karma and plenty of karma, and souls that work on a personal level and on the collective level. The perfect system or school, meant to help you grow, is a reality where you have always been in charge.

HOW YOUR SLICE OF THE UNIVERSE IS CREATED

No two people live in the same world—your slice of the matrix is entirely, irrevocably, and undeniably your own. In fact, you are projecting it forth with your body day in and day out.

Projecting forth your personal slice of reality happens with the help of the thymus—a seemingly unimportant gland located in your upper chest area. Also called an "upper heart" in spiritual circles, the thymus is point zero—the inception point of your reality. One of the critical functions of the thymus (that you will not find in any medical texts of today) is the ability to process your emotions. The thymus is the organ most connected to your Emotional Body and thus is most in tune with how you are feeling at any point in time. The thymus is also your center of compassion and understanding, of yourself and others. It is probably one of the most underrated human organs; it almost single-handedly projects your reality forward. You see, the magnetism of your emotional state gets amplified within the thymus and fills it like a vessel. Your emotions are frequently driven by the thoughts, actions or emotions of others. Those external stimuli are what impacts your world the most. The thymus takes an amalgamation of your feelings and projects it forth, right from the center of your chest area and into the future.

Technically, the thymus reduces your feelings to a frequency and then reflects that frequency into the outside world; it is the director and the producer of the movie of your life. This process is constant and dynamic. It doesn't stop for as long as you draw breath. Imagine having a projector inside of your chest that shines a light on your path and scripts your movie as you go along. This analogy is exceptionally close to what is happening in actuality. It all begins with the thymus—your point zero, the genesis of everything true in your life.

Energetically speaking, the thymus is the steering wheel of your vehicle (your body). It has a spin and a rotation to it—it is always in movement unbeknownst to you, and its movement determines your reality. The thymus moves like a rotating spiral. Imagine that the point where the organ is located in your body is the center of that rotation. A healthy rotation of energies is represented clockwise, parallel to the floor (horizontal). An unhealthy rotation is counterclockwise. When your thymus is rotating counterclockwise, you are attracting negative circumstances into your orbit and are generally moving further away from your ideal path, not toward it. One of the easier ways to fix your outside circumstances is to flip the rotation of your thymus and make it clockwise. This rotation switch also helps unlock manifestation if you haven't made much progress despite the exercises in this book. This rotation is exactly what we'll be addressing in the practice session today.

PRACTICE: USING THE THYMUS TO TAKE CONTROL OF YOUR FUTURE

Any time you feel low, close your eyes, and focus on the area of your thymus. Focusing on your ideal outcome while rotating your thymus so it moves in a clockwise direction is a very quick and simple way to get back into alignment. We'll explore this practice in detail below.

1. Take a comfortable position and close your eyes.
2. Focus on the upper chest area of your body—right in the middle where the thymus is located. Imagine your thymus is like a mini galaxy with a dark center, and it is rotating.
3. If you are not feeling optimal today, start rotating your thymus area in a *counterclockwise* direction. The thymus also helps you control time and jump around the various lifelines and possibilities. When you rotate it counterclockwise, you can return to a particular point in the past and upgrade to a different lifeline. Keep rotating your thymus area and think back to the most recent time you felt truly happy, aligned, and on the path. Return to that day now. Allow the thymus to rotate counterclockwise until it is ready to stop. When it does, you are perfectly aligned with that happy day.
4. Now think of what you are trying to manifest. Think of the most ideal, most perfect outcome. As you do that, start rotating the thymus area in a *clockwise* direction, faster and faster. Allow the spin to take on a momentum of its own. Imagine how you are being transported to your ideal outcome—to a perfect point in the future where you already have what you want. Clockwise rotation of the thymus allows you to move forward and align your current lifeline with the one where what you want is already present.

You should be able to notice an almost instant shift in your mood and perception. Enjoy!

PART III

MANIFESTING ON A PLANETARY LEVEL

The last part of this book is devoted to the very few of you working on manifesting things on the planetary level. Star seeds, warriors of light, and everyone who feels like they came here for a bigger purpose—please stay tuned. The keys to manifestation we'll be talking about are Ph.D. level and are not for the faint of heart. Most of the concepts discussed in the following chapters are lesser known, but that doesn't make them any less effective, and perhaps it makes them more so. Here is to building a better world together.

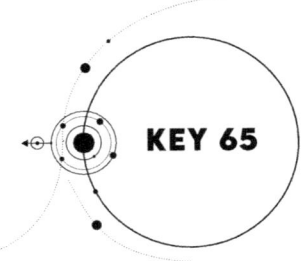

KEY 65

MANIFESTING THROUGH AN EGREGORE

An *egregore* is an energetic entity created consciously or subconsciously by a group of people whose thoughts are aligned (also see Key 28, page 52). An *egregore* is thus a collective thought-form of a group of people united by or focused on the same idea. The energetic field of planet Earth is full of *egregores* of every shape and size. From the *egregore* of an apartment building to a political party to a celebrity, collective energy forms are abundant and omnipotent. When you join an organization of any kind (like a school, gym, or medical institution), you start contributing your energy to the betterment of the *egregore* of that organization, whether you realize it or not.

Egregores are not inherently good or bad—they just are. Yes, they rely on human energy to sustain themselves, which implies that in interacting with one, we tend to lose energy. However, there tends to be some sort of payback through the virtue of this interaction—whether it's a feeling of belonging to something greater than yourself or some other tangible or intangible benefit. An *egregore*'s strength and power depends on how many people are "feeding" it with their energy, as well as how often they do so. Thus an *egregore* of a national sports team with high rankings will be much more powerful than a local school sports team. Level of fame is directly correlated to the number of thought-forms that exist in the vicinity of planet Earth around a particular individual. *Egregores* can stay strong or erode over time. Energy is a fleeting currency—it requires maintenance. That's why the *egregores* of certain movements disappear over time while others get stronger.

By definition, most *egregores* are much stronger than one human, precisely because they are powered by many. Thus, enlisting an *egregore* as your partner in manifesting something can be an incredibly lucrative endeavor.

It is important to note that *egregores* don't have consciousness outside of their collective intention—the intention of their adepts. For example, generally speaking a medical institution will stand for health while a college would stand for education and knowledge. Each *egregore* thus has a very particular vibration—it becomes an endless well of the energies it represents and stands for while being almost barren as far as all other energies are concerned. When you are manifesting something for the collective, you could leverage the energy of an *egregore* to help you achieve what you want. Through the virtue of its existence, an *egregore* accumulates energy. You could think of it as the equivalent of your savings account. That energy is saved for a rainy day—such as fighting a rival *egregore* or drawing on survival needs in case the livelihood of an *egregore* is threatened.

On top of that, an *egregore* may donate a portion of its stored energy to a cause that is aligned with its mission. For example, there is one collective *egregore* of yoga for planet Earth. So if you have a dream of building a yoga studio, you may want to request assistance from the yoga *egregore*. If your personal mission aligns with the intention of the *egregore*, you will get an incredible ally in the creation of the studio.

PRACTICE: FINDING YOUR SPONSORING EGREGORE AND ENLISTING IT IN YOUR MISSION

Below are the main steps of enlisting an *egregore* to help you achieve what you want.

Step 1: Finding the right *egregore*

This part is about finding an *egregore* whose purpose is already connected to what you want to do in the world. Chances are, there are a few that already exist.

In a meditative state, make an intention to see all the *egregores* aligned with your mission (what you are trying to create in the world). You should see them as large globes or spheres of energy. They may be plentiful or very few—the quantity doesn't really matter. Examine the globes of energy you are seeing. Is there one that catches your eye the most? Perhaps it's bigger or glows brighter than the rest? There are many options for you to choose from, but there is one *egregore* from the ones you see that has already selected you and is open to collaboration. Focus on the *egregore* that you like the most. Zoom in on it. Trust your gut feeling on this.

P.S. Sometimes, you know exactly what *egregore* you need to talk to. If you have clarity, just allow yourself to find this *egregore* in time and space. Ask the Universe to reveal this *egregore* to you so you can establish a connection with it.

Step 2: Connecting with and enlisting the *egregore* as a sponsor

Once you have zoomed in on one of the *egregores*, examine it closely, feel into its energy, and explore its surface. Is there anything unique about what you are seeing? What is its true shape? What colors does it contain within? You can ask the *egregore* for its name. Trust what comes to you in response to this question, don't doubt what comes through. Before enlisting the *egregore* in your cause, you need it to opt into helping you. This is a free will Universe, and even collective consciousness can make choices. Share what you want to create in the world with the *egregore* the way you would with a friend and ask for assistance. Then place two cups on each side of the *egregore* and denote one as meaning "yes" while the other as meaning "no." Ask the *egregore* to fill up one of the cups with its energy. If the *egregore* wants to help you, it will fill up the "yes" cup.

If this *egregore* doesn't want to help you for some reason, don't despair. Simply repeat step 1.

Step 3: Establishing a permanent donor relationship between the *egregore* and your desired outcome

Now that the *egregore* is open to assisting, let's move forward to the most critical aspect of this practice. Imagine that your desired outcome is a sphere of light—although potentially really small at this point. See how this sphere appears right next to your sponsoring *egregore*, which is a much larger energy structure. See how a bridge of light is formed between the two structures, and through this bridge, energy is starting to flow—from the sponsoring *egregore* into your smaller sphere. Let the smaller sphere become saturated with the energy of its bigger kin. Watch as the smaller sphere is slowly starting to expand, powered by this newly found energy stream.

Step 4: Creating an anchor to increase the flow of energy

Now that the flow of energy has been established, your most important next step is to ensure it continues to flow. Create an anchor for yourself—something in the physical world, like an object or a symbol that you encounter reasonably often—as a reminder that the energy flow needs to be restarted again. An example of a symbol could be 11:11, a white rose, a black cat, or anything else that resonates with you. Create an intention for yourself that every time you encounter this object or symbol in your daily life, for a quick second you will get back to this meditation and restart the flow of energy through this bridge of light. Just like a newborn, your desired outcome is still in its baby form and requires intentional and frequent nurturing. So make sure you feed it often by remembering to connect it to the energy it so desires.

Happy Manifesting!

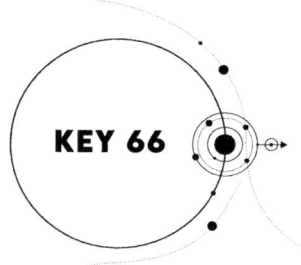

KEY 66

ACTIVATING YOUR MERKABA

The *Merkaba* is one of the aspects of your light body—an extension of your auric field and a significantly underleveraged part of your being. It is an integral aspect of your sacred geometry arsenal. Understanding how to work with it can enable you to manipulate your personal timeline, help alter your personal gravity field and accelerate your manifestation potential.

Merkaba is a Hebrew word that stands for "chariot" and comes from a combination of three Ancient Egyptian words (Mer—ka—bah) that mean light, body, and Spirit. You should think of your *Merkaba* as the fastest (speed of light fast) part of your light body—your most potent resource when it comes to energy work, interdimensional travel, and manifestation mastery.

The *Merkaba* is a spatial representation of the Star of David (see Figure 27) and consists of two inverted pyramids, one facing upward and the other facing downward. The upper pyramid represents the Divine Conscious Principle—the power of action, intention, forward movement, achievement, and the act of giving. You should think of it as the Pyramid of the White Sun—it represents your personal connection to Higher Realms and manifestation potential.

FIGURE 27: THE MERKABA

The lower triangle is the Divine Subconscious Principle and represents the power of intuition, vulnerability, inward movement, insight, and the act of receiving. You should think of it as the Pyramid of the Black Sun—your doorway into the greater mysteries of existence, the larger interconnectedness, and the depth of knowledge. When the two Suns come together in a movement of two inversely rotating pyramids, your light body becomes fully activated and ready for use.

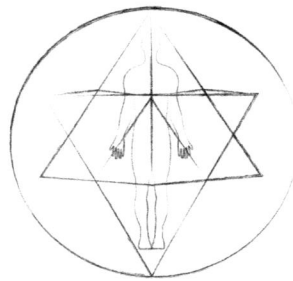

FIGURE 28: THE MERKABA AND THE HUMAN BODY

This sacred geometry powerhouse creates its own center of gravity—the point from which stems the figure's movement. When overlaid on the human body (see Figure 28), the gravity center falls into the heart area—most often in the area of your thymus gland, or your higher heart. This makes the *Merkaba* a true wonder to work with. The activation of your connection with your *Merkaba* feels like an altered consciousness state where Universal oneness is perceived as a physical sensation in the body. The *Merkaba* enables your heart-to-heart connection with the rest of creation—and from this connection, you can draw power for true and meaningful change as well as a greater understanding of what already exists.

The heart space connection is the truest connection that exists: it is a form of telepathic communication with the Universe—the spiritual "I see you" exchange.

The *Merkaba* can be used for numerous things, including:

△ A deep cleanse of all of your light bodies and your auric field.
△ A connection to various aspects of higher consciousness—up to Source energy.
△ An alignment with your energy in a way that better enables you to manifest the life you want.

The *Merkaba* is also a connective layer—it is a sort of interstitial tissue that merges your individual self with the fabric of the rest of the Universe. Your *Merkaba* enables you to interact with the world around you in the most impactful way. When properly using your *Merkaba*, you become "visible" for the rest of creation and start playing at higher levels.

PRACTICE: ACTIVATING AND MANIFESTING WITH THE MERKABA

In today's practice session, you learn how to activate your *Merkaba* and use it to amplify your manifestation force.

Step 1: Activating the *Merkaba*

1. Close your eyes and take a deep breath in.
2. Imagine that the upper part of your body is encapsulated in an upward-facing pyramid. The pyramid's tip should cover your head, and the pyramid's base should align with your knees.
3. Imagine another pyramid facing down. Its tip should stretch a few inches below your feet. The base of the pyramid should align with your chest area, slightly above your heart.
4. Slowly, start rotating the top pyramid clockwise. Breathe in deeply. As the pyramid is rotating, speed it up enough so that the lines become blurry, and the only thing you feel is movement in the upper part of your body. As it happens, a pillar of light emerges, straight from the top of the pyramid, and connects you to the heavens. This upward stream of energy is proof you are doing everything right.
5. Now, while the top pyramid is rotating, focus on the bottom pyramid. Start slowly rotating it in the counterclockwise direction. Allow the pyramid to gain momentum and rotate faster. Whenever ready, allow both pyramids to go as fast as the speed of light. Trust your body to know exactly what this speed feels like. And as this happens, you should feel light particles traveling around you at record speeds. As a part of this rotation, a downward stream of light should also be created.
6. Imagine that the upper stream is connecting you to the energy of the White Sun, and the bottom pillar is connecting you to the energy of the Black Sun. Powered by these two sources, your *Merkaba* is now activated.

From here, you may choose to speed up certain things in your life or slow them down—whatever works. To speed up a particular event or circumstance, align it with the energy of your *Merkaba* and allow the *Merkaba* to take the event over with its energy. Given the *Merkaba* moves at record speeds, anything that gets inside its field also speeds up. To slow something down, reverse the rotation of your *Merkaba* for a few moments. The top pyramid should move counterclockwise (and create a downward pillar), while the bottom pyramid should rotate clockwise and create an upward pillar of light. Whenever something gets into the inverted *Merkaba* energy field, it slows down, or its manifestation may be completely derailed (think: stopping or reversing the effect of a disease).

Step 2: Manifesting with the Merkaba

7. Focus on your desired outcome—whatever you are trying to manifest in the physical. Create a *Merkaba* around this object. Rotate the two pyramids until you see particles of light creating a field around the object—the field should resemble a flying saucer in shape (see Figure 29). Now that this potential future has been activated, all we need to do is align it to your personal rotation axis and the speed of your personal *Merkaba*.

8. Take a few moments to activate your *Merkaba* by starting to rotate both of the pyramids. Whenever you reach high speeds, imagine that the two pillars of light of your *Merkaba* are aligned with the vertical axis of the *Merkaba* of the object you are trying to manifest. Align their collective rotational speed by willing the second *Merkaba* to match your speed. When that happens, you can increase your own *Merkaba* in size to engulf the smaller *Merkaba* of your desired outcome. You should imagine one major *Merkaba* field encapsulating a smaller *Merkaba* field. However, both should be aligned around the same center axis.

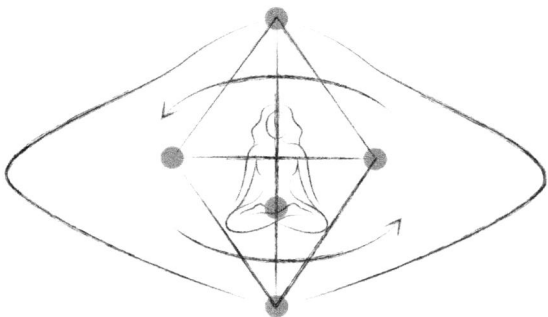

FIGURE 29: THE MERKABA IN MOTION

9. Feel free to stay here for a few moments.

This is a pretty powerful activation and will enable you to speed up the manifestation of that which you desire, or even enable it in the first place.]

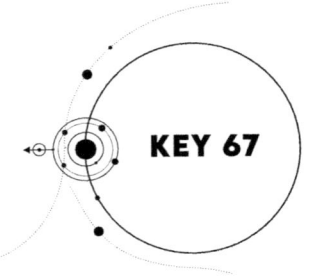

THE SACRED FLAMES FOR MANIFESTATION

The Sacred Flames are the formative energies of the Universe. Imagine that the Creator of the Universe once had a crayon box that created everything in existence. This box of crayons, not dissimilar to the color range of the rainbow, represents the many faces of heavenly fire. The Sacred Flames are the many aspects of Source energy—all unique and multifaceted, more ancient than life itself, and containing the keys to the world's mysteries. Understanding the different aspects of heavenly fire enables you to recreate your life from a higher perspective using the tools of divinity itself. Literally nothing is impossible for the energy of the Sacred Flames—the alpha and the omega, the inception point and the toolbox of creation. The energies of the Sacred Flames are exactly that—sacred—and thus they don't work well for selfish desires that operate against the highest good of all. However, if your heart is pure and your intentions true, you will hardly find better allies than the many flames of heavenly fire.

WHITE FLAME

The original Heavenly Flame, the White Flame, was once a true beginning of everything—the first stroke of a brush in a grand painting. It is also a flame that later split itself into all the other flames while still preserving its integrity. The inception flame of the Universe, the White Flame is a flame of purity, freedom, service, choice, intention, and all aspects of manifestation. The White Flame is in itself perfection. It is the most selfless of all flames and forever insists on the purest truth there is: we are all one, and we rise and fall together. If you are seeking to manifest something on the planetary level and for the highest good of all beings, the White Flame is one of your best bets.

VIOLET FLAME

Probably the most famous of the flames, the Violet Flame is a flame of transformation and transmutation. It represents the energy of change and movement itself, enabling you to get from point A to point B with as few obstacles as possible. Nothing is impossible for the power of the Violet Flame. It provides the freedom to move in any direction you choose and get away with it. This aspect of heavenly fire can be instrumental in helping you achieve goals in any aspect of life—there is no task too big or too small. It is thus very forgiving and non-judgmental energy. The Violet Flame can help you transform anything, from your thoughts to your finances to your circumstances. This flame also helps you align with your highest good—a gentle companion and a wise teacher.

GOLDEN FLAME

The Golden Flame is the breath of life flame. While the White Flame gives birth to all living things, the Golden Flame is responsible for sustaining and nurturing life. Without this energy, sustaining life over time would be an impossible endeavor. Call upon the Golden Flame when you need to bring something from its current state into the state of perfection. The flame of identity inception, a higher-dimensional flame, the Golden Flame is responsible for imparting identity on all living things. It once gave an identity to you also, so you could experience this world from your unique vantage point and make it a better place for all.

The flame of resurrection, creation, and creativity, the Golden Flame is a master of restoration. It has the power to bring something from a suboptimal form back into its original God-given state. As a high-dimensional flame, the Golden Flame only acts in accordance with your highest good as defined by Source consciousness.

RED FLAME

A flame that thrives in third-dimensional worlds, perhaps more than any other flame, is the Red Flame. It is a flame of inspired action, passion, raw expression, and achievement. The Red Flame offers agility, speed, and scale to anyone who works with it. It holds within itself the power of the raging forest fire—all-consuming and devilishly fast. It enables ideas to catch and spread globally. It is also the energy that inspires and drives revolutions—out with the old, and in with the new. The Red Flame can help to create something from nothing and manifest it in the physical. It has the potential to light a fire under the bellies of a lot of people—whole generations if necessary. While it is challenging to sustain this flame over time, if you play to its nature and allow it to come in spurts, you may not wish for a better companion. Blazing and scorching, the Red Flame is here to make your wildest dreams come true. If you can tame it, that is.

PRACTICE: WORKING WITH THE SACRED FLAMES

Any flame that you want to activate looks just like that—a flame of a particular color. Each flame dwells within the temple devoted to preserving it and keeping it alive. Each flame has its guardians and many helpers who are happy to work with you if you choose to activate it.

Start getting to know each flame by visiting the etheric temples devoted to them. Each flame will be located right in the middle of the main hall of its namesake temple. Approach the flame and bask in its energies. You can even walk through the flame, absorbing its energies and asking the guardians to activate the power of the flame in your body. It is a great honor to work with heavenly fire, and it is only bestowed on the select few. Treat it as such, and you can never go wrong with using the energy of the flames.

White Flame Activation

Make sure to spend enough time in the etheric temple of the White Flame and connect to its energies. To activate the White Flame within your body, imagine how a small portion of the original White Flame is detaching itself and is floating toward you before finally settling itself in your crown chakra—right above your head. Feel how this simple action is creating a ripple effect throughout your body. Feel the pure heavenly energies entering your bloodstream and becoming one with who you are. See how your whole body is glowing with the brilliant white light.

Now focus on what you'd like to manifest. Shrink that image into a sphere the size of a large apple and allow it to enter your aura through the crown of your head—the exact place that the White Flame entered your body earlier. Allow the energies of the White Flame to anchor your desire within your body and within the Universe. This anchoring sets in motion the Law of Attraction ("like attracts like"), only tenfold, as the energy of the White Flame is a great amplifier.

Violet Flame Activation

Allow some time to connect with the energies of the Violet Flame in its etheric temple. Approach the Violet Flame and take a small portion of it into your palm. Allow this aspect of the Violet Flame to float into your body and settle into a spot that is most connected to your end goal. For example, if you are looking for love, allow the flame to settle in your heart center. Create an intention and ask the Violet Flame to assist you with something specific—the more direct you are, the better. The Violet Flame requires full clarity to help you manifest what you want.

If you are manifesting a lofty, long-term goal, imagine a path that connects you today (point A) to your desired outcome (point B). Now palace mini Violet Flames along that path—like a thousand torches lighting up your way. Trust that the Violet Flame will show you the best possible path and remove all obstacles along the way.

Golden Flame Activation

Golden Flame works best when you already have planted the seeds of what you want.

In your mind's eye, focus on those seeds and the early fruits of your labor. Yes, they might not be exactly what you want yet, but they are something. Now imagine that right beneath those seeds and early sprouts, there is a Golden Flame of heavenly fire. And as that flame burns bright, your sprouts are starting to grow. Watch as the seeds of what you want are taking root and expanding rapidly. Watch as exactly what you want is being sprung forth from those seeds. See how the energy of the Golden Flame is accelerating the lifeforce of your creation by a thousandfold; see how it is making your creation better, stronger, and healthier. You can enlist the energy of this flame as your long-term partner in this mission—it will help you nurture and sustain your seeds day in and day out.

Red Flame Activation

Once you spend some time in the etheric temple of the Red Flame, you are ready to activate it within your life. The best aspect of the Red Flame related to manifestation is the ability to inspire you into action—the kind that feels exhilarating and beyond exciting. The Red Flame provides the thrill of making things happen.

To accomplish this connection, imagine the guardians of the Red Flame gift you two mini Red Flames to take with you on your journey. Place one flame below each of the soles of your feet. In a meditative state, imagine how your feet, powered by the Red Flames, are now carrying you with speed and agility toward your desired future. See how nothing is impossible for this ancient force, and achieving your goal is simply inevitable.

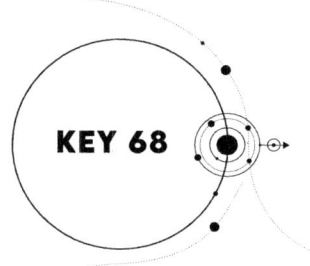

KEY 68

CREATING YOUR MANIFESTATION DOUBLE

At any point in time, your Higher Self has several projections—or life-streams—emanating from it into a myriad of worlds, both low- and high-dimensional. Such splits enable your oversoul to accomplish learning and expansion with as much momentum as possible. Splitting a single stream of energy into multiple smaller streams is very natural to your soul—you can think of it as the oldest trick in the book.

As a projection of your Higher Self, you have access to a similar toolkit by association. You can create an energetic double of yourself and task it with helping you accomplish any goal you set your mind to. There are two ways to accomplish this—splitting your current energy stream OR calling on your energy reserve to make a double from scratch.

Using your energy reserve is a preferred route since it doesn't tap into your current resource, but rather uses an extra resource that your Higher Self has allotted for a proverbial "rainy day." Generally this resource is tapped into if the soul undergoes an intense or traumatic experience, whether planned or impromptu. This resource could also be called upon if a soul undertakes additional challenges for the incarnation, ones that were not part of the original "to do" list. It is not always possible to draw from that energy pool, though, as it is closely guarded by Spirit, and you need special permission to use it. In any case, splitting your own resource is definitely something you have the full power and authority to accomplish.

There are many benefits to having an energy double, including:

△ Your energy double is not a corporeal being—it is an energy structure. Therefore, it never gets tired, or hungry, or sick, or stressed. It works day and night tirelessly; it needs no rest and requires no pep talk. It is just like you, only better.

△ Your energy double is a programmable entity—it literally becomes obsessed with the mission you send it on. This tunnel vision provides an incredible amount of focus. And things we focus on always grow.

- △ An energy double enables you to accomplish your goals faster—whatever you are doing, your energy double is busy helping you manifest your heart's desire.
- △ The energy double requires little upkeep and tuning. Once created and charged, it will not stop until the goal is accomplished. It is a dog with a bone.

SIMPLE RULES FOR CREATING AN ENERGY DOUBLE

This practice is in the realm of energy magic. And as you know, all magic comes with a price. I recommend referring to this tactic ONLY if you wish to manifest something on the planetary level and with the greater good in mind. Otherwise, this tool could backfire and create more negative karma for you and your family tree than it's worth.

Don't attempt this tactic if you often experience low energy or are seriously ill. Both of these are signs that you need your full energy stream for the next step of your journey. Being able to split your energy is a luxury. Make sure you do not create repercussions for yourself beyond what you can currently handle.

Make sure to return the double back into the stream once its "job is done." You can do that by simply setting an intention and creating a declaration along the lines of "I order my energy double to return to the greater stream as soon as my intention is complete, unless I say otherwise." Make sure to set that boundary right after you create a double so you don't forget. While having loose energy doubles floating around without purpose is not necessarily damaging in and of itself, you always want to have a tight grasp on all of your energy, especially if you require it for another purpose later on.

PRACTICE: CREATING YOUR ENERGY DOUBLE

Make sure you attempt this practice when you are full of energy—ideally, when the Sun is in its prime; noon would be perfect. Make sure you are well rested and don't feel sleepy. This practice can tax your energy, so pick a day when you don't need to do much or go to work/study. You'll also need some quiet time afterward to replenish your energy.

1. Close your eyes and focus on your breathing.
2. Center your focus on the White Sun—its rays and its warm caressing energy. Imagine that its energy is entering your body freely and removing any toxins and impurities that don't belong there. Imagine that your body is a temple, and the Sun is doing a full spring cleaning—a gut renovation of your body and your organ systems. Feel every cell of your body fill up with the healing golden glow—the power of your great Celestial Father.

Step 1: Creating a double from the energy reserve

3. Take a few deep breaths and imagine that there is a gilded well right in front of you. The well is amply guarded. It feels like something precious, ancient, and powerful beyond measure dwells within its depth. Even the air around it is filled with mystery. This well contains your energy reserves: this energy doesn't belong to any particular incarnation, but rather is shared between your multiple incarnations. The management of this well is under the full control of your Higher Self.
4. Approach the guardians of the well. State your intention clearly—let them know that you have come to partake in the resources of the well and you would like to create a manifestation double for yourself.
5. Ask for the guardians' permissions to take from the well. One of the two things will happen—either you will be granted access, or you won't. If the access is denied, don't despair. Simply move to the next step. If the access was granted, rejoice! This approval is a great sign indeed—this means your Higher Self believes you are on the right path and indeed deserve additional help and resources.
6. Approach the well and dip your hands in it. Feel the warm golden waters of your personal higher energy stream. It should feel both familiar and unknown at the same time. Pick up some of that energy and start making an exact replica of your energy body. An energy replica has the same shape and size as your body, but instead of being made of flesh and bone, it is made of intertwining silver and golden threads.
7. Watch as this energy structure is created next to you with the help of the energies of the well.

8. Allow the form to take shape; the process will run its course naturally. Just wait it out with patience. You will feel it in your heart when the work has been completed.

Step 2: Splitting your stream (if Step 1 was unsuccessful)

9. If you weren't able to access your reserve, this step is for you. Examine your body inside of your meditative state. What you need to uncover is your energetic imprint. When you look at your body, do you see it made of flesh and bone? If so, imagine that it was made of energy instead—your personal energy stream that would represent the wholeness of who you are at soul level. Instead of flesh and bones, you should be witnessing several colored threads that weave into each other and form a beautiful energy structure. Let your energy body fully reveal itself. When that is accomplished, imagine creating a perfect copy of that energy body—similar to how you would copy and paste things on a computer. As an end result, you should have two equal bodies right next to each other.

Step 3: Charging your double

10. Congratulations: now that your energy double is created, you need to charge it with a particular intention. Focus on your heart's desire—exactly what you are attempting to manifest.
11. As you envision that as clearly as possible in your mind's eye, imagine that there is a stream of consciousness that connects you with your double. Imagine that your intention, the imprint of your desire, is being passed to your double telepathically. Imagine that a stream of energy enters your double through its crown chakra—a master receiving center.
12. As your intention is uploading to your double, watch the vibrations of your double being altered to match your heart's desire. Allow your double to get saturated with those vibrations. Thanks to the Law of Attraction, your double will start attracting people, circumstances, and events that are vibrating at that same frequency. Remember that your double is essentially your copy, so

whatever it attracts, you also attract, because you are one and the same even when separate—two sides of the same coin.

Step 4: Declaring your intention

13. It is imperative to solidify your intention with a declaration, which is also known as a spell. While you don't have to use these exact words, the following represents a good example of a declaration that works:

    "From this day forward, I command my energy double to work tirelessly to bring forth my desired outcome. I ask it to use all of the resources at its disposal to manifest and accelerate my desired future. I ask it to charge the space around me so that what I want can come swiftly and without delay. I ask it to become a master magnet and rearrange the energetic field around me to become a vibrational match to what I want to attract. And I order that as soon as my energy double's work is done and what I want is manifested, my double can fully recede to where it came from and be rejoined with the rest of my energies for future missions."

14. Allow yourself ample time to come back from this meditation. This is deep energy work, so please do not rush the process.

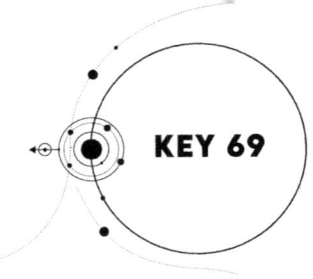

KEY 69

ASSEMBLAGE POINT

Each of us inhabits our personal slice of the Universe. You might want to think of it as a cell in a large honeycomb of this time-space reality. Many factors determine what your personal cell looks and feels like—from your ancestral settings to the thought loops you are running to your personal comfort zone (See also Keys 32, 54 and 60, pages 146, 244, and 267.)

YOUR PERSONAL VANTAGE POINT

Your assemblage point is another important input into the formation of your reality. The assemblage point is your personal vantage point, the angle from which you perceive your life and everything that happens in it. Humans tend to have a fixed, default assemblage point—you tend to be born with it and stick to it unless dramatic shifts happen during your life. The simplest way to understand the concept of the assemblage point is to realize that it tends to be fixed within one of your major chakras (see Key 7, page 47). So for instance, there are people who perceive this world from the root chakra level and others who perceive it from the throat chakra.

While temporary shifts in perception and thus your assemblage point happen, you always tend to revert to your default setting. A lot of your life energy tends to accumulate in or around your assemblage point, so whether or not you are aware it, you have a main chakra that runs your life. Shifting your assemblage point is an advanced practice and a curious exercise for anyone attempting to live a more mindful life. But today, we'll explore how the position of your assemblage point can help you manifest more easily.

ASSEMBLAGE POINT IN THE SOLAR PLEXUS CHAKRA

The manifestation from this assemblage point is focused, intentional, and full of force. It takes dispersed energy and reorders it into a focused, targeted stream as if you were masterfully aiming an arrow to hit the bull's eye. While it's not a high-vibrational space, manifesting worldly things from here would be fairly easy.

ASSEMBLAGE POINT IN THE HEART CHAKRA

This assemblage point lives in harmony and balance with everything else in existence. Don't ever underestimate the power of the heart to bring about your perfect future. Since it represents your point of connection to everything in the Universe, manifesting from this assemblage point enables you to tap into the power of the collective for the greater good of all. It's perfect for planetary missions, larger-than-life goals, and ambitious projects, as well as any undertakings that are meant to bring about better harmony for everyone.

ASSEMBLAGE POINT IN THE THROAT CHAKRA

This assemblage point connects you to the potent force of your personal truth and the path that you came here to walk. It activates the entirety of your resources, anchoring the full spectrum of your soul gifts and enabling them to manifest into the physical. The throat chakra assemblage point is a shortcut to the power of Logos—the creative force of the word of God (see also Key 58, page 260)—through your personal slice of it. This space is where your true commitments lie, but it is also the seat of your personal godliness. This point connects you to the greater vision of who you could be: it gives you access to deeper wisdom, deeper knowledge, and the finality of understanding. This assemblage point is a true manifestation powerhouse and a much-hidden gem.

As mentioned earlier, each one of you has a default assemblage point. And while it may be quite hard to alter your assemblage point permanently, you could temporarily travel between the various points to open gateways to more productive manifestation.

PRACTICE: MANIFESTING THROUGH THE ENERGIES OF THE ASSEMBLAGE POINT

Sometimes it may be hard to determine which assemblage point you should be using to optimize the outcome of your manifestation practice. In this session, we will take the guesswork out of the equation and use all three points simultaneously.

1. Focus on your breath and close your eyes.
2. Start by centering your assemblage point in your solar plexus chakra. Imagine that there is a little elevator traveling up and down your chakra system on the inside of your body. As it moves up and down, your focus goes with it. Imagine that the elevator travels to your solar plexus chakra and makes a stop there. Notice how your perception may change. It may feel like you are instantly more alert and ready for action. You may feel a slight tingling sensation in your abdominal area.
3. As you perceive the world from your yellow center, focus on what you are working on manifesting. Imagine it as a globe of light. Picture your solar plexus chakra is feeding this globe of light with a stream of yellow energy. As the globe becomes more saturated with color yellow, it becomes heavier, more defined, and more real than ever before. Stay here for a few moments and allow the energy transfer to run its course.
4. Now watch the elevator move up your body toward your heart center and then stop right in the middle of your heart chakra. Notice how it feels to be in this center—allow your attention to dwell here, uninterrupted by any other energies. See yourself merging with the rest of the world—as if you can no longer tell where you end and everything else begins. Feel the magic of your heart space. This is a very healing, soft, and pleasurable place to be. You can feel the effervescent emerald energies taking over your entire body.
5. For a moment, focus on the sphere that you have just fed with yellow light—your desired outcome. Imagine how a stream of emerald light is leaving your heart space and entering this sphere to power and charge it with the loving energy of your heart center. Allow the sphere to take as much of this energy as it needs. You will notice the stream runs low when the sphere doesn't require any more energy.

6. Lastly, get back to your elevator and travel to your throat chakra. Allow your full attention to go directly to your throat area. Settle here and stay for a few moments. How does being here, in this assemblage point, feel? Do you perhaps feel expanded? Do you feel like you might be floating in the ether? Can you feel higher vibrational energy entering your body? This center allows you to connect to the truth of who you are—your vastness, greatness, light, and endless resources. Stay and bask in these energies.

7. When you are ready, send a stream of sapphire blue energy from your throat chakra to the sphere of light that has been powered by yellow and emerald energies. See how the only energy that has been missing from the sphere is the sapphire blue. Notice how this energy is the exact sustenance that your dream has been thirsty for. Sustain the stream for as long as the sphere is accepting new energy. The flow will dissipate when the sphere has been changed completely.

8. Picture your sphere of light as being nurtured by all three points simultaneously. Since you have established this flow of energy, from this day forward, the sphere can tap into any of the three streams whenever it requires sustenance.

9. Take the sphere into the palms of your hands, feel it pulsating with life. Drop the sphere into the soil below your feet and watch it grow—watch it become exactly what you wish it to become right in front of your eyes.

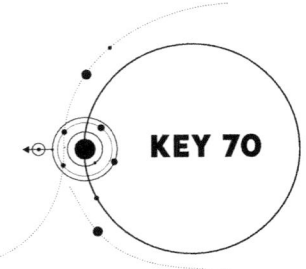

KEY 70

LEY LINES, AXIS MUNDI, AND PLANETARY ALIGNMENT

The concept of alignment has become a bit of a buzzword in spiritual circles. Aligning with your path, aligning with your Higher Self, and aligning your chakras into one coherent pillar of light—all these are the various forms of alignment around achieving a heightened state of being.

At its core, manifestation is energy work. This work includes massive upgrades to the various energy systems of your body—your Etheric Body, your Emotional Body, and your Mental Body. Once those upgrades are complete, the only thing remaining is taking massive action in the physical, powered by your newly found heightened and aligned state.

When you are manifesting things on a personal level, using your individual resources should be enough. Manifestation on the planetary level is a whole new game altogether. Your own devices are simply not enough. The good news? We are living in a world where all aspects of reality are intrinsically interconnected. You are a link of a grandmaster chain: you are as impacted by the whole as the whole is impacted by you. And by consciously plugging yourself back into the system in exactly the way that counts, you may be able to unleash the force of the collective.

ENERGY CENTERS

In this chapter, we'll be discussing planetary alignment. This type of alignment is a spiritual master move. It requires a reasonable level of health and vitality in all of your energy centers, as well as an understanding of how the puzzle works together. The latter, I am happy to help with.

LEY LINES

Our planet has an intricate system of energy vessels that permeate its core and cover its perimeter—not dissimilar to a human circulatory system. Most of the planetary energy that exists in its purest (unmanifested) state travels along these ley lines at hyper speed, beating to the drum of the energetic heart of Gaia. This is a well-choreographed planetary dance that, while invisible, is intricate and impressive. Like blood vessels, ley lines vary in diameter and output—you have your major vessels that pump large amounts of energy, and you have your smaller ones that are only responsible for a modest share.

The planet uses energy as required to manifest healing for itself on various levels—physical, energetic, emotional, and mental. This healing happens all the time, and major resources are dispatched to places that are undergoing a crisis. Ley lines are strongest at the convergence points; just like two or more massive highways coming together, the energy potential for those spots is quite extraordinary. Some examples of the points where ley lines converge are famous heritage sites like Stonehenge, Easter Island, the pyramids of Giza and Teotihuacan, Mount Fuji and Mount Olympus as well as certain temples, like the Temple of Jerusalem. Massive amounts of planetary energy are coursing between the ley line convergence points throughout the planet. These intersections are the busy energy hubs through which the neighboring territories may receive an energy boost. Since ancient times, the ley line convergence points have held special significance for humans. People with the Sight would note the mystical experiences and visions connected to these points. Some ley line convergences have become the spots of pilgrimage (Mecca and Machu Picchu) while others remain a mystery to unravel (Glastonbury Tor and the Bermuda triangle). Generations upon generations of humans are drawn to these places since they are subconsciously attracted to the energy vortices they represent.

AXIS MUNDI

Axis Mundi (also known as the cosmic axis or world axis) is a mystical concept that represents the proverbial planetary center—the shortest distance between Earth and the heavens. Axis Mundi is a shortcut between the low and the high dimensions: it is a point of connection between the mundane and the magical, or the expected and the

Divine. The concept of Axis Mundi is deeply connected to that of the tree of life in Christian, Cabbalistic, and Nordic traditions. The one that conceives of the mysteries of the tree is the one destined for enlightenment. And yet, you don't need to mediate under the fig tree for 49 days in a true Buddha fashion to partake in the mysteries of the Axis Mundi. You simply need to be willing.

Since ancient times, people with the understanding knew that there are many Axes Mundi. The fixed ones rest in the places where the ley lines converge. Those paths are the more permanent kind—once established, it takes a cataclysm to unmake a point of convergence. Other Axes Mundi are of temporary nature. Those come and go with the times to support strong rulers, bountiful civilizations, or powerful mystics and disappear upon their demise.

One of the greater hidden truths, however, is that when properly aligned, each human becomes an antenna into the Higher Realms: they are the perfect pillar of light and the point of connection between the mundane and the high-vibrational worlds. And from that state, many things that may have felt impossible become not just possible, but probable. The impossible becomes manifested.

PRACTICE: BECOMING THE AXIS MUNDI

Becoming the Axis Mundi is the next step on your journey of manifesting at the planetary level. It is easier than you may think, and today's practice will help.

1. Close your eyes and settle into your breathing.
2. Imagine Earth below your feet. See how the surface of the planet is covered with vertical and horizontal lines filled with golden light. These lines are like a grid on the surface of the planet.

Notice a vertical axis that goes through the very center of the planet. Alongside this axis, there are many ley lines and many energy arteries running up and down, accumulating the planetary power around this point of connection. Notice how this axis is infinite—stretching up and down as far as the eye can see. Imagine that your own body is located alongside this planetary core, right along this axis. As the axis is entering your body, all of your chakras light up with the power of a thousand Suns and emanate true white light (see Figure 30).

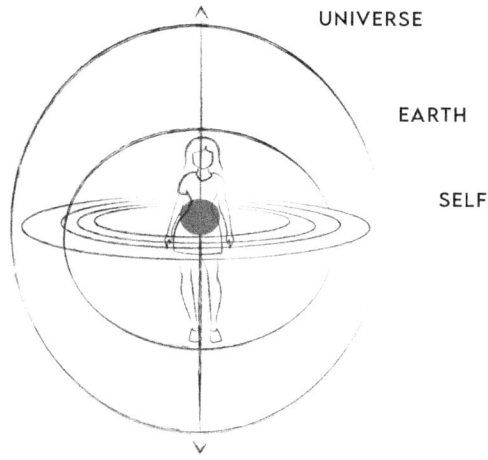

FIGURE 30: AXIS MUNDI, CONNECTING US TO THE REST OF EXISTENCE

1. Feel the energy coursing through all of your chakras, building a pillar of light from your base chakra, stretching beyond your crown chakra, and floating into your higher chakras.
2. Follow this upward pillar that flows through the Earth's center and now your very own center. Zoom out and see how this same pillar is running through the very center of the Milky Way—the very center of its rotational movement. See how this pillar is penetrating the dark womb on our galaxy, as heavy as a million Suns and as dense as matter itself. Allow yourself to align fully with this wise galactic force.
3. If you feel called, zoom out again and go with me to the next level—the level of the Universe. As you Zoom out of your home galaxy, notice that you are now aligned with the very center of the Universe—a Central Universal Sun, or the energy we call Source. As you look around, you see a myriad of galaxies spinning and floating around, each one with its unique destiny and vibration.
4. Breathe in deeply here. Notice how calm it feels to be fully aligned with the entirety of the Universe. Notice how you are both infinitely small and infinitely

large at the same time. And from this point, know without a trace of a doubt that your wishes matter—they matter at the planetary level, at the galactic level, at the Universal level, and most importantly, they matter at the level of Source energy. Feel free to speak about what you would like to create freely. May the power of the Great Logos be on your side, today and always.

Feel free to follow this alignment practice with any other practice in this book for amplified effect.

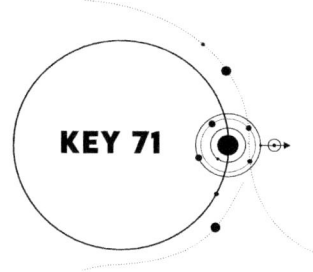

KEY 71

ON ANCHORING

Any time you incarnate into this time-space reality, an anchor is created. An anchor enables the energy of your Higher Self to plug into both the matrix and a physical body so you can have a happy and healthy incarnation. If it weren't for the anchor, the energy of your Higher Self wouldn't be able to attach to a low-vibration planet like Earth—the difference in frequency is just too great. An anchor exists between dimensions, or rather, across all dimensions at once. It is a true wonder of creation.

Once an incarnation is complete, the anchor is maintained, in essence trapping a portion of your energy to a past life. Some anchors are much needed even after an incarnation is completed; it is a spiritual bookmark. It marks important lives in case your soul wants to explore or rewatch them in the future or process some learnings at a later date. Anchors are also necessary for your cornerstone incarnations—lives in which you establish an important quality of yours. Anchors enable you to keep this quality for many incarnations to come and refer to it whenever you need it.

However, not every anchor is useful. Most of the lives you have lived could be considered middle-of-the-road, forgettable incarnations that only contain moderate learnings and minor forward movement. While in the grand scheme of things this aspect of anchoring is unavoidable, it represents a suboptimal use of your energy. For instance, you might be low on energy here, but that energy may be fully available if you borrow it from a less important past or parallel life. Think of this energy absorption as spring cleaning—you toss out the old so that the new can come in. This process is essentially sophisticated energy recycling. And it fits within the laws of the matrix completely—after all, this is a free will Universe, and thus you get to decide if you could use more energy and even get it whenever you want.

ON PARALLEL LIVES

Chances are, you are living at least a few parallel lives. Those parallel lives are always prime targets when you want to free up energy.

There are two types of parallel lives. The first one is a life sponsored by your Higher Self, and it's happening at the same "time" as your current incarnation, but in a place different from where you are. It may be a life in another city or even another planet, but it uses a parallel stream of energy from your Higher Self.

The second type is a rendition of your current incarnation, but one where you made a different set of choices. So these parallel lives would be of a similar version of you—same body, same parents, same place of birth, but only under a different set of circumstances. Depending on the complexity of your life, you may have thousands of parallel splits of your current incarnation. This is a way for your Higher Self to get the most out of the incarnation. Upon the completion of an incarnation, an optimal stream is selected from all the parallel streams. That is the stream that gets uploaded into the *Akashic* field—the memory bank of the Universe. The rest of the streams get erased.

Most parallel lives are disposable because they don't lead to your desired outcome and your desired future. However, despite being dead ends, they don't get erased automatically while your incarnation is in progress. And yet they are still taking up energy—the energy you could use to create the life of your dreams. There is no harm in collapsing these anchors and reclaiming that trapped energy for more productive use. About 90 percent of parallel lives are completely disposable and should be cleaned up in a way that you clean your house. A clean energy field is a prerequisite to a happy and productive life.

PRACTICE: COLLAPSE ANCHORS AND FREE UP ENERGY

We'll explore how to collapse anchors and free up energy in the practice session today (also see Key 6, page 43). Whenever you undertake cleaning up past or parallel lives, it is important to ask for assistance from your spirit guides. They can lead you to the lives that no longer serve you so you don't accidentally remove a useful anchor.

1. Close your eyes and settle into your body. Breathe in and out deeply. Repeat three times.

2. Imagine you are floating in a vast ocean. The ocean feels very familiar—like you have bathed in it before. It is very warm and pleasant, and you know that you can trust its wisdom and waters completely.
3. Ask your guides to show you a life—past or parallel—that is no longer serving you and can easily be collapsed and harvested for energy. A life will be shown to you like a bubble of light that floats on the surface of the ocean. Each life has an anchor attached to the bubble's surface—that anchor connects it to the bottom of the ocean.
4. As you get closer to the bubble, simply pull the anchor up to the surface of the ocean and then burst the bubble. When it bursts, the energy trapped inside will start floating upward since it is no longer locked into this reality. Create a net of light in the sky that will be able to capture this freed energy.
5. Repeat this process two more times with other lives so that you can free up a significant amount of energy.
6. Now gather all of the newly collected energy from the net and into an empty glass vessel. Imagine that your current incarnation is also a bubble—and your physical body is located right in the middle of it. Bring the glass vessel with the freed energy inside of your bubble.
7. Once the vessel is inside, allow the energy to spill out and rejoin the energy already in your bubble. From here, declare an intention that this new energy should be used to fortify your manifestation and enhance your creative stream.

The power of your word is critical here—unless you designate that this energy should go toward manifestation, there is a chance that it will naturally flow elsewhere. Make it a habit to distribute your energy consciously to projects and goals that truly matter to you. This conscious attribution is what being a modern-day alchemist is all about.

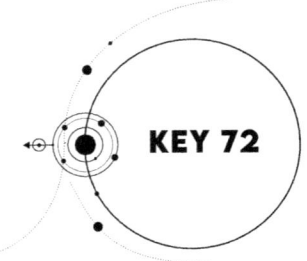

YOUR OWN MANIFESTATION CODE

To the one pure of heart and pure of intention, the Universe has a special gift—the one thing to amplify everything you do and to manifest everything you are meant to become. This gift is called your Manifestation Code, and it is crafted specifically for you by the Universe. Your manifestation toolbox may be vast, but nothing could ever compare to working with your Manifestation Code. The crown jewel of your arsenal, your Manifestation Code is the closest thing to the unique vibration of your Higher Self here on Earth. It is your gateway to the depth of the resources your Higher Self has at its fingertips. Manifestation in the Higher Realms is instant. And while the vibrations of our planet do not allow for instant manifestation at this point in time, with your personal Manifestation Code, you could come close.

WHAT IS YOUR MANIFESTATION CODE?

We live in a mathematical Universe—the Universe of Chaos and the Universe of Order. A world where most things can be reduced to a numeric frequency and everything is defined by a set of mathematical equations. No wonder your key to unlocking manifestation is a code—a string of numbers and symbols that defines who you are at a deeper level. Your Manifestation Code enables you to align with the best version of you, whatever that may look like. It enables you to flow in unison with the rest of creation and be supported by a tailwind instead of having to fight your way through thorns and obstacles. You should think of your Manifestation Code as your secret weapon—it can amplify your creative potential by as much as ten times. The good news? You don't have to be intuitive or psychic to download the codes. Truly the only thing required is the purity of your heart and intentions plus faith that something like this is even possible.

WORKING WITH YOUR MANIFESTATION CODE

Once you have activated your Manifestation Code (please see the ritual in the practice section later in this chapter), you can start working with it. You don't need to know the exact sequence of numbers or symbols that represents your code—simply know that it is a stream of golden light emanating from your body.

Once your code is activated, you can charge different objects with it to enlist them in your mission and enable them to help you. You could charge your vision board with your Manifestation Code, for instance. Just imagine a stream of golden numbers is emanating from your fingers and penetrating your vision board to charge it with your unique energies. The vibration of the Manifestation Code is extremely active—this is pure and potent creative energy. It is never idle, so as soon as an object is infused with it, it becomes an active helper in your manifestation journey. You can similarly charge the clothing you wear, the food you eat, the water you drink, and even the content you consume with the energy of your Manifestation Code. The more you work with this energy, the more magical your life shall become. Try infusing your goals with this energy. Simply write your goals down on a piece of paper and allow the golden manifestation stream to saturate the page. This will ensure your goals are achieved quickly and precisely.

PRACTICE: ACCESSING YOUR MANIFESTATION CODE

This practice should be done overnight. It requires an invocation before going to sleep and an invocation in the morning upon waking up.

Objects you'll need

- 1 white candle
- 1 gold candle
- 1 Vogel crystal
- 1 stick of *Palo Santo*
- Jasmine essential oil
- Clary sage essential oil

Preparing for the ritual

Fill a small bowl with distilled water. You can use regular water too, if you perform a cleansing ritual with it. Add seven drops of clary sage essential oil and seven drops of jasmine essential oil to your water bowl. Mix well.

Conducting the ritual

This ritual is best done half an hour before going to bed on a day when you don't have to be up early in the morning.

1. Clear your space by smudging some *Palo Santo*. This will help you get in the right state, as well as provide some energy clearing.
2. Light the two candles you have prepared for this ritual. Place the white one in front of you to the left and the golden one in front of you to the right.
3. Get into a comfortable seated position. Close your eyes for a few moments and focus on your breath.
4. In your mind's eye, imagine standing in a beautiful field. Above you is a cloudless periwinkle-blue sky. Everything about this place feels serene and magical. Look into the sky and open yourself fully. Surrender to this moment.
5. Watch as a stream of golden light is formed right above you, and as it forms, small particles of light start falling over your body, washing over you like a Divine shower. Allow those energies to penetrate your body and light you up from within. Stay here for a couple of moments.
6. Open your eyes and focus on your candles. The white color symbolizes purity, Divine intention, undiluted potential, and God-given grace—the vibration of being blessed. This is the energy you need present for the duration of this ritual so Divine blessings can come more easily to you. The golden candle represents cosmic abundance, the state of perfection and attainment, the transmutation of any blocked negative energy, and overall prosperity. It is the energy of truly thriving, not just living. This energy is a very high-vibrational frequency that is quite rare on planet Earth. The energy of the golden candle is paramount to aligning your current vibrations with those of your Higher Self—a prerequisite for the work we are doing today.
7. Place the bowl with the essential oils in front of you and dip your fingers in it. Close your eyes and imagine that your Higher Self is standing right in front of

you. Imagine that it is smiling at you and blessing you for this ritual. Open your eyes, take your fingers out of the bowl, and lightly touch your temples and then the area of your third eye, anointing yourself. If it feels good, you can sprinkle the essential oil mix onto your hair lightly—you cannot go wrong here.

8. Take your Vogel crystal with both hands and place it at a point between the two candles, but in a way that the three objects form a triangle. Make sure the thicker end of the crystal is facing downward and the thinner is facing upward; this placement enables you to create an upward stream of energy that goes up to the heavens and straight into the higher dimensions. Vogel crystals are Divine tools—they enable you to focus your energy stream and amplify the power of your intention by more than a thousand times. They are truly magical and extremely underrated.

9. As you hold the crystal, imagine how the energy is starting to course through the triangle you just created. It starts with the white candle—the first point—then moves through the Vogel crystal and culminates with the golden candle. As you are doing this, imagine a pillar of white light is forming and emanating from within your triangle. You are now fully connected and ready for the invocation.

10. Place your left hand on your heart while holding the crystal with your right hand. When ready, say the below invocation out loud:

Dear Universe,

Thank you for bringing me to this point in my life and for trusting me with this ritual. I do not take this trust lightly. Today and with your blessing, I would like to activate my personal Manifestation Code. I have done my inner work and believe I am deserving of this blessed gift of yours. With the greater good in mind, I ask you to unlock and upload my light Codes of Manifestation into my body. So shall it be.

11. Anoint yourself with the essential oil mix one more time—the temples and the third eye area. Place some of the oil on your Vogel crystal to accumulate the power of your intention within it.

12. Before going to bed, place the Vogel crystal underneath your pillow.

13. The codes will be uploaded into your body as you sleep—this is when the veil between worlds is at its thinnest and your spirit guides have easier access to you. Trust the Universe to do right by you. The essential oil mix we used enables dream state magic—your dreams this night may be extremely vivid

and potentially even lucid. You also may experience some physical symptoms at night—such as feeling hot or experiencing chills. This is completely normal—your body is going through an upgrade. In the morning, make sure to write down any insights you may have gotten during the night. Sometimes your spirit guides may choose to send you messages during this time. Whether or not you remember what happened during the night, rest assured that the codes have been uploaded to your body.

14. In the morning, be grateful for the work that has transpired overnight. Close your eyes and place both hands on your heart, one over the other, and repeat the below invocation:

Dear Universe,
I thank you for uploading the light Codes of Manifestation into my body. Thank you for granting me extra strength, power, and resources to pursue my dreams. Thank you for being on my side today and always. So shall it be.

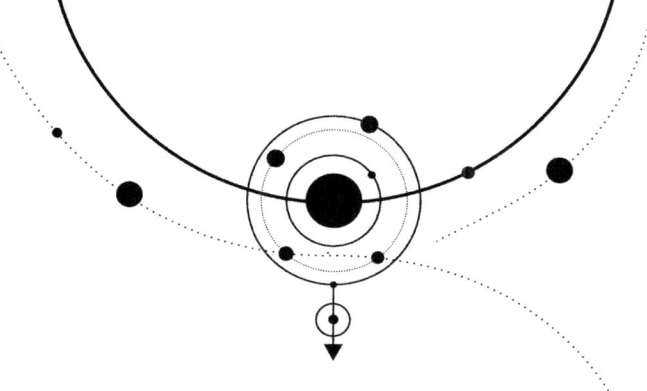

PARTING INTENTION

Alas, my friend, we have reached the final moments of our time together. Thank you for coming on this manifestation journey with me. It has been my honor to guide you thus far. I know your path doesn't end here; it is merely just beginning.
May you find everything you are looking for.
And through that, realize that it is by expressing who you are truly that you become indelibly happy.
May you shine your light freely.
May your light touch others.
May you go on many more adventures that fill you up, enrich you, and make you stronger.
And if you ever wish to reconnect again, I'll be here.

With much love,
Mariya

ABOUT MARIYA

My life changed forever the week I turned 31, the week I had my awakening. That week and seemingly out of nowhere, my clairaudience opened up. For the first time in my life, I was able to hear my Spirit Guides. Their messages were deep and very on point - they spoke of the mysteries of the world, of life beyond the veil and of humanity's place in all of this. Since then, my life has been a stream of activations - of discovering more of my abilities and owning my spiritual path. I have found that I have a deep connection with my Higher Self and can easily channel her wisdom, which my husband and I turned into a podcast called Conversations with my Higher Self. Over 100 episodes and tens of thousands of downloads later, I am being called to expand once again. Hence this book - the first of many. This book came to me as a calling. The moment I answered the call, I knew how many chapters the book was destined to have, I knew their names and started receiving a daily stream of wisdom which I humbly recorded here. I used to define myself as an entrepreneur, that label felt very safe and described me well, since I co-founded and have been running a beauty startup for many years now. However, my true calling is being a scribe for Spirit, my true calling is to hear and record the messages that I get for the greater good of all. I am also called to teach manifestation—the Art of Creation—as it is one of the mediums that brings humanity closer to divinity. Thank you for coming on this journey with me and I hope that you join me for many more.

Please stay in touch!

Visit **www.thisismariya.com** for more channeled material from me, including my podcast.

IG: @ThisIsMariyaOfficial

Most importantly, there will be a follow-up book. If you would like to get an alert when it comes out, sign up for my email notifications at **www.thisismariya.com**

Printed in Great Britain
by Amazon